The Happiness Animal

Will Jelbert

For Happiness Coaching & Personal Training for Happiness
visit: www.happinessanimal.com or email the author:
w@happinessanimal.com

For my family, and other animals

Contents

<u>Chapter 1</u>

before you begin

A man's as miserable as he thinks he is

Seneca

Education is not the learning of facts, but the training of the mind to think

Einstein

WE ARE ANIMALS, trained. How we exercise our muscles determines the strength of our happiness. How do you get a healthy body? You give that body two treatments: healthy diet, and, healthy exercise. But for healthy happiness, you only need one treatment: healthy exercise. It is easier to be happy than it is to lose weight. I found this out the hard way.

My first job was working as a translator for Reuters. Translating French and German into English did provide me with three different ways to look at the same piece of information, three different ways of thinking, but it didn't teach me much about happiness. I had a degree specializing in the origins of Modern French Thought, and although that kept me interested in philosophy, it didn't teach me much about happiness either. Almost a decade into a great career with Reuters, promotions, holidays around the world with a beautiful wife, and relocation to a place in the sun, I was deeply unhappy. Then things got worse. My marriage was dead and divorce loomed its ugly head. I started drinking, partying, sleazing - all heavily. I was caught between alcoholism and the pretensions of a playboy. Then things got worse. One afternoon I had a near-fatal bike accident, which resulted in an eight hour operation to reconstruct my face, and a year of follow up surgery. I no longer recognized myself. I couldn't understand who I was or what I was doing. I took months off work, lost my ability to plan and prioritise, and became a case study for both Obsessive Compulsive and Post Traumatic Stress disorders. I became the psychology patient with four therapists. I made a full recovery, learned a lot about managing anxiety, but it didn't teach me much about happiness. I was still unhappy, or numb. I decided to go on a journey to escape my apartment, my city, my job, and so I went, alone, on a three-month drive around the remotest parts of outback Australia. Nature often struck me with awe, but the journey itself didn't teach me much about happiness. So I moved into a penthouse apartment next to Sydney Harbour Bridge, ate out in the best restaurants, and you got it, it didn't teach me much about happiness. I had the ultimate bachelor lifestyle. I was living the dream, but I wanted to wake up. All my experiences had one thing in common: I could take momentary pleasure from them but they didn't make me happy. I had learned, at least, what didn't make me happy, but what was I missing?

In 2001, I had stumbled on a dark-green book in my parent's bookshelf on their farm in Cornwall. Age had frayed and worn the book's spine, where the once golden, now darkened letters read: 'Self Control And How to Secure It, by Paul Dubois.' I took that book from the farm that day, and it has remained in my possession ever since. But I didn't start reading it until about ten years later when I stumbled on it again. The book did not directly teach me about happiness, but it did provide me with a lot of clues to where I could learn about happiness. The author made references to books, which he said were guides to the innermost workings of the human soul. So I got started on his reading list. I read the old, and I mean really old, beginning with the writings of Seneca.

Born in 4 B.C. in Spain, Seneca moved to the Roman Empire where he became the adviser to the then Emperor of Rome, Nero. Before attending to his own poisoning (Emperor's orders), Seneca had in his philosophical writings, secured himself a place as one of the greatest thinkers of Ancient Rome, and of all time. His letters to his friend Lucilius are still relevant to every human being. Seneca was my happiness game-changer and I acknowledge his influence by opening every chapter with a quote of Seneca wisdom. Next on the reading list was the slave Epictetus's manual, and Marcus Aurelius' *Meditations*. While these ancient books still had relevant advice on how to be happy, my reading list needed updating to include the latest findings from psychologists, scientists and bestselling authors in the field of happiness, on the off chance that someone had something new to say about happiness in the last two thousand years. Which brings me to an important point:

Why would you read this book when you could read one of the other highly-acclaimed, happiness bestsellers like *Flow, Flourish, How Pleasure Works, The Happiness Hypothesis, The How of Happiness, The Secret, Authentic Happiness, The Happiness Project, Stumbling on Happiness, or, Stop Thinking, Start Living?*

What this book has that these others do not, is the direct experience of the exercise that strengthens your happiness. Dan Gilbert is open about the limitations of his book, *Stumbling on Happiness*, and he makes them clear in his preface: 'this is not an instruction manual that will tell you anything useful about how to be happy'. *The Happiness Animal* will tell you everything useful about how to be happy. Here, I take the latest psychology and scientific research on happiness, and support my own work with the core ideas presented in the abovementioned books. Although each of these books has its own unique angle, insights, and discoveries of science and psychology, no book fully captures the importance of exercise. My approach to writing *The Happiness Animal* is to create the only book you will ever need to exercise happiness. If you've ever had any of the below thoughts, your Happiness Animal's muscles will benefit from some exercise:

1. If I had more time, I'd be happier
2. If I had more money, I'd be happier
3. If I had a new job, I'd be happier
4. If only I could get ___ or ___ I would be happier (fill in the blanks)
5. I am tired of feeling dissatisfied after, or at the time of, things I consider pleasures
6. I could be happier
7. I am unhappy, at least sometimes
8. I want to feel more alive
9. I used to feel more alive
10. Expectation is the mother of my disappointment

If you answered yes to one or more of the above, then keep reading. Of course, if you're happy all the time, then stop reading. Here. But if you've had things, events, holidays, or people, which you thought would make you happy, but didn't, then keep reading.

What I quickly discovered when I introduced the exercises - first to those I knew, then to my happiness training clients and then, to the thousands of others online around the world - is that what makes people happier is universal. It is universal that all people, regardless of their taste, class, country or background, see the same two images when they look at the below. Some see a vase first, and some see two faces first, but all people can see both faces and a vase.

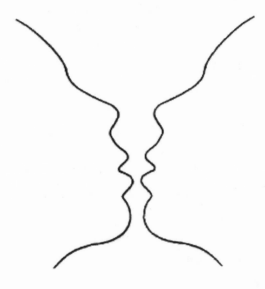

It is universal that human beings are born with two eyes, two ears, and one nose, and it is universal that human beings are born with a Happiness Animal. The origin of the word Animal is 'Anima', which means 'spirit'. What is also universal about this spirit, this Happiness Animal, is that everyone can exercise exactly the same five muscles to make it strong.

What's the name of the exercise?

When I was thinking of a name for the exercise, I decided it should give you an immediate understanding of what you do and how it makes you feel. Let's start with how the exercise makes you feel: it does the opposite of demoralizing you. But in the English language there isn't really an exact opposite of the word demoralizing. If you take off the negative 'de' part of the word you are left with moralizing, but when you look up moralizing in a dictionary it gives you the following definitions:

1. Comment on issues of right and wrong, typically with an unfounded air of superiority.

2. Interpret or explain as giving lessons on good and bad character and conduct.

Interestingly, neither of these definitions mean the opposite of demoralizing, and chances are you wouldn't want to read my book if I had 'an unfounded air of superiority'. That's not the look I am going for. Moralizing turns out to be demoralizing in every sense. I needed a new word. So I asked the question, other than making your Happiness Animal stronger, what is the other key benefit of this exercise? The answer is the same for this exercise as it is for physical exercise: you feel more alive. So, with a remit of creating a name that both evokes the opposite of demoralizing, and the feeling of being more alive, I created moralive®.

OK Jelbert, so you've written the book on how to exercise happiness but do you practice what you preach, and are you happy?

I think the most important credential I have is that I am happy, most of the time. The second most important credential I have is that what I have written in this book has worked for me personally. Before I was able to help anyone else I had to help myself. Writing this book was the most logical way for me to create a reference guide for my own happiness. When I was done resolving my own Happiness Animal's issues, I began to notice, to varying degrees, that my personal problem – that was not a mental illness but more a feeling of being stuck and languishing in life – was something that I had had in common with all my family, friends, co-workers and most other people I met.

I started running personal training for happiness sessions. My clients confirmed that the exercises strengthened their spirit, their Happiness Animal, and with the help of my clients I was able to tweak the exercises for the best possible workout of each of the five Happiness Animal's muscles. And the results I started getting from my clients blew me away. Some of my clients were coming to me with more than just a languishing dissatisfaction. Some were just plain unhappy. When one of my clients, Jamie, first came to me, she was suffering from minor depression, anxiety, obsessive compulsive disorder and paranoia. This was her feedback after a few sessions of exercising her Happiness Animal: 'Years of chronic illness have severely affected me physically, emotionally, and spiritually. One day I felt compelled to search for something, anything, to help me rediscover my carefree, once happy, confident self. I was led to Will. After meeting with Will a few times for one-to-one sessions, I feel like 'my inner self' has awoken from a long sleep! I am so grateful to him for using his Happiness Animal to help others!' I immediately knew that it was my responsibility to share the benefits of *The Happiness Animal* with as many people as possible.

And so you begin…

You don't have to be serious, to be serious about being happy. But if you're curious, read on and give your Happiness Animal a workout.

Part I – What you think makes you happy (but doesn't)

Chapter 2

What you think makes you happy (but doesn't)

If sensuality were happiness, beasts were happier than men; but
human happiness is lodged in the soul, not in the flesh

Seneca

Animal's Anecdote
The hotel room

Ko had booked the suite at the Royal Clarence Hotel, imagining the two of them in bed together again. He had ordered Dom Peringon to be delivered an hour after Charlotte's arrival. He wanted to impress her with the best the hotel had to offer. Lounging nude on the suite's sofa, or bending her over the mahogany desk. What Ko had imagined, had obscured the reality that he now had a girlfriend. Imagination had also blocked the fact that Charlotte had a boyfriend, and that Ko and Charlotte's relationship had been nothing more than extroverted friendship for the last year. But the idea still attracted Ko: the idea of sleeping with a twenty-two-year-old opera-singer, the idea of sleeping with a model, the idea of sleeping with a soprano.

Ko swiped his key-card and opened the door to his suite. He saw a bed, and a bath. Where was the desk? Where was the sofa? The room was tiny. At least the view was good. Exeter Cathedral filled both his windows. He pulled open one of this sashed windows, bent his neck down and poked his head outside: Straight ahead, above the green, Ko looked into the full body of the Cathedral. Below, in the cafes of the yard, he heard cups clink as they slid on saucers. Ko wanted coffee. Ko's phone pinged it's notifier for a new email. He looked at the screen and saw it was a message from his bank, warning him that he had exceeded his overdraft limit and would be charged a fee next month.

Ko pulled his head back inside and looked at his room's floor, which sloped down into one corner as if the room was sliding into the wall.   Ko viewed the subsidence more as dilapidation and less as charm. He was paying three hundred pounds a night and expected to pay at least two hundred pounds for dinner at the Michelin starred restaurant, Michael Caine's, downstairs. 'Michael Caine doesn't give a shit about this hotel,' said Ko. He looked at the 1990's grey plastic box straining at its black-metal wall-fixing: the pre flat-screen, seventeen inch television, which stuck out from the wall more than the size of its screen could justify. Ko searched for the remote control with a pained expression, pacing the room, opening the drawers and checking the cupboards, his Sesame Street eyebrows pinching his nose. 'What the fuck,' he said, when he realized he'd already been looking for ten minutes. When he found the remote control and pushed its buttons, which were sticky from accumulated snack residue, he was only able to click through five channels and the reception was poor. The tiny TV was a disappointment. Ko sat on the bed that filled the room like a marshmallow filled a shot glass. He wanted the bed to marshmallow him. It had nothing on the four-thousand-dollar King size that he used to sleep on in his waterfront apartment in Sydney; the bed he sold to his ex-girlfriend, Cynthia, when he moved out, and the same bed that the salesman had told him had been bought by former Miss Universe, Jennifer Hawkins. The suite bed disappointed. He missed his bed, but Cynthia he craved. Ko began rustling through the complimentary basket of local products that the hotel provided. He munched nuts, crisps, chocolates, and he moderated his dissatisfaction. He did not moderate his eating, as the hands of his Tag watch approached 4 o'clock. Ko washed off the chip's flavour-you-can-see from around his lips, and applied a fingertip of matt paste to his hair. He felt only half-satisfied with his appearance but the time to tweak it any further had passed. He had to run to the station.

Charlotte was visible a hundred metres away from the entrance to the train station. She wore Jackie Kennedy Onassis sunglasses and a faux fur coat, and her bouffant dominated high above her pursed, glossed, lips. Her pose imposed on Ko. And he admired her look, admired the Jackie O's, even if she neither intoxicated him, nor sent signals to his horn.

'Charlotte. Great to see you,' said Ko.

Charlotte and Ko took a taxi back to the hotel, where Ko carried her over-packed bag into his suite. Charlotte's eyes widened as she noticed Ko's suitcase next to hers on the floor.

'There's only one bed? Is this my room?' asked Charlotte.

'Yes – no, sorry. I've already asked at reception. I booked a suite with twin beds so they must have made a mistake. I'm still waiting to hear back. They said they'd call me but I'll go down and ask now,' said Ko, shuffling his feet back and forth around a semi-circle on the floor.

Charlotte followed him downstairs to reception, ever present, like the examiner in a driving test.

'Sorry, I'm in suite 24, and I thought I'd booked a suite with twin beds?' said Ko.

'I'm sorry for any confusion Mr Ko, but all of our suites are King Bed only,' said the receptionist.

'Are there no twin rooms in the hotel at all?' asked Ko.

'The hotel does offer family rooms but unfortunately, all our family rooms are fully booked this weekend'

'Can I book a separate suite for Charlotte?' asked Ko, 'we are not a couple, that's why I booked a twin suite,' he added. Charlotte may have been a better actor than Ko. Ko was a better liar.

'We do have one of our comfortable rooms available Mr Ko', said the receptionist.

'I'll take it'. Ko's mouth was a straight line. He had stopped blinking.

'Will you be settling the account for the additional room with the same credit card we have on file for you Mr Ko?'

Ko felt pretence crushing him. This was a cash blow on an excess and, he had just resigned from his only source of income. He no longer had a job. It frightened him. Ko felt a tightening wrap the band of his face that glasses would have covered, but Ko didn't think he needed glasses.

Animal Analysis

What you think will make you happy, often, is different from what will make you happy. That's the crux of this chapter. Before you can exercise your Happiness Animal, you first need to accept that what you think will make you happy, won't. Why was Ko unhappy at the hotel? It was because he didn't get what he thought he wanted. But also, when Ko got the things he wanted, he didn't want them anymore. They were not what he expected them to be. What Ko got did not make Ko happy.

Your first instruction of the book

Before you move to chapter three, your first instruction is: **use this chapter to clean your slate.** Your journey through the remainder of this book will be made easier if you first wipe off the following happiness myths:

- **Ko's myth no. 1: Money will make you happy**: There is a common theme in Ko's anecdote that life will be better if he spends a lot of money on things like the suite, or a four thousand dollar bed. Loss of money through unexpected spending triggers negative thoughts: the 'cash blow' of having to buy the extra room for Charlotte. Ko thinks his credit card and his buying power are important to his happiness and Ko is not alone. In a survey published in the American Economic Review in 2011, 2,699 participants were asked to consider the following scenario: Either choosing a job that paid US $80,000 a year with good working hours and a full night of sleep, or, choosing a US $140,000-a-year job with long working hours and only six hours of sleep. Most participants chose the higher-paying job. What would you choose? How much money do you need? How much money is enough? You need money, but studies conducted by Stanford and Harvard Universities, have shown that once you meet a threshold that covers your basic needs, more money beyond that threshold will not make you any happier. According to Harvard Professor Dan Gilbert (the bestselling author of *Stumbling on Happiness*) the threshold in the USA is US $40,000. Cost of living varies by location, but the point is that once you cover basic needs, any increase in your cash levels will not have an impact on your happiness. So why do most of us pursue more? The founder of Positive Psychology, Martin Seligman explains that we might believe we are better off with more money but the reality is that more money won't impact our happiness: 'The truth is that your judgment that your circumstances are better goes up with income, but not your spirits.' What's the point of 'better circumstances' if you don't feel any happier? During the researching of this book I used up all my savings, maxed out my three credit cards, had to sell my kayak, my watch, my coffee machine to pay the bills. Finally I believed that if I sold my house and got the money from that, that I'd feel happier. I sold the house, paid off my debts and had enough money to finish the writing of the book. Paying off my debts did mean that I had less to worry about, and it solved a problem, but getting the lump sum of cash itself didn't make an ounce of difference to the strength of my happiness (Animal).

- **Ko's myth no. 2: Things will make you happy:** Ko's desire for a sofa and desire for a desk is created by thoughts that these things in themselves will make his life better. But, according to many studies and experts in the field of happiness, including

Oddly Enough – winning the lottery won't make you happier
In studies, lottery winners, a year after winning are no happier than a control group of people who did not win.

University of Illinois psychologist, Ed Diener, 'materialism is toxic for happiness'. Studies show that an increase in material wealth and goods in America has had no effect on the wellbeing and happiness of its people. Using two measures of subjective happiness, a study by W.B. Russell in *Advances in Consumer Research*, found that materialism is actually negatively related to happiness i.e. the more materialistic you are, the less happy you are. Another study published in the Journal of Consumer Research demonstrated that people who believe that acquiring material possessions (such as buying a house) is an important life goal, have lower life satisfaction scores. What is more sinister, materialism correlates with serious psychological issues such as depression, narcissism and paranoia, a correlation exposed by researchers Kasser and Ryan, who published their findings in *A dark side of the American Dream*.

- **Ko's myth no. 3: Luxury and Comfort will make you happy:** Ko doesn't just want a hotel bed. He

Time to Define:
Enjoyment vs. Happiness
Enjoyment is a momentary feeling and almost always is triggered or stimulated by something external through one of the five senses. Enjoyment is closer to pleasure than to happiness. The Oxford Dictionary defines enjoyment as: *[mass noun]*
- **1** the state or process of taking pleasure in something: *the enjoyment of a good wine [count noun]* a thing that gives pleasure: *one of his particular enjoyments was campfire singing*
- **2** the action of possessing and benefiting from something.
Happiness is an internally created emotion, and can be independent of what is external. Happiness is eudaimonistic. Literally translated from the Greek eudaimonistic means 'of good spirit'. Eudaimonia is still used to this day in Greece as the word for happiness.

wants a bed that marshmallows him. Ko reacts negatively because the television channels have poor quality reception. Ko wants perfection. But, luxury, comfort and quality do not make you happy. First they make you comfortable, and then they make you bored. Chasing

> **What about health?**
> There are no myths about health in *The Happiness Animal.* That's because health and exercise have an important role that you will read about in part II

luxury, comfort and quality amounts to nothing more than chasing the material. Of course, there are some bare necessities of human existence – the kind of physiological needs represented in Abraham Maslow's hierarchy of needs: you don't want to be too hot, cold, tired, thirsty, hungry or in pain. But being at just the right temperature does not strengthen your Happiness Animal's muscles. When I moved to the USA I thought I'd be happier doing my research by the swimming pool, lying back in a sun lounger. Rather than feeling happier, what I felt was emptiness in the distraction. It wasn't supporting my purpose.

> **What's love got to do with it?**
> You may be wondering where's the myth about love? Ko craves Cynthia, and crave, was the strongest emotion of the anecdote, the strongest amount of unfulfilled want. Craving someone is not the same as loving someone. We will take a closer look at love in Chapter 9.

- **Ko's myth no. 4: Appearances will make you happy:** Ko is attracted to the idea of Charlotte's model looks, and her pursed, glossed lips. He also attaches value to Charlotte's imitation of looks, from Jackie O' sunglasses to a coat that imitates the look of fur. As far as height goes, Ko thinks more is better: the bouffant maximizes Charlotte's visual impact. But are a tall body and a pretty face a source of happiness for either holder or beholder? Is appearance linked to happiness? The USA is the number one country in the world for total spent on cosmetic, appearance enhancing products (skincare, makeup, toiletries and hair care). But according to the Satisfaction With Life Index

(SWLI), the USA is ranked only 23rd in the world. Japan, the second biggest spender on cosmetic beauty products is one of the lowest ranked countries in the world (ranked 90th against the SWLI). What is more notable is that the two countries with the lowest spending on cosmetics – the Netherlands and Sweden – have two of the highest SWLI rankings (7th and 15th respectively).

- **Ko's myth no. 5: More time will make you happy**: Ko took more time than he had anticipated finding the remote control. He wanted more time so he could apply the finishing touches to his hair. Ko does like to be busy but busy conflicts with a desire for more time. There is a fine line between occupied, and pre-occupied. Neither one makes you happy, and nor does having time to kill. The fact is you can't increase the amount of time you have in this world. But you can exercise awareness and moderation in how you use your time. As you will experience in chapter 8, it is how you use your time and how you exercise awareness of your time – and not how much time you have – that has an impact on your happiness. Having more time could actually make you unhappier, depending on how you use that time. Research by Wharton Professor, Cassie Mogilner has proven a paradox that destroys the myth that more time will make you happier: The paradox is that the more time you 'give away' to the people you care about, the more time affluent and the less rushed you feel.

- **Ko's myth no. 6: Your job will make you happy:** Having just resigned, Ko has lost confidence in his actions. Why then, did Ko resign from his job? Why would you resign? According to the founder of Brazen Careerist, Penelope Trunk, whose career advice runs in two hundred newspapers globally, the capacity of your job to make you happy is small, but that it isn't a reason to quit working. Trunk not only says that if you have a positive outlook, you will make the best of any job, but also, that you don't need to depend on your job to give your life a greater sense of meaning.

What I personally discovered was that my happiness at work could be strengthened by improving my relationships at work, more than by the work itself. True, you can enjoy some jobs more than others: if you find a job where your skills match and evolve with the challenges that you face, you are more likely to find yourself working in 'Flow'. Mihaly Csikszentmihalyi has written an entire book on the subject. 'Flow' happens somewhere in between stress (anxiety) and boredom. It happens when you feel challenged but not so challenged that you become overwhelmed. To enjoy your job, and find flow you need to feel that you are able to meet the new challenges. The enjoyment happens when you become so immersed in the activity that you forget about – or lose – your self. If you can find 'flow' in any job you are almost guaranteed to enjoy it, but enjoyment is not the same as happiness. As we will discover in chapter 5, it's more the dropping of the self, or more specifically the dropping of your ego, which is linked to an improvement in the health of your Happiness Animal, than is your job.

- **Ko's myth no. 7: Location, location, location will make you happy:** Ko's view is that the better his hotel room, the better his time with Charlotte will be. What matter to Ko are the location and the view: opposite Exeter Cathedral, above the cafés and the green. Beautiful surroundings bring pleasure, yes, but is that pleasure happiness, or is it distraction from what is, or what isn't, inside? As Professor Dan Gilbert writes in *Stumbling on Happiness,* many Americans believe that moving to California will make them happier. But it has been proven by Nobel prize winning psychologist, Daniel Kahneman that Californians are no happier than anyone else. When I was alone in Hawaii or Sydney Harbour with a balcony overlooking the ocean, I was often more anxious than happy. If you think a lot about problems, you'll still think a lot about problems wherever you are until you are able to find freedom from being a passenger on your trains of thoughts, and until you are able to start driving the trains. That's why there is a whole chapter in this book dedicated to exercising awareness (chapter 8).

- **Ko's myth no. 8: Prestige, fame will make you happy:** Ko chose Michael Caine's 'Royal' Clarence Hotel for a reason. When Ko read that the restaurant was Michelin-starred, his thoughts associated with other thoughts of prestige, and his desire to eat there increased. Buildings, homes, restaurants, hotels, all have their own prestige attachments. Why would Ko stay in a room with a view of a house when he can stay in a suite with a view of a Cathedral? Ko wanted to buy the same bed that Jennifer Hawkins had bought from the same store. Ko is attracted to the idea of Charlotte, the idea of an opera singer, of a soprano, because of the associated prestige but does association with prestige make you any happier? One of the most quoted American writers in history, William Arthur Ward, says no:

Oddly Enough: Internal happiness with external furniture
'The more we seek satisfaction in material goods, the less we find them there' says Richard Ryan, professor of psychology at the University of Rochester.

'Greatness is not found in possessions, power, position, or prestige. It is discovered in goodness, humility, service, and character'. Philosopher Jim Spiegel also believes that prestige and fame are negatively correlated with happiness. Spiegel calls the American celebrity machine 'a soul-eating monster'. Prestige and fame are not good for the health of your Happiness Animal, but associating with (or attempting to associate with) people of prestige can be even unhealthier for your Happiness Animal. And since 2007, with the advent of social media, unhealthy associations have gone viral. A study by Utah Valley University found that pictures of smiling faces which Facebook users tend to plaster over their pages, cumulatively convey a debilitating message to others. The more perceived prestige, the more demoralizing your association with the Facebook friend can be. This post-Facebook dissatisfaction is caused by a psychological phenomenon known as 'correspondence bias', in which we draw false conclusions about people based on limited knowledge. According to researcher Ms Chou of Utah Valley University, 'looking at happy pictures of others on Facebook gives people an impression that others are "always" happy and having good lives'. Comparing yourself to the imagined lives behind the 'picture perfect' images often leads to an injured ego, and thoughts (and then feelings) of envy and jealousy, both of which demoralize the Happiness Animal.

Time to Define: **Pleasure vs. Happiness**

Pleasure is a momentary feeling and almost always is triggered or stimulated by something external through one of the five senses. Pleasure is hedonistic in that it is sensually self-indulgent.

Happiness is an internally created emotion, which has less to do with self-indulgence and more to do with connection with existence, and more specifically connection to others. Happiness is eudaimonistic (of good spirit).

Your own happiness myths

It's a good warm up exercise to notice and accept what your own happiness beliefs are before we move any further into the book.

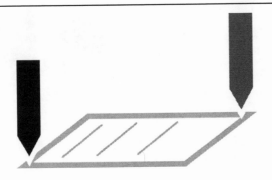

Pens with benefits

Your benefit: You will use this list again when you reach the end of the book. The list will give you your own reference point of how happy you think you are now vs. later.

Instructions

Use the space below to make a list of the top five things that, if you got them, would make you happier than you are now. Take no more than two minutes.

1. _____

2. _____

3. _____

4. _____

5. _____

Look at your list and decide the following: Are your top 5 internal (i.e. non-material, non-monetary, non-physical), or are they external? Start with a total of 100% and deduct 20% for each of your answers that relate to getting something external. What % are you left with? Your thinking is_____% happy (enter your % in the gap). OK, it's a very simple illustration, but it is important to be aware of how much you are currently looking to external dependencies for happiness. Here's why: happiness is an internal emotion and trying to build happiness externally is like going to IKEA, walking around all the display-

Phone a friend:
Ask a friend to give you their top five things that would make them happier. Do you see any similarities with your own answers? Are their answers more external or more internal?

rooms (with a break for meatballs), to buy things with a short pencil and fill a truck with furniture that you won't even be able bring inside your home. The only home you'll find happiness in, is in your Happiness Animal, your being, your spirit. Don't worry if right now your thinking is not focused on happiness internally. You are not alone. I ran a global online survey and asked five thousand people, what one thing would make them happier. The breakdown of what they said would make them happier appears in the following chart:

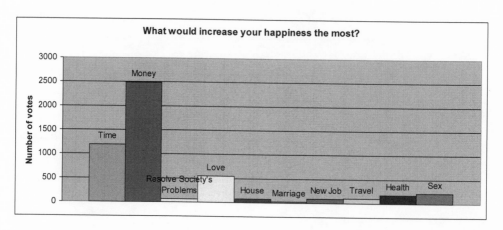

While it is encouraging that some think there is happiness to be gained by helping others (resolving society's problems), they represent a low number of responses: only 1%. Moreover, the majority of those polled say the top two things that they think would make them happier are:

1. More money (50%)
2. More time (24%)

There was, however, one person who told me that there are no things that could make her happier. Nothing. She was the exception, but is the majority always right?

Getting what you want is what you want?

The saying 'be careful what you wish for' exists for a reason. What Ko thinks he will want before he arrives at the hotel, is different to what he wants when he arrives at the hotel. By the uncomfortable conclusion at the hotel reception desk, Ko would have preferred to not be at the hotel at all. The reason for Ko's mismatch between expectations and reality is that you cannot accurately predict what you will feel or want, regardless of whether that's in a future that is five hours or five years away. Yet we all think we can predict what our feelings and desires will be. These predictions are what psychologists call 'Affective Forecasting'.

Expectation lays the disappointment egg

What came first, the expectation or the disappointment? If your expectations are not met with what you thought you wanted, then you'd be normal if you felt something other than happiness. Ko expected to find a desk and a sofa in his suite. When he opened the door, he cracked the egg and out popped disappointment, all bones and no feathers. When things don't live up to your expectation, it can be worse than not getting what you want. All expectations need conditions – even if you expect it to be sunny today, being sunny is the condition – and a good rule of thumb about conditions of happiness is as follows:

If you give conditions to what you want, then what you want will not make you happy. If you have to say 'if' to happiness, the answer is no.

The experiences and material things in Ko's anecdote have brought him the opposite of happiness. First, there is regret and then there is fear. Whether to gain material things, or to gain experiences that depend on material things, Ko has had to make financial sacrifices, financial losses. The things Ko bought gave him feelings of buyer's remorse, and remorse had an impact on Ko's self esteem as well as creating physical anxiety in the tightening around his head. Would it have made Ko happier if he had focused less on increasing what he had, and focused more on decreasing what he wanted? It is clear by the conclusion of Ko's hotel room dilemma, that he is feeling something other than happiness. In moments, the lie about the room, the lie about his intentions with Charlotte, and the subsequent avoidance of the truth, exercised Ko's muscle for anxiety, and destroyed his peace of mind. Ko acted on thoughts of desire for external things and external pleasures, and started a battle that turned peace of mind into war of mind. The result was a demoralized and unhealthy Happiness Animal.

Time to Define: **Affective Forecasting** is predicting how you will feel (and react to things, people, events) in the future. Most of the time we make affective forecasting errors. It happens for 3 reasons:

1. Faulty memory: You often remember things as making you happy when, if you had been asked at the time, you might not have felt happy.
2. Your future happiness depends less on the present than you think.
3. Affective forecasting is controlled by the newest part of the brain (frontal lobe), a recent addition in the context of human evolution and, is still evolving.

When you say you wish you'd ordered the salmon instead of the steak, when you wish you hadn't bought that muffin, it's your affective forecasting, in error: you don't want what you thought you would want.

Oddly Enough: Barbara Houseman, director and coach to actors (including Joseph Fiennes and Kenneth Branagh) says one of the fastest ways to bring about change is paradoxically, to stop trying to change anything. But simply be aware of what you are doing and notice unhelpful habits and this awareness alone will set in motion a change.

- What you think will make you happy, is not the same as what will make you happy.

- You cannot create internal happiness with external furniture.

- If you have to say 'if' to happiness, the answer is no.

- External pursuits can turn peace of mind into war of mind.

- The things you think will make you happy change. You will discover that what does make you happy is universally consistent.

Coming Up Next...in Chapter Three

You will take a look at what makes you think, to answer the question: Why do you think things will make you happy?

Chapter 3

Why do you think things will make

you happy?

(if they don't)

We are born for happiness but not with happiness

Seneca

Because human beings were shaped by evolutionary processes to pursue success, not happiness, people enthusiastically pursue goals that will help them win prestige. Success in these competitions feels good but gives no lasting pleasure.

Jonathan Haidt

Animal's Anecdote

From fried chicken to divorce, I got my education

It is nine years before Ko met Charlotte. Ko is sitting to the right of his friend and colleague Gareth, at a table of fourteen people at the Waterside Meadery Restaurant in Penzance, a small town in the toe of Cornwall, on the foot of England, kicking the Atlantic. Ko tears off a piece of crispy skinned, deep fried chicken breast and a snail trail of fat runs over the edge, the ulnar border, of his hand.

Too hot to eat, he thinks. *But the skin's so crispy and the meat's so juicy and it smells so bloody good.*

'Happy Birthday G,' Ko says to Gareth as he cheers him with a glass of Cornish mead. He downs the glass of mead and then pours another from the communal bottle. 'You ready to get air tomorrow?' Gareth asks Ko. Gareth has recently become Ko's companion on his now almost daily, after-work kite buggying outings to the park near the pub where they spend many weeknights and weekends sitting by the canal with beers and live music, after a couple of hours of getting dragged around the grass in a three wheeled buggy by a giant kite. Over the past three summer months, Ko's arm muscles have almost doubled in size from the kiting. It is 2001 and kite surfing and kite buggying are still new sports. Ko, in his early twenties, thinks that if he keeps practicing every day he'll soon be good enough to become a serious competitor. Moreover harnessing the power of nature for a thrill ride has been giving him more daily enjoyment than he can remember.

As Ko gets stuck into the meal he feels the mead's warm anaesthetic run through his neck, his forehead, and his back. He feels his stomach ballooning, reducing his lung space.

I'm getting full, he thinks, licking fat from his fingers.

He looks at the people he's sharing the table with: some are mutual work colleagues and friends of Gareth and Ko, some Gareth's casual love interests. He looks up from his plate, and through the dim cavern of the restaurant he sees the smiling eyes of a woman, lighthouses blinking at his eyes. She is sitting at a table with her parents, but Ko only sees her.

Gareth notices who Ko is looking at, and sees her smiling back at Ko. 'That's Rachelle. Her brother's PJ – you know PJ from school. She was in the year down from us,' says Gareth.

Gareth waves and smiles at Rachelle and Ko follows Gareth's lead, releasing his slippery clutch on a wave.

'I'll introduce you mate,' says Gareth.

'Really? You're friends?' says Ko.

'Let's go clubbing,' shouts Gareth.

Gareth's group screech their chairs back on the wooden floor, get up, and shuffle with banter and jibes towards the door. Gareth steps closer to Rachelle's table with Ko a couple of metres in tow, his eyes directed at Rachelle's, blinking back.

'Rach! You have to come out with us, it's my birthday,' shouts Gareth.

Rachelle laughs and looks at her parents.

'Is it ok if I go with them?' Rachelle asks her mother.

When the group exits onto the street, Ko moves closer to Rachelle and introduces himself. Ko feels freed, by mead, from inhibitions.

'So you've just graduated? Congratulations. What did you study?' asks Ko.

'French and German,' Rachelle says.

'So did I. Where are you living?' asks Ko.

'At the moment I'm staying on the farm with Mum and Dad.'

'Your parents are farmers as well? They might know my parents or my grandparents.'

Ko smiles at Rachelle and Rachelle smiles back as they walk up the street behind the rest of the group.

'Do you have a job lined up now you've finished Uni?' Ko asks.

'No, but I need to find one soon. Gareth mentioned that you two work together,' says Rachelle. Her eyes widen, pausing position, for the play of Ko's response.

'Yes, I got G a job and I got a referral bonus for introducing him.'

'Ah, so that's the real reason he's keen to get me a job, I see,' says Rachelle.

'And at the moment we do have a German speaking vacancy,' says Ko. They take the bus to the nightclub on the other side of town and they aren't long inside the club's lounge before Ko pulls up a stool next to Rachelle and clinks his glass against hers.

'Don't forget the eye contact,' Ko says. The words come out of his smile, quickly and firmly. His hand slides across the table, steadily yet lightly over the top of hers; he checks her expression, her smile remains; he stands up, and still holding the top of her hand, steps around to his left, leans forward, lowers his head towards hers, and kisses her opening lips. 'What are you doing tomorrow?' asks Rachelle.

One month later Rachelle has an interview at Ko's workplace in Devon. Ko offers Rachelle the spare room in his apartment for the night before her interview. The spare room remains spare, but Rachelle gets the job. From the day Rachelle starts at work, Rachelle and Ko spend every night together. They stop going out as much, staying in to watch episodes of *Grand Designs* and *Location, Location, Location*.

'That place is seriously cheap. We could get a run down cottage, give it a coat of paint, and make some money,' Rachelle says.

'I got a letter from HSBC last week. I have a graduate account with them, so they'll give me a hundred percent mortgage. We wouldn't even need a deposit,' says Ko.

'I saw an advert in the Express & Echo. HSBC say they'll beat any other mortgage by half a percent,' Rachelle says.

'That's a big saving,' Ko says.

The next day on their lunch break they walk past an estate agents' window on their way to the deli to buy sandwiches.

'No harm in looking, I suppose,' says Ko.

'Look at this place in Tiverton - it's only ninety thousand. We could get a mortgage for ninety thousand,' says Rachelle.

'Why don't we have a look?' says Ko.

On Saturday morning, Ko and Rachelle are the second couple to arrive at the viewing. The first couple know the estate agent, and have already made an offer before Rachelle and Ko finish looking.

'That place was perfect for us,' says Ko.

'Yes, I'm gutted. I can't believe how fast you need to move on places. I guess we can't really mess around too much,' says Rachelle.

'Let's have a look at the little cottage between Tiverton and Exeter. That was cheaper,' says Ko

'Call home first and see what our parents think,' Rachelle says. 'Anyway I'm not sure if they'd be too keen on the idea of us living together before marriage.'

'You both have our full support in whatever you want to do,' says Rachelle's mum.

Three weeks later Ko carries Rachelle across the threshold of their new house. Ko pulls out a bottle of champagne and then runs upstairs. When he comes back down, Rachelle sees an unfamiliar look in his eyes, the look of a boatman waiting for the anchor he's dropped to stop slipping, drifting, and catch. Rachelle is sitting on one of their new Ikea chairs as Ko puts his hands down on the floor and kneels.

'Rachelle, I know we've only been together for a few months but will you marry me?'

Rachelle's 'yes' is a sob, a laugh and a sigh. She cries across her smile. 'I have to tell Mum,' she says.

Saturday, the next morning, they go into Exeter city centre, to the newsagent, WH SMITH, where every bridal magazine catches Rachelle by the eyes. Rachelle clutches gloss while Ko shuffles behind wondering both what he has ignited in Rachelle, and why he isn't of the same tinder. When they get back to their house, Rachelle begins scrap-booking photos of table designs and dresses, while Ko feigns curiosity, enthused only by the Pritt Sticked images of beautiful women. He is mid-way through a copy of Cornish Brides magazine when he spots a 'Wedding of the Year' competition. 'Rach, look. We could win this. Almost everything except the reception is paid for and we'd be in the magazine just for entering the competition,' Ko says.

Rachelle's mum takes photographs of them kissing in the straw barn. They submit their entry and all they have to do is get the most votes based on their photographs and the story of their romance. As soon as the magazine comes out with the phone number for Ko and Rachelle, the couple sends an email to the hundreds of employees at their office. Rachelle and Ko are counting on their votes. Ko and Rachelle accrue a phone bill seven times higher than normal, but they win the competition and are announced by the local MP at a gala dinner. It is after the prize-giving that the full details – and the full limitations – of prizes are revealed: the specific wedding cake supplier, the dresses, the suits, the photographer, the wedding cars and, the wedding planner, who also happens to own the dress shop.

'She's really pissing me off. She keeps changing what I want,' says Rachelle. 'I wish you hadn't been such a cheapskate and entered this bloody competition in the first place,' says Rachelle. Eighteen months after they first met over fried chicken, they are back in Penzance to marry. A week after their honeymoon, Ko waits until Rachelle has fallen asleep next to him in their bed, and then creeps out. It's 10 pm on Wednesday night. He picks up his jeans and buttons up his work shirt, unlatches the front door and runs across the road into the warm babble of the village regulars, who smoke into the vapours of the Castle pub.

'Look out. Ko's back,' says the landlord.
'Two pints of Stella please John,' says Ko.

'Who's the second one for then Ko?' asks the landlord.

'No point in ordering twice, is there?' says Ko.

He picks up one of the glasses of beer and downs it in six seconds. And then starts on the second.

'Another two?'

'Yes please,' says Ko.

Six pints and an hour and a half later, his thoughts are reduced to how he crosses the road and how he slips back into bed. Rachelle mutters something unintelligible to Ko and then they both fall asleep.

The next evening, Ko and Rachelle are watching *a place in the sun* on TV.

'I wish we could live in Australia, but now we're tied to the house and we have to think about our jobs,' says Rachelle.

'Yes but we could rent the house out. We did when we were in India,' says Ko.

Two days later Ko emails the manager of the Sydney office. Based on their respective work experience, not only Ko, but also Rachelle, is offered a job and a relocation package and by April 2006, they find themselves at desks in Sydney.

'You guys coming out for the leaving drinks at Metro tonight?' asks Grant, one of Ko and Rachelle's new colleagues.

'Yes, great,' says Ko.

Ko joins the party late to find Rachelle at a table with a group of twenty-somethings, huddled together in laughter and mischief eyes.

Ko's eyebrows furrow his forehead.

'Can I get a pint of Coopers Red and two tequila shots,' says Ko to the bartender. Ko downs the three drinks, and behind the huddles of other groups, no one notices.

It's December and a summer night in Sydney and Ko and Rachelle are on their way home from work. At circular quay the QE2 is arriving as the Queen Victoria is leaving and Ko and Rachelle stare at the floating block of lights from their seats on the Mosman ferry.

'Can we go on a cruise this Christmas? I've always wanted to,' says Rachelle.

'But we said we would go up to Queensland to visit my cousins and do the road-trip over Christmas Rach. We've bought the four-wheel-drive now,' says Ko.

A cruise is too expensive and it's for old people, thinks Ko.

Day three of their drive north from Sydney and Rachelle's face is turned away from Ko as she stares out the window, fifteen kilometres into a four-wheel-drive track through the rainforest. A tear breaks the levee and darts across Rachelle's cheek, where it eventually slows to rest. 'I wish you had listened to me. You knew I wanted to go on a cruise. Instead we're being thrown around in a car all day in the middle of nowhere. This is hell. It's not a holiday. You never listen to me,' Rachelle says.

Ko feels trapped, trapped by his decision to drive at Christmas, trapped in the rainforest, trapped in the marriage. The thoughts of entrapment paralyse his voice box and his neck stiffens as pressure builds on his chest. 'I feel like I want to kill myself,' says Ko.

Two months later, Rachelle finds her own apartment and Ko helps her to move out.

'Do you think we should get divorced?' asks Ko, with a cup of tea in his hand, on one of his regular visits to Rachelle's new apartment.

'I don't know if we can in Australia?' asks Rachelle.

Later, while sitting on Rachelle's new Ikea sofa, Ko and Rachelle Google divorce on Rachelle's new laptop and find an online application form.

Animal Analysis

The question and title of this chapter is 'Why do you think things will make you happy?' but you need to shorten the question to widen your answer if you want to appreciate its full panorama. Remove the last four words and you are left with: 'Why do you think things?' In this chapter you will look at three reasons why you think things. The first reason is links, more specifically, the links between the things you think. From this point on in the book I will refer to these links between your thoughts as: 'thinking links'.

What are thinking links?
Thinking links connect one thought to the next. Thinking links are created by the order in which you receive information through your senses, which creates an association of one thought with the next thought. Thinking links are also created when new thoughts match thoughts with things in common from your memories. For example when you see two letters together on a packet of CC's chips and the CC matches the initials of someone you know, or someone you remember. Ko might have captured the following thinking links during his meal if he had written down his thoughts as they came to him in order: *This meat is juicy (touch tells me)> the chicken smells good (smell tells me)> this chicken is too hot to eat (touch tells me)> will have to wait before I can put the chicken in my mouth (memory tells me)> I need something else to do while I wait (memory tells me)> I am looking around (seeing tells me)> I see Gareth smiling (seeing tells me)> He's smiling because it's his Birthday party (memory tells me)> Time to cheers him (memory tells me)> I'll pick up my glass and aim to touch it against his> Drink> Meade feels warm> Warm > What's the temperature of the chicken now?> Feels cool enough to eat> Eat> Eat> I normally get food on myself when I eat> Is there grease on my face?> Better wipe it> Eat> I'm feeling full> Should I stop eating?>*

Yes, I will stop eating> I feel good> What now?> Will look around> Who's that woman over there on the other table smiling at me?> Smile

The more time that passes, the harder it can be to remember your thinking links, but often with timely retrospection it is possible, and it can help you to understand or even to troubleshoot why you have done things. Think about, for example, how you came to pick up this book today. What were you doing or thinking immediately prior to that action? And prior to that? Can you remember anything specific about what happened before you picked up the book? Something generated an attraction to the thought of picking up the book, even if you saw the book lying on the floor and it annoyed you, is it not still true that you were attracted to the idea of tidying which attracted you to the thought of picking it up? Whether you planned to read or were just tidying, one thought linked to the next and now you are here at the end of this sentence.

Gareth told Ko that Rachelle was a friend, so Ko associated Rachelle with friendship. Ko's conversation with Rachelle revealed that they had both recently graduated with French and German degrees. The degree was another thinking link that connected Ko to Rachelle. Through dialogue, they discovered that they had both gone to the same school. Another thinking link was created when Ko discovered Rachelle's parents were farmers, the same as Ko's parents. The impact of these links in quick succession was to create multiple common associations and connections with Rachelle in Ko's thoughts, and vice versa. They both felt immediately connected.

Who's in charge of my thinking links?

Your thinking links are controlled by attraction, and by association. Attraction creates new thinking links, and association links to pre-existing thinking links. What controls the attraction and association? Education, but education is not just what you learnt at school. Education is everything you have seen, heard, felt, tasted, smelt or remembered, and it is the order in which you have seen, heard, felt, tasted, smelt and remembered. Education is the sum of your thinking links. It influences your attraction to new thoughts, and to new thinking links, which in turn, associate with your education:

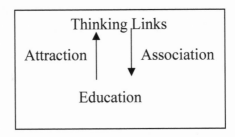

If Ko captured all the thinking links he created between the night at the restaurant and submitting the online divorce application, he could map out a chain of thinking links, associated actions, and the attraction that led from the fried chicken, not only to his marriage, but also to his divorce.

Got your education? Or did your education get you?
When it comes to thoughts you are what you eat. And what you eat is your mind diet, your education of life. This education of life is brought to you by the following food channels:

- **The senses:** everything you see, hear, touch, taste and smell, and the order in which you see, hear, touch, taste and smell. For example, Ko learning through touch and the subsequent sensation of pain, that if food is very hot, he does not put it in his mouth. 'Such collections of simple ideas as we have observed by our senses to be united together, do really exist together,' said the philosopher, John Locke. But education through the senses doesn't stop with the senses. The new thinking links from the senses interact with associated thinking links that you have already accumulated, and it's this interaction between old and new thinking links, that creates your current thinking model. We use, says Harvard Professor Dan Gilbert, 'a combination of sensory information and pre-existing knowledge to create our perception of reality'.

- **Formal Education**: When you say the word 'education' to anyone, there is a good chance they will think of schools and universities. Ko's degree in French and German taught him how to construct sentences (and thoughts) in other languages, but a lot of formal education is based on memorising, more specifically memorising information that's prescribed in the form of a course. Just as you rely on your doctor to prescribe medicines for a medical condition, you rely on professors and teachers to prescribe information for a learning condition; it could be a perceived or real condition to gain entry into, or progress within a career, a post-graduate degree programme, or the prescription required to get a certificate.

- **Education at leisure:** Whatever attracts your interest based on your existing education, and leads you to reading, watching or listening to things you associate with that attraction (including the very book you are reading at this moment).

- **Education by social proof (SP):** Wikipedia defines social proof as: 'a psychological phenomenon where people assume the actions of others reflect correct behaviour for a given scenario...and is driven by the assumption that surrounding people possess more knowledge about the situation.' Social proof, however, isn't restricted to observing behaviour in others and assuming that's the correct way you should behave. Social proof pervades through several channels, not all of which are visible or related to behaviour. It makes sense to expand the

Wikipedia definition to include the following channels through which social proof (SP) operates:

SP1. **Perceived opinions and beliefs of family and friends:** Rachelle imagines her parents' belief that Ko and her shouldn't live together until they are married, and as Rachelle gives voice to this belief, she creates a follow-on social proof feed into Ko's thoughts. Social proof is fed both by real beliefs and opinions that are expressed by others, and by imagined beliefs and opinions that are not expressed by others. There is an imagined belief that Rachelle's mum is against pre-marital co-habitation. The reality is that Rachelle's mum is in favour. When Rachelle's Mum expresses this support, Ko and Rachelle go ahead and buy a house together, but the social proof in Ko's imagination influences Ko to propose before they spend their first night in the house.

SP2. **Cultural and religious beliefs, traditions and rules:** Your beliefs stay alive when they go unquestioned and unchallenged. Some of these beliefs can be proven by psychologists as false or unhealthy,

Oddly Enough
Contrary to what Bill and Ted might say, Alexander Dumas was not a dumb ass. When he wasn't busy writing *The Three Musketeers* he asked the people of France an important question: Why is that while children are so intelligent, men are so stupid? The answer, he decided, is education.

You are weaker physically if your body is unhealthy due to diet, and lack of exercise, and you are of weaker spirit if your Happiness Animal is unhealthy due to mind diet and lack of exercise. Your mind diet is your education.

yet we don't question them. Nor do we question the system that perpetuates the beliefs. For example, the cultural belief that acquiring wealth, property and belongings through work will make us happier. Professor Gilbert says our belief is false, but it continues to exist because it benefits the economy: 'the production of wealth does not necessarily make individuals happy, but it does serve the needs of an economy, which serves the needs of a stable society, which serves as a network for the propagation of delusional beliefs about happiness and wealth. Economies thrive when individuals strive, but because the individual will only strive for their own happiness, it is essential that they mistakenly believe that producing and consuming are routes to personal well-being. False beliefs that happen to promote stable societies tend to propagate because people who hold these beliefs tend to live in stable societies, which provide the means by which false beliefs propagate.' Ko and Rachelle's cultural beliefs were that they 'should' accumulate wealth and 'should' buy their own house. But cultural beliefs are not limited to wealth and property: There are also – often unspoken – pervading cultural beliefs about differences between men and women. Gender stereotype beliefs may not seem like they are influencing you, but at a subconscious level they can even censor and influence your memories. This is what Dan Gilbert calls the 'stereotype proof of memories'. For example, in a study that asked participants to think about how they were feeling a few months earlier, when volunteers were prompted to think about their gender, female volunteers remembered feeling more intense emotion, and male volunteers remembered feeling less intense emotion. For the others in the survey who were not asked to think about their gender, both males and females reported feeling the same levels of emotion. Yet, when the concept of gender was introduced females recalled feeling more stereotypically feminine emotions like sympathy and guilt, and males recalled feeling more stereotypically masculine emotions like anger and pride.

SP3. **Media**:

> *Noun* **(**the media**)** the main means of mass communication (television, radio, and newspapers) regarded collectively.

You can add social media to the Oxford definition above: the media in which we are all journalists and editors of our own publications - publications read by our hundreds of friends or followers. But there is one medium that still holds more social proof power over Facebook: television. Television is a more trusted medium than the internet, mainly for the reason that it has been around for the length of most people's lives, whereas more than half of us still remember living pre-internet and pre-smartphone.

Media-reality feedback loop of thinking links

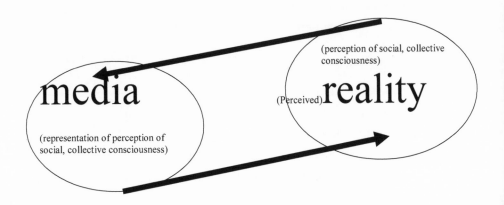

Almost everyone has access to a television, but not everyone has signed up to social media. The US Supreme Court states that 'broadcast media (has) established a uniquely pervasive presence in the lives of all Americans'. Both the Channel 4 show that Ko watched that glorified the home buying process, and the show that put a photo-shopped shine on what it's like to have a place in the sun, planted thoughts and associations in Ko and Rachelle that attracted them to buying a house, and to moving to another country. Similarly if things are presented in newspapers and magazines in an attractive way (focusing only on the positive attributes of a scene in a photograph , and excluding any negative surroundings such as scaffolding, traffic, heat, smells, humidity, and rowdy individuals) they have a strong power of attraction to readers. True, you shouldn't believe everything you read in the newspaper, moreover, you shouldn't believe everything you see in the media. Ko and Rachelle were attracted by the digitally enhanced, idyllic scenes on the covers of wedding magazines. Inside one such magazine they found details of a competition, with the prize pool portrayed as a silver bullet to remove their financial doubts, and any other obstacles to getting married. If they could win the competition, it wouldn't just be any wedding. It would be 'the wedding of the year'.

The media: The mirror

Social proof not only influences an individual's thoughts, but also feeds the creation of group opinion and beliefs that are then represented in the media. The media acts as the mirror to our communal mind. It's no coincidence that there are so many newspapers around the world with the name: 'The Mirror'

Why is education important to happiness?

Weaknesses in your education can lead to weaknesses in your thinking which, in turn, lead to unhealthy thinking. Unhealthy thinking is demoralizing thinking. These weaknesses in education are best imagined as cracks through which your thoughts can tumble, and demoralize into pools of unhappiness. The pools of unhappiness are brimming with the chatter of negative thoughts. But the weaknesses in education are not caused by not going to school or university. Not having formal education doesn't mean a weaker education of life. In fact, the opposite can be true, and a university education can be just as unhealthy a mind-diet as watching television advertisements for three years. The good news is you don't need to go to university to have a strong Happiness Animal.

It's all about want

Want's domination of Ko's thinking left Ko weak when it came to thinking about others, and about how to be considerate to his wife. The media also gave both Ko and Rachelle more things to want. A house, a place in the sun, a four-wheel-drive, a cruise. Want thinking dominated their marriage and weakened their Happiness Animals. Their Happiness Animals were sick, demoralized by selfishness. Rachelle wanted to go on a cruise. Ko wanted to use his new four-wheel-drive. The more the media talked about divorce, the more celebrities got divorced, the more Rachelle and Ko thought about divorce, the more Ko and Rachelle were attracted to the idea of divorce. From the moment they met until the moment of divorce, Rachelle and Ko were puppets to their thoughts associated with attraction, to their thinking links of want.

Why can thinking be an effort? The chore of indecision

Ko's thinking indecision took the form of despair at not knowing which direction to take, not only physically with the four-wheel-drive in the rainforest, but also, mentally with the impasse in the relationship with Rachelle. The idea of turning around attracted Ko as much as the idea of trying to continue, and so he found it difficult to decide. Painfully difficult to decide, because he was literally being torn apart inside as the two courses of action played tug of war in his mind. With hindsight, Ko thought he *had* had a choice between two holiday options: the four-wheel-drive, or, the cruise, which with the benefit of hindsight he thought would have avoided the relationship impasse with Rachelle. The reality however, was that this choice did not exist. There was no indecision in Ko's mind between going on a cruise or going on a four-wheel-drive holiday, because there was no attraction in Ko's thinking to the idea of the cruise: Ko didn't associate going on a cruise with pleasure; if Ko saw the word 'cruise', it would fire thinking links to the image of his grandfather, who had been on a QE2 cruise and had puked for the entire two weeks. 'Cruise' fired another thinking link in Ko associated with thoughts of not being able to control the journey. Ko was attracted to control. Ko's attraction, based on his history and thinking links, was to thoughts of breaking a journey wherever something attracted his curiosity, and to thoughts of talking to local people, sometimes to thoughts of striking up romance. The word 'cruise' would also fire other thinking links created by what he had heard from those around him at work and at play: cruises were for old people who couldn't walk far; cruise ships were full of retired people. When he thought of retired people, it fired associations (thinking links) to thoughts about people he wouldn't be able to relax around, people he would have nothing in common with. Of course, the real problem wasn't the lack of choice between a cruise ship and a four-wheel-drive. The real problem was the lack of relating between Rachelle and Ko. Ko had not considered Rachelle's thoughts. Ko had no thinking links to thoughts that the drive would make Rachelle unhappy because he associated the four-wheel-drive with adventure and pleasure. He had not questioned whether Rachelle would make the same association. He hadn't questioned Rachelle because he had no awareness of the connections between associations, thinking links and education – or that thinking links even existed. But they do, and Rachelle's were as follows: 'Cruise' links to images of sexy, bikinied bodies with suntans, laid back on sun-loungers, reading books on the sundeck; reading links to pleasure, a thinking link created in Rachelle's childhood while her parents worked on the farm and she escaped with a book to a life of stories with romance.

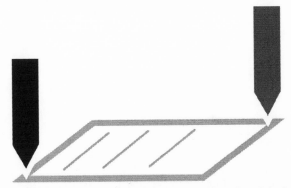

Pens with benefits – breaking the chains that bind you

If you are feeling under pressure, stressed, trapped, or down in the dumps, use that feeling as your trigger to break your thinking links with this simple exercise. The way to break thinking links is simply to become aware of them. There's a lot at stake because thinking links, if unchecked, lead your thoughts to demoralizing destinations.

Your benefits:

1. Awareness of how each thought you have links to the one that precedes it and the one that follows, and that when you say you have lost your 'train of thought', you are just unaware of the carriage you are in.

2. You get to break your demoralizing thinking links.

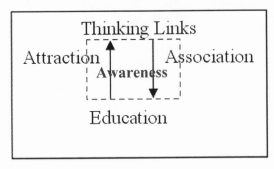

Instructions

1. Get a blank piece of paper and a pen.

2. Close your eyes and pay attention to your breathing. Are you breathing all the way out or is it still possible for you to scrape a little more air from the bottom of your stomach?

3. Stop paying attention to your breathing and wait for the first thought that comes into your mind.

4. Write down your first thought.

5. Capture every thought that follows in the next two minutes. Separate each individual thought with a '>' e.g. my stomach just rumbled > am I hungry? > what can I eat? > do I have something in the fridge? > the fridge is too cold > Do I need to get a new fridge?

Still having problems breaking the thinking links?

Practise this simple, walking-down-the-street exercise to become instantly aware of what you are seeing and what you are thinking. **If you have a voice notes function on your phone, you can use your headset to avoid embarrassment of appearing as if you are talking to yourself.** When you vocalise thoughts, you become aware of them. You turn subconscious detail into conscious detail. Awareness of your thoughts can stop you from being the puppet to your thought-strings.

Instructions

Phone a friend

Record your next phone or face to face conversation with a friend for 2-3 minutes. Type up the dialogue from the recording and read it back to yourself. What you are reading are the thinking links and associations that are combined and created when two people have a conversation.

This combining of associations and creation of new thinking links is naturally more harmonious between some people than it is with others.

1. When you next go for a walk, take your phone and headset with you and start recording a voice note

2. Say out loud, every thing you notice, and every thought that results e.g. what thoughts do you have immediately after seeing an ad on the side of a bus for a new 70 inch television, a piece of grey plastic on the pavement, or a newspaper rolled up by someone's door?

3. When you get home, pull out the paper and pen, play back your recording and transcribe the thoughts you recorded.

Too self-conscious to do the above?

Instructions

1. Choose the first question that enters your head and write it down at the top of a piece of paper.

2. Write your thoughts and associations as they occur, without editing. The secret of effective stream of consciousness writing is to *keep writing and write like no one's reading.*

One of my favourite scenes in the film, *Inception* speaks to the power of attraction and association of thoughts:

Dom Cobb: *What is the most resilient parasite? A bacteria? A virus? An intestinal worm?*

Dom Cobb: *An idea. Resilient, highly contagious. Once an idea has taken hold of the brain it's almost impossible to eradicate.*

And Dom Cobb is almost correct. Almost. An idea is almost impossible to eradicate. An idea takes hold of the brain. Freedom of thought is impossible. But even if an idea is almost impossible to eradicate, freedom **from** thoughts and freedom from ideas is possible. And that freedom comes with experience. That experience comes with exercise. How does Ko attain freedom from demoralizing thinking? By exercising awareness. Awareness changes attraction, and attraction changes education. So far, Ko has no awareness because Ko's education has only taught him what, not how, to think. Ko needs a new kind of education: an education that explains how he thinks. Once he has that foundation of awareness, he'll be ready to exercise his Happiness Animal. You, yes you, are already way ahead of Ko if you have read to here in the book. So for you, it's exercise time.

- Winning a competition won't make you happy.

- If you are feeling unhappy, use that as your trigger to break your thinking links: Stop what you are doing and write down how you got to the thought you are having. Accept that that thought makes you unhappy, scared, worried or whatever feeling it makes you feel.

- There is no freedom of thought, but there is freedom from thoughts. It's called awareness.

- Attraction decides your education and education decides your attraction and both are connected by your thinking links.

- When it comes to thoughts you are what you eat. And what you eat is your mind diet, your education of life.

- Education without awareness can weaken your thinking and weaken your Happiness Animal.

- Exercise of five muscles strengthens your Happiness Animal against the weaknesses of demoralizing thinking and indecision.

Coming Up Next ...It's time for you to begin the exercises that guarantee to strengthen your Happiness Animal.

Part II

Exercising The Happiness Animal

Chapter 4 – Introduction to the muscles of The Happiness Animal

No one can lead a happy life, or even one that is bearable, without the pursuit of wisdom, although even the beginnings of wisdom make life bearable

Seneca

What are all your tribulations but exercises for the training of your reason?
Every exercise of our proper natural instincts ought to be esteemed a form of pleasure

Marcus Aurelius

What's your idea of happiness?

I ran an online poll of 700 people globally, asking them to choose the best definition of happiness from six descriptions. The list of definitions I provided was not intended to be exhaustive, but the results surprised me. One of the definitions – trust and confidence – was something I had picked up from an online dictionary. Trust and confidence are represented in the Happiness Animal's honesty and courage muscles, and trust and confidence were what the majority of those polled voted for as the best definition of happiness.

Then it struck me that if only two of the five Happiness Animal muscles are already on their way to representing the best definition of happiness, imagine if the definition was widened to include the other three muscles. The dictionary definition would read something like this:

Happiness

noun.

A feeling of trust, confidence, kindness, honesty, awareness, courage and love.

Oddly Enough

'What people enjoy is not the sense of being in control, but the sense of *exercising* control in difficult situations' – the words of Mihaly Csikszentmihalyi, author of Flow, expert in the field of 'optimum experience' and whose name is prone to the occasional spelling mistake .

Try imagining what that would feel like. If you had to summarize that feeling in one word, what would that one word be?

Why exercise?

Go back to Einstein's quote at the beginning of Chapter 1: 'Education is not the learning of facts, but the training of the mind to think.' As we have seen, education literally trains (creates trains of) our thoughts into thinking links of attractions and associations. If education is the training of thinking, then exercise is the training of experience. Unhealthy education can make any human being slave to unhealthy thoughts and unhealthy associations, a slave with little space and little time to exercise her Happiness Animal. And so her Happiness Animal's muscles begin to waste away. This part of the book provides you with nature's own organic exercise equipment; equipment designed specifically to strengthen your Happiness Animal. It doesn't matter how little time or space you have, or how much of a slave you are to work, or to your spouse. It doesn't matter if you're in prison or in a palatial resort, the exercises in the next five chapters will both strengthen your Happiness Animal, and free you from unhealthy thought slavery.

How to approach the exercises

- Each of the following five chapters contains five exercises.
- There is a chapter for each of the five muscles of the Happiness Animal.
- In addition to the five exercises you will find 'phone and friend' and 'pens with benefits' activities scattered through the five chapters.
- Every obstacle you face, every frustration and everything that causes you pain or suffering is an opportunity to strengthen your Happiness Animal. That's because every obstacle provides an opportunity to exercise your Happiness Animal.
- No obstacles in your life at the moment? You will still benefit from the exercises. Just as an athlete needs to train regularly to stay strong, so does the Happiness Animal. Just as an athlete builds cumulative strength with regular training, so does the Happiness Animal.
- Many exercises involve interaction with other people, exercising how you relate and connect to others. If you can't meet people face to face because you live somewhere remote, use Skype. If you don't have Skype, use the phone. If you don't have a phone, write a letter. The maximum benefit of the exercise is obtained when you meet with people face to face.

- Approach the exercises with curiosity and trust yourself to find what you need. You will develop an awareness of which exercises help you the most.
- You don't need to read the next five chapters in order but it helps. Reading the chapters in order will show you how each muscle interacts with the others.
- Short on time? Try during your breaks and your breaks will become the happiness hotspots of your day. Even better, try to incorporate exercises into your work with other people. This will benefit both your Happiness Animal and your performance at work (as well as increasing your job satisfaction). You don't need to make time for the exercises. You can choose to apply them to what you are already doing each day.
- Approach all the exercises with an open mind. Try not to think about whether new ideas are right or wrong, but use curiosity to put exercises to the test of your own experience by curiously trying each one out and then noticing how you feel.
- Some of the exercises will seem so simple that your first reaction may be to judge them as naïve or stupid. Put them to the test of your actual experience before you pass your judgements.

Introducing the five Happiness Animal muscles

Five animals represent the five muscles of the Happiness Animal as follows: dog – honesty; dolphin – kindness; penguin – tolerance; koala – awareness, and lion – courage.

Each animal was voted unanimously (by thousands of votes) as the best representation for each respective muscle in a global online survey I ran in 2012.

Choosing which muscle to focus on

The chapters that will be most useful to you specifically will be the chapters that apply to the muscles you rate as your weakest. These are normally the muscles you have exercised the least. Giving your weakest muscles a workout will give you and your Happiness Animal the maximum health benefits. Often this involves using muscles you have been avoiding using for a prolonged period of your life. To help you identify which muscles you will benefit from exercising the most, spend five minutes to answer the six questions that follow:

1) Rate yourself on a scale of 1-10 against the following muscle behaviours with a rating of 10 signifying that you exercise the behaviour consistently, regularly and without exception.

a) Honesty

1   2   3   4   5   6   7   8   9   10

b) Kindness

1   2   3   4   5   6   7   8   9   10

c) Tolerance (including patience)

1   2   3   4   5   6   7   8   9   10

d) Awareness (including self-control and moderation)

1   2   3   4   5   6   7   8   9   10

e) Courage

1   2   3   4   5   6   7   8   9   10

2) What thing, situation, or person is making you unhappy, worried, or frustrated the most?

_____

3) What is it specifically about this thing, situation, or person that is making you unhappy, worried, or frustrated?

_____

_____

_____

_____

4) Look at each of the Happiness Animal's muscle cards that follow. Which of these muscles would help you the most with the thing, situation or person that's making you unhappy, worried or frustrated?

_____

_____

Muscle 1 - honesty

Definition: SHIFT: Sincerity, Harmony, Integrity, Frankness, and Trust. Unpretentiousness, egolessness.

The opposite? Dishonesty, insincerity, lies, egocentricity, falsity, deceitfulness, fraud, two-facedness, imitation.

Benefits: Peace of mind, simplicity of being, develops character, courage, credibility, trust and authenticity. Self-discovery.

Suits situations: Where there appears to be a gain by lying; where there is a temptation to people please or conform; relationships.

Muscle maxim: That which is false troubles the heart, but truth brings joyous tranquillity (Rumi).

Quick fix? Start your sentences with either 'I notice' or 'I imagine'. Be aware of the difference between what you notice and what you imagine.

Muscle 2 - kindness

Definition: An intention of: warmth, respect, recognition, appreciation, consideration, gratitude, empathy, compassion, generosity, helpfulness, spirit.

The opposite? Selfishness, meanness, coldness, cruelty, inconsiderateness, apathy, unfriendliness, greed, miserliness, narrow-mindedness, egocentricity, schadenfreude, jealousy.

Benefits: Reduces stress & loneliness, counteracts ageing, scientifically proven to make you happy. Increases solidarity, connects you to others.

Suits situations: Any interaction with other people where you can anticipate another person's wishes, or where you can give a benefit.

Muscle maxim: There is no choice between being kind to others & being kind to ourselves. It is the same thing. (P. Ferrucci)

Quick fix? If someone looks rushed let them go before you in a queue

Muscle 3 – tolerance

Definition: Tolerance of fpoes (fear, pain, others, events, self). Patience, indulgence, calmness, awareness, curiosity towards opinions, beliefs, things, people, situations & self. Using the five senses to question imagination.

The opposite? Intolerance, impatience, apathy, ignorance, reflex-reaction, frustration, irritability, anger, madness, hypochondria.

Benefits: Reduces: frustration, anger, fear, anxiety, loneliness & separation, ignorance. Increases: sense of belonging, peace of mind, learning, curiosity, creativity, authenticity.

Suits situations: Disagreements; unplanned, early or late people & situations.

Muscle maxim: To understand all is to forgive all.

Quick fix? Notice what you notice with your senses vs. what you imagine.

Muscle 4 – awareness

Definition: Noticing, self-control, temperance, sensing, being present, acceptance, freedom, focus, fidelity, authenticity, identifying sources of inadequacy.

The opposite? Ego, unconsciousness, distraction, greed, excess, decadence, lust, infidelity, wastefulness, corruption.

Benefits: Stops you from being consumed by anything you consume. Allows you to be more than what you do. Better health.

Suits situations: When something or someone attracts or distracts your senses. When thoughts demoralize you, or trigger unintentional actions.

Muscle maxim: If you wish to enrich someone, do not add to their riches but lessen their desires (Epicurus)

Quick fix? Ask: What is my intention right now in this moment?

Muscle 5 – courage

Definition: Noticing, accepting & facing fear, authenticity, acting consciously, selflessness, love, approachability, taking responsibility.

The opposite? Cowardice, shyness, despair, discouragement, reclusion, intimidation, avoidance, denial, shirking.

Benefits: Confidence & Trust define happiness. That's what 67% of people said in a global poll on the definition of happiness.

Suits situations: Times of uncertainty; when you meet (new) people.

Muscle maxim: It is not because things are hard that we lack confidence, but things are hard because we lack the confidence (Seneca)

Quick fix? Notice your fear. Name it. Accept it. Describe the physical sensations your fear gives you, & how they subside once you accept them.

5) Does the Happiness Animal muscle you chose match the behaviour you rated yourself as weakest against in question one?

_____

6) What could you do differently that would introduce more of the Happiness Animal muscle behaviour with the person, situation or thing that's making you unhappy, worried or frustrated?

_____

_____

_____

_____

_____

If you have answered the above questions you are already aware of which muscles may be the weakest in your Happiness Animal. As a head's up, here is the order in which we will exercise the five muscles of The Happiness Animal over the next five chapters. You will discover that this is the natural order of how one muscle is connected to the next.

Chapter 5: Honesty – moralive®1

Chapter 6: Kindness – moralive®2

Chapter 7: Tolerance – moralive®3

Chapter 8: Awareness – moralive®4

Chapter 9: Courage – moralive®5

Get ready to exercise…Get ready to feel more alive…Get ready for happy time.

<u>Chapter 5</u>

moralive®1: honesty

Telling the truth is like an exercise and diet program that works
to improve your strength and resistance over a period of time

Brad Blanton

That which is false troubles the heart, but truth brings joyous
tranquillity

Rumi

Things that deceive have no substance. Falsehood is a flimsy
mask and if you look hard you can see through it
Pride prefers a mask to her own face

Seneca

Animal's Anecdote: 'Insincere hugs'

Doug paddled his kayak onto Balmoral beach and pushed himself out of the cockpit, stepping onto the wet sand. As he walked past two girls sunbathing he gave them a smile and a 'hey' on the way to the kiosk to buy a coffee and a sandwich. The kayaking had relaxed his muscles, the sea air had cleared his passages, but he hadn't slept last night and his eyes were dry and heavy. He needed a coffee. The kiosk doors were closed. A sign read *coffee machine closed for repairs – apologies for the inconvenience.* Doug sighed as he turned around. A boy on a plastic tractor pushed himself along the beach walkway past Doug. The child flopped and dragged his legs around like propellers on the ground. Doug was struck by the purity and simplicity of the boy's intention. He roamed freely, was innocent of the dangers of the road. He raced towards the end of the walkway and the wheelchair access, onto the kerb. Doug saw from the child's propulsion that he had no intention of stopping. The sense of movement fired an instinct of urgency in Doug. He bounded from his pause and sprinted to cut off the child's path onto the road. A car driver's eyes bulged as he drove past Doug and the boy. It was only when the driver had pulled level with Doug that he had registered the boy's presence down below. Doug towered above the boy, who sat like a spring winding up with tension against Doug's resistance to allowing him to move forwards on his plastic tractor. 'This is a road. It's dangerous. It's dangerous because cars are driving down here and they might not see you,' said Doug. The boy looked up at Doug like he was trying to solve a puzzle. 'Where are your mum and dad?' Doug asked, as he looked around. The boy looked like he was going to propel past Doug, who shuffled to block the boy's path, as if trying to stop a calf from escaping a farmyard.

'A car might hit you if you go onto the road. It's dangerous,' Doug said, staring at the boy's eyes.

'It's better if you go back that way. You can have more fun,' said Doug as he pointed at the park. The boy relaxed his puzzled look, pushed himself one leg at a time to turn around and then accelerated back onto the walkway towards the picnic area. Doug felt a foreign feeling in his stomach. In the picnic area Doug saw a man near the boy, who he assumed to be the boy's father, wipe the boy's nose. The foreign feeling grew in Doug. A ball of tension inside his stomach spread to his shoulders. A new necessity in Doug dictated that he walk over to the man he assumed to be the boy's father. The father did not acknowledge Doug's presence until Doug piped up a 'sorry to bother you' and then a slightly louder 'excuse me, is this little fellow your son?'

The man registered that Doug was talking to him, and turned from his picnic with his six friends to look at this unexpected intruder. The group fell silent in frowns directed at Doug.

'Yes,' said the father.

Disdain in the 'yes' compressed Doug's chest, spring loading his diaphragm muscle and as he released it, out flew his truth:

'Your son was about to wheel out into the road over there.' Doug pointed over in the direction of the road.

A twitch to the eyebrow disturbed the flatness of the man's expression, but he remained silent.

'I spoke to your son and told him it was dangerous, but I think you should know that he was about to go out into the road,' said Doug.

'I didn't see that. I must have missed it,' said the man. He frowned. He jutted out his lower jaw and appeared to close his eyes as he looked at the ground.

The man said nothing further but shifted position in his fabric folding chair. Doug felt the conversation at an end, and walked away with a mixture of concern, bemusement and shock. Nausea, accompanied him on his paddle home.

That evening, Doug was shuffling bread, jam and the kettle in the kitchen, stepping around his housemate, Mia who was preparing something in a roasting tin.

'It was a strange feeling, saving a boy's life,' said Doug. Exaggeration sucked the fullness out of his feeling. The more he spoke, the more hollow he felt. 'It was like two different realities hit a T-junction and if I hadn't decided to go to Balmoral today, that boy could be dead now.'

'Some people really shouldn't be allowed to have children,' said Mia. She stared at Doug as if urgency could never exist when she was talking to him.

'Can I have a hug please?' Neediness in women repulsed Doug, perhaps more than anything else. He thought it had something to do with natural selection. Neediness, he thought, was tantamount to weakness. Mia's arms were not just open. They were reaching for him, ready to cling. Doug lent towards Mia, and felt increasingly uncomfortable as he lied to her with his body. He knew his body would be turning her on as she wrapped herself around him. He asked himself, *how much longer will be enough?*

It felt like a minute had passed already. Doug had no grip on Mia, no desire for any body warmth from her. His palms were light, his finger tips straining away from her back. Mia pressed her waist against Doug's and he felt the pressure of her stomach muscles. She moved her thigh forward so it rested against Doug's crotch. She had already succeeded in seducing Doug twice in this way. And not following up sex with soft conversation and hugs would see Mia descending into a bi-polar freefall. Seduction by Mia had post-coital, time commitment consequences. He looked down and saw her skirt had revealed an inch or two more of her silky thigh as she moved it forwards. His mouth opened a little, watering around the sides of his tongue. He felt warmth rush between his legs, and the warmth of Mia's face on his as it moved closer. He turned his head and noticed the clock on the wall. It was already 6pm. If he went to bed with her now he wouldn't be able to leave her until 8, and even then she would begrudge him for not spending the evening with her. Mia slid her hands down Doug's back, as she clung tighter. Doug focused his thoughts on escaping as soon as the first opportunity arose, rather than let his body react any further to her heat. He lowered his arms, slowly prised her away and took a half-step back, turning his body towards the door. Mia reacted by half opening her mouth, with surprise and disappointment that the hug had ended.

'Back to the to-do list,' said Doug, smiling and shuffling hastily towards the door to allow no time to register Mia's reactions.

'See you later,' he smiled, and bounded up the stairs to his room. He closed the door behind him and released a long breath, dropping his shoulders and leaning his head back against the door.

In his room, Doug played out what he could say to Mia in his head. *I'm just not that into you; I like you as a friend; we have shared some moments of connection, and you are attractive, but I'm not in love with you.* Doug looked at the to-do list on his whiteboard on the wall. His project of buying coffee machines from Italy and selling them in Australia had some outstanding actions. He remembered that he had to get a refund for the coffee machine that he'd imported from his supplier in Italy. The machine sprayed water when he switched it on. The seller had requested Doug post the machine back before he would issue Doug the refund. Doug had thought there must be a better way not to lose money by paying for postage so although he had told the seller he had posted it back, he had actually dropped the machine off at a coffee machine shop, Jet Black Espresso, for a quote to be fixed locally. He clicked on the eBay messages tab. Another message from the seller read: *I have refunded you the 140 Euros. Have you posted the broken machine?*

Doug clicked on reply. *Yes, please let me know when you receive the machine.*

Doug picked up his phone and called Jet Black Espresso.

'It might take a while as we need to check whether we can get the parts in from Italy. The quote will cost you \$80 but you can offset that against the cost of our repairs,' said the store rep.

Doug's thoughts dominoed.

If they can't repair it, I won't be able to sell it. If they can repair it, how much is it going to cost on top of what I've already paid? I think the supplier already doesn't think I've posted it. If I lose his trust, he might not sell me any more machines and I'll lose my business. How long will it be before he finds me out? I could have posted it back to Italy for the same cost of that quote. I can't lie to him anymore. Shit. I don't think he believes I have posted it back. And the bloody machine hasn't been posted at all. What if he hasn't sent me the other two machines I have just bought from him? I'm going to lose everything.

Doug was sat staring down at his desk playing the monologue of his own thoughts, a monologue that had a sudden change of scene when his phone started playing Lana del Rey's *Yayo*. It was the notification of a text message from his housemate, Mia: *You seemed to be in a hurry to get away from me. It would be nice to spend some time together soon.*

'Fuck. I can't do this anymore,' said Doug.

Sure, is it OK if we just hang out as friends? he replied to Mia.

Doug heard her door slam downstairs and knew that she'd be stomping around in typical Mia fashion for a few hours but that she'd get over it. eBay was still open on Doug's laptop screen. Doug wrote a message to the supplier: *The post office has returned the machine to me today because they said water was leaking out of it.* Doug opened up the machine. He saw that a copper pipe had cracked off from the boiler and this was where the steam had been escaping from. He took a photograph of the cracked pipe and emailed it to the coffee machine supplier. He felt that the sending a photograph also sent away the burden from his mind. Doug wrote another message: *I will send you your refund back now. I found out it's too much to send the machine to Italy again so I will try and get it repaired locally instead.*

Doug felt the connection between him and his supplier had been restored. He sat back in his chair, and felt the warmth of unburdened tiredness.

Animal Analysis

What's honesty got to do with happiness?

Less than five percent of those polled in an online survey I ran said honesty was the weakest of their five Happiness Animal muscles. But were they being honest? I say with sincerity that honesty is the most critical of The Happiness Animal's five muscles because no other muscle can be exercised without it. Honesty creates the harmony that holds the Happiness Animal's five muscles together, and when I am frank with you, it's easier for you to trust my integrity. My intention for this chapter is transparent in the words I have used in the last two sentences. The SHIFT (**S**incerity, **H**armony, **I**ntegrity, **F**rankness, and **T**rust) is about to hit the fan. When you make the SHIFT, you connect to all of your Happiness Animal's muscles: You can be aware when you are honest about how much you have; you can be kind when you are so genuinely; you can be tolerant when you are honest objectively; and you can be courageous when you have trust in the truth.

Sincerity (moralive®1.1)

Sincerity is the first of the virtues. The lie is the weapon of the weak. Respect for truth is the virtue of adult humanity.

Paul Dubois

So you tell the truth? But are you sincere? More than just telling the truth, sincerity is when you connect with the words you speak. It is a passionate pursuit of the truth. If you are sincere, you are

Time to define: Sincerity
The root of the word is **sincere**, which means without wax, as in honey without the wax. Sincerity is purity and sincerity is simplicity. Sincerity is an attitude of earnestness, and earnestness is an attitude of intense conviction.

necessarily curious. And for good reason: To find the truth you need to ask where it was last seen. Then you ask questions that will help you locate it now. But when you start to see your first glimpse of the truth, you need to be transparent about what you see. Otherwise truth will make an instant getaway. The only way to get a firm hold on truth is tell everyone clearly and with urgency where it is so they can help prevent it from escaping. You need to radio for assistance. And you need to call for back-up now.

The importance of being earnest

Piero Ferrucci asks: 'When are we kinder? When we hide our warmth, our dreams, our wonder, our humour, or when we reveal them?' Sincerity leads you not only to truth, but also to kindness.   Exercising your Happiness Animal with sincerity is the best way to learn, the only way you can grow and the only way you can create something authentic. It's done by telling the truth as you see it, by contributing your unique piece to the infinite jigsaw puzzle. If you are looking for a meaning to your life, or the purpose of your existence, this is getting pretty close, if not hitting the nail on the head: You are created to be you. The purpose of your existence is to be you well. The only way to be you well, is to be honest. Truly

Oddly Enough
An 'earnest' also means a sign or promise of what is to come. Is it possible that the more sincere you are about something, the more likely that something is going to happen?

you. In *The Happiness Project,* Gretchen Rubin writes that one of her own happiness commandments is 'Be Gretchen'. If you only have one happiness commandment, make sure it's 'Be _____'.

When to exercise with sincerity (moralive 1.1)

The answer to the question of when to exercise with sincerity is simple: Every day, without exception, unless your life depends on it –

but wait – your life does depend on it. There is nothing wrong with being a simple person. Simple doesn't mean stupid. It means you tell it as you see it. Nothing else needs adding. No seasoning. Einstein said: 'Everything should be made as simple as possible but not simpler.' Sincerity is a simple diamond, and no matter how many times you wear it, it will always enchant others and remain unblemished. Insincerity, on the other hand, is cheap superglue for a cracked, plastic mask. The more we wear the mask, the more the plastic cracks, and the more superglue we need to hold our mask together. Once insincere, you are more likely to keep being insincere. The reason? You do not want to admit your first insincerity so you use more insincerity to cover it up. The only way out of insincerity is throwing out the plastic mask, and showing your diamond to the world. Your instincts are genuine, unfiltered, unmasked and unpretentious actions. Doug's and the car driver's reactions were honest reactions dictated by natural necessity to protect a child. That's easy. But once the need for instincts has disappeared, the old mask is grasped for, like a comfort blanket or a new handbag, an air kiss, a false hug, or a lie to avoid the truth.

Glamour is plastic
In the greedy pursuit of presenting the appearance of progress and personal gain, you more often see masks of vanity, than unmasked sincerity. Nowhere else in the world is this more visible than in the corporate world of acronyms and abbreviations, where KPI names are replaced as often suits, and where there are more vice-presidents than there are countries in the world. The same masks of vanity appear in the restaurants that use French words to dress up Colorado potatoes with jus served by a waiter on minimum wage, wearing a costume from Downton Abbey. And you find the same masks of vanity in the bars where you pay to reserve kabanas and well-dressed servants. Venice might be the best place to buy a mask, but it has nothing on Sydney or Los Angeles for mask wearers. A Nigerian tells me that the most insincere country in the world is not the USA, but Nigeria.

According to the latest report by Gallup, Nigeria is also rated the second most corrupt country in the world. Is it possible that a corrupt government necessitates insincere citizens? I would encourage any sociologists to investigate the links between insincerity and corruption, but if you are seeking out the biggest insincerity hotspot of all, head straight to your living room. If you are like most people, you have a television. TV is take-away, on demand, insincerity, and it's on tap 24 hours a day, 7 days a week. When I was filming for an Australian 'reality' TV show the producers asked us to wear the same clothes for days in a row to create the illusion that everything had been filmed on the same day. If you don't believe that television is an all-phoney illusion, then please join a studio audience at your earliest possible convenience. In Scandinavia, many of the television channels broadcast in English, and, as a result many Scandinavians speak perfect English even though it's not their first language. Worldwide, all television channels broadcast insincerity, and as a result everyone who watches television learns to speak perfect insincerity, even though it's not their first language.

The baby is the daddy
Small children, who have not yet been exposed to the falsity of interpretation, association, hidden meanings, politics, and plain bullshit, are naturally more sincere than adults. Children learn to be themselves using their senses before they learn to be themselves with all the bullshit. The problem, as Brad Blanton, author of *Radical Honesty*, explains is as follows: 'Every adult has a whole raft of values they think should be taught to children.'

These values are based on abstractions, generalizations, evaluations, summations, assessments and principles. One by one these adult generalizations, evaluations, assessments and principles permeate the child's existence and distract the child away from their senses and into the new world of their mind. Yet by default, children are the closest of all of us to being true human beings. Children are human beings who still live and experience life primarily through their senses, and with happiness, as it is with education, there is no substitute for experience through the senses. Experience is the only way to feel your Happiness Animal, and to feel it getting stronger. Children have the happiness advantage of pure, sensory experience. Why do adults tell their children 'these are the best days of your life'? Your Happiness Animal thrives when it exists independently of abstractions, generalizations, evaluations, summations, assessments and principles. The founder of Gestalt therapy, Fritz Perls said that 'principles are substitutes for an independent outlook'. Your Happiness Animal accepts no substitutes. Your Happiness Animal only thrives when you live your life honestly, with an independent outlook.

The necessity of sincerity

Doug noticed danger, which activated his instincts and his senses. His experience was one of noticing how close the car was to the child and noticing that the child was moving towards the road. He saw what was happening and he acted with pure intention. In the moment of danger he didn't think 'I wonder where that child's parents are' or 'I can't say anything to that boy because he is not my child'. Similarly, the child focused only on feeling the exploration of the world around him, through his eyes and ears, and his vision of the world from two feet off the ground. To prevent disaster, Doug had to talk to the child in a clear language, language the child would understand, the language of sincerity. And sincerity was pure, unadulterated, instinct. I use the word unadulterated here for good reason. When something pure is synthesized for adults, it is no longer pure. Purity has been tampered with. Clarity has been doctored. 'The great enemy of clear language is insincerity,' said George Orwell. The great friend of clear language is sincerity. The only route to clear language is to use your senses, rather than interpretations, as the primary source of information. It all starts with an intention of sincerity.

Exercising sincerity (moralive®1.1): Be sincere with me dear

Based on exercises for 'Connecting the Range' that appear in the book *Finding your voice* by Barbara Houseman. Barbara is a coach to both Joseph Fiennes and Kenneth Branagh. Reproduced in part with the permission of Nick Hern Books.

Exercise for connecting your voice to your truth, so you speak sincerely. Internally, we may remain as expressive as when we were children, but this inner expression can become 'unplugged' from our outer expression. We may shut down out of fear of being too passionate, too revealing or too emotional. Or we may mask feelings of depression or tiredness or sadness or boredom – exaggerating the pitch movement in our voice so we seem happier or more upbeat than we feel. Either way, our movement around our pitch range fails to truthfully reflect our thoughts and feelings.

We are often not aware of having made a decision to disconnect in this way. So, now, it can be very frustrating, since we don't understand why the life of our internal voice does not show through in the life of our external voice. Another cause of flatness or exaggerated movement in the voice can be lack of trust. One of two behaviours occurs when we lose trust: either we become tentative or we become over-effortful. If we become over-effortful, the voice will tend to be over exaggerated in its pitch movement since we will not trust our thoughts and feelings to be expressed by the natural movement of the voice and will therefore 'help' everything along. A further cause of disconnection can be that we are not connecting with what we are saying or with the person we are saying it to. This can happen both with our own words and with text. We need to see the pictures or images behind our words and, then, we need to *want* the person we are addressing to see the same pictures and images. This is not a question of thinking about what you are saying or trying to *explain* it to your listener. It is about being present with the words and images and with the person you're speaking to. This may sound horrendously complicated but it isn't and when you make this connection you become utterly simple and yet utterly engaging!

You start by exercising your connection with words to fully and authentically colour how you say them.

Instructions

1. Sit comfortably, somewhere that is quiet and private.
2. Take a piece of text a small phrase at a time, sometimes you may even take one word at a time. The reason for this is that, if you take more than a few words at once, you will find yourself only connecting with some of the words, usually the 'so called' more important ones. Whereas, if you take a few words at a time you can connect with every word. This does not mean that you will end up stressing every word, but rather that each word will have its own place and colour within the whole, which leads to greater variety and greater subtlety.
3. Take the first phrase and repeat it quietly, but not whispered, three times. Just let the words register. Don't try to find different ways to say them, simply let the words sink in.
4. Then, move on to the next phrase and say that three times through, again letting the words sink in and register.
5. Continue in this way, saying each small phrase three times and then moving on to the next.
6. Don't string all the phrases together, just say each one three times and then leave it and move onto the next.
7. There is no need to try and achieve anything in this exercise, just receive the words and let them guide your voice.

Now it's time to share the pictures with the listener. Use the energy of your communication to bring life and authentic

colour to your speech. The following steps are all about connecting with your listener.

Sincerity is about two connections: firstly connecting with the words, and secondly connecting with your listener. It is these two connections that will bring your full range into play in a truthful and exciting way. You need a partner for the following steps.

8. Sit comfortably opposite your partner
9. Start to speak a piece of text to your partner. Focus on talking rather than acting the text. Put all your attention on your partner and on wanting to communicate with them.
10. As you are talking, your partner listens and honestly questions any part of the text where they don't get the picture. Here is an example of how the exercise might work using some of dialogue from 'Pentecost' by David Edgar.

> YOU: When she came back
> PARTNER: When she what?

11. You then need to answer by repeating the particular bit of text questioned, but you can't raise your voice or emphasise the word (or words) more to get the images across to your partner. You need to really connect with what that word (or words) mean for you, what they conjure up and then share that.

> YOU: came back

(If your partner feels they have received the picture, you can move on, otherwise they may ask again)

> YOU: at first it looked quite normal
> PARTNER: When did it look quite normal?
> YOU: at first

(Again, if your partner feels they have received the picture, you can move on, otherwise they may ask again)

    YOU: it looked quite normal

PARTNER: Looked quite odd?

    YOU: quite normal

    YOU: And as it was the morning

PARTNER: The evening?

    YOU: the morning

    YOU: it was no surprise to find the door open

PARTNER: It was a shock?

PARTNER: it was no surprise

    YOU: to find the door open

PARTNER: to find the shop door closed?

    YOU: to find the door open

12. Your partner has a big responsibility here to not just question you arbitrarily but to really pick you up when they feel that they haven't been communicated with.

13. Your responsibility is not to take the easy way out and simply raise your voice or emphasise the word more, but rather to really connect with the word and share that.

Harmony (moralive®1.2)

I would rather you brought about some harmony in my mind and got
my thoughts into tune
Seneca

Truth is the agreement of thought with its object. Harmony is the agreement of representations in our minds (thoughts) with the things that have been represented. Harmony in an orchestra comes about when the objects – the notes – are expressed in synchronicity by each musician in the orchestra. Everyone in the orchestra sees and expresses the same note at the same time with their unique instrument, breath or hand movement. Harmony in your thoughts comes about only when you produce a sound which resonates with both the object of your thoughts and your expression of that thought. Resonance between thought and your expression of thought happens only when you tell the truth. Harmony in your Happiness Animal happens when what you express resonates with what you feel. If you see and feel a G note and you play an F, you will be out of tune. Seeing and feeling a G note, and playing an F is lying. Doug was out of tune when he told the supplier he had posted the coffee machine when he knew he had not.

Sen says: Honesty is harmony in the mind.

When to exercise harmony (moralive 1.2)

The world is out of tune. The world is noisy. The world is full of the sounds of words that don't resonate with people's thoughts. And it's out of tune because it's not using the language of the senses. Instead it's using copies, fake plastic copies of true sounds. These fake plastic copies are all the abstractions, generalizations and evaluations, summations and assessments that are taught to us as soon as we enter childhood. It is the language of advertising, the language of glossy magazines, and the language of television. It is the language of egos. It is the language of false identities and of hiding behind job titles. It is the language of lies. And it is a language that we now speak more fluently than the language of sincerity that can resonate with our senses. Instead of feeling the high definition of our senses resonate within us, we have been muffled by so much plastic gloss that we barely vibrate.

The English vocabulary is full of abstractions, generalizations and evaluations, summations and assessments but there is a drought of words that relate to the senses. Let me test this out on you now: what is the sound equivalent of the word: visualize? A word for this wasn't even invented until someone realized there wasn't a word in 1975, when they created 'aurelate' – which is a word that is still not recognized by my laptop's spellchecker. What about a word like visualize, for imagining the feel (touch) of something? A word for imagining the taste? For imagining the smell? I didn't know aurelate was a word, and I had never used it, yet words like visualize and aurelate are the language of your senses, the language of being, and the language of your Happiness Animal.

The curious case of harmony

Harmony can exist between thoughts and actions, and between thoughts and intentions towards people. Curiosity is the tuning tool that you use to find the resonance that creates harmony. Curiosity for harmony is no different from experimenting with the tension on guitar strings. Be curious and notice the result. Lying, on the other hand, does the opposite of tuning yourself in. Lying creates noisy interference that you force yourself to listen to, on full volume, at point blank range. Make that closer than point blank. The noise of lying scrapes inside of you. If your alter-ego forced you to turn your television up to full volume and then pull the antenna out of the back, with only the harsh noise of the interference snow remaining and then forced you to sit with your ear up against the speaker for as long as that alter-ego existed, wouldn't you consider that to be torture? Yet lying is no different. Lying is self-abuse, an attack of self-harm at your core, an assault that demoralizes you through discord, disharmony, and discomfort.

Lie detectors are like electronic tuners. When you lie your brain's activity is out of harmony with what you say. Lie detectors work because our brains tell the truth by default and unnatural brain activity is required to lie. And it's this additional activity that is detected by the lie detector.

Be kind. Tune up.

In order to be kind, you have to learn to look after your own harmony first. Otherwise you will produce noise and that's unkind to you and to your neighbours. If you lie to 'protect' yourself, the unnatural noise you create can only resonate with a Trojan horse. And not the kind that harms laptops. Once it slips inside your mind, the Trojan horse will do some serious damage to your sleeping Happiness Animal. The Trojan horse will systematically destroy your peace and harmony of mind. It was such a Trojan horse that violated Doug when he gave Mia the hug of false intimacy, the lie of body language, that created disharmony with his true feelings, and the interference allowed the Trojans in. The result of the Trojan attack this time: repulsion, nausea. Doug knew he did not want a true intimate relationship with Mia. In that moment, he was nothing more than a stand-in actor, a liar that was not, in truth, attracted to the warmth of her body. Doug had no resonance between his thoughts and his actions with Mia, and this lack of resonance was caused by non-disclosure of his true sound. He thought and F and played a G. Doug's lack of harmony was not limited to his personal life: it also spilled over into his business life. The lie about having posted the coffee machine when he hadn't posted it tugged at Doug's thoughts like a screaming child. How can you listen to an F when you are playing a G? He couldn't think about his regular routine or selling coffee machines because his mind was full of the noise of disharmony, of interference, of the Trojan attack. The Trojan attack, prevented Doug's ability to do business. Disclosure restored it.

Non-disclosure disagreement

Non-disclosure disrupts the harmony of social relationships. It creates blockages in relationships, blockages that get in the way of connecting well with others. Disclosure is critical to harmony in your thoughts, relationships, and Happiness Animal. It is also critical to your health. In his book, *Opening Up,* social psychologist Jamie Pennebaker reports on a study he conducted that proved the health benefits of disclosure.

He asked study participants to disclose their secrets, by writing about the most upsetting or traumatic experience of their life. Over the next year, those who wrote down their disclosure story recorded a lower incidence of ailments requiring the treatment of a doctor or hospitalisation. Their disclosure restored harmony in their mind, which had a physiological effect of increasing harmony in their bodies. By disclosing, the participants exercised the honesty muscle in their Happiness Animal. But let me be clear here about what disclosure is: Disclosure is not venting. Disclosure is sense making, so that you fit what happened to you into part of the harmony of your overall story. As Jonathan Haidt explains, 'you have to use words and the words have to create a meaningful story'. The story is of when and why, and what good you can derive from it, what lessons you have learned. The next step is disclosure to others, to cherish and grow the network of people you can open up to. You are about to try it for yourself.

Exercising harmony in disclosure (moralive®1.2): Writing the wrong
Adapted from an exercise that appears in *The Happiness Hypothesis* by Jonathan Haidt.

Instructions
1. Take a blank piece of paper and write for five minutes about 'the most upsetting or traumatic experience of your entire life. If you have never experienced trauma, write about something that upset you or something you are ashamed of, or, a deep regret. Preferably choose an experience you have not talked about with other people in much detail, if at all. You don't have to show what you write to anyone other than yourself.
2. The next day, continue writing about the experience for another five minutes. Don't edit or censor yourself. Don't worry about grammar or sentence structure; just keep writing.

Write about what happened, how you feel about it, and why you feel that way, and in whatever order you like.

3. Repeat for several days until you have nothing further to write.

Tip: If you hate to write, talk into a voice recorder on your phone. The crucial thing is to get your thoughts and feelings out in words without imposing any order on them – but in such a way that, after a few days, some order is likely to emerge on its own.

4. If the experience involved another person, ask the other person to meet up with you as a favour to you.

5. When you meet up with the other person, notice any bodily sensations associated with your anxiety or fear of disclosing what you are going to disclose to them. Where do you feel tension? Your stomach? Your forehead? Your shoulders? Your hands?

6. Tell the other person that you are doing this to exercise your honesty muscle, an exercise in disclosure for the benefit of your own happiness.

7. When disclosing your story, take your time. Speak slowly and notice any bodily sensations you have as and when they come up. If the other person reacts to what you say, notice your own body's reaction before you react verbally. Tell them how you are feeling throughout the disclosure. e.g. 'I notice my hands are shaking' or 'I'm feeling tension in my stomach'.

8. If resentments and/or appreciations come up continue this exercise with the exercise of expressing yourself (moralive®1.3 - page 90).

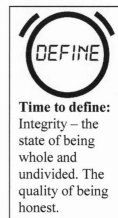

Time to define:
Integrity – the state of being whole and undivided. The quality of being honest.

Integrity (moralive®1.3): Why copy the Mona Lisa when you can create a masterpiece?

Authenticity is the key. It is the key to being undivided. Is it better to be half you half of the time or all you all of the time? Authenticity, being truly you, ensures integrity. You are authentic when you are true in communicating your view, your piece of the infinite puzzle of life. This happens when what you say is in harmony with what you sense, and your expression of what you sense, resonates your essence. You say it as you see it. You don't choose longer words when you talk to someone who you perceive to be highly educated, and you don't dumb down what you say to people who you perceive as uneducated. If you look at a painting and all you see is a yellow block, you say 'I see a yellow block' rather than 'that's an interesting colour theme'. Your essence does not lie in your mind, your essence exists in your senses. The origin of the word 'essence' is 'esse' meaning 'to be'. Interesting the German verb 'essen' means 'to eat'. If you exist through your senses, then you literally are what you eat (and smell, touch, taste, hear, see). Your existence, your sensory diet that forms your essence is unique. You do not exist in principles, abstractions, generalizations and evaluations. Your being's authenticity is created and channelled through your senses. You can use your senses to rediscover your essence, to rediscover your existence, and then give it to the world using your mind as a tool to select the words and colours and materials that resonate what you feel. That is authenticity. Giving it is an act of creation. It is a creation of integrity. It is Art.

When to exercise integrity (moralive®1.3)

Always, unless your life depends on it – but wait, your life does depend on it. The simple truth is: You are not you if you are not you. You don't exist. To speak the truth with integrity, you speak the truth in a way that resonates with your being, with your essence, that is to say, you say it as you see, hear, touch, smell and taste it – whatever it is. Do you remember the last time you were at a party where two women discovered they were wearing the same dress? Why were they embarrassed? But why did they both choose the same dress? Is it really a surprise when we look to what other people are doing, liking, finding fashionable, that we end up looking identical? And yet your mind's response to being discovered as inauthentic is one of embarrassment at best, or shame at worst. But your mind is also telling you to choose a dress that will fit in with what other people think to be 'a good look'. Your instinct does not consider what you perceive other people will perceive to be 'a good look'. Your instinct is authentic. Your mind's compulsion is to worry about (and attach meaning to) what others will think and say about you. But is being afraid of what others say a good enough reason not to be you? The next time you are tempted to change your outfit or to lie because you are afraid of what others will say, the next time you are tempted to save face, or put someone down because you know someone else has a problem with them, just remember one word: integrity. Your existence is at stake.

Oddly Enough
It's so simple…
Einstein coined what has become a no-brainer: 'Everything should be made as simple as possible but no simpler.' Sincerity, being pure, without wax is the way to integrity. Without integrity, you can forget about being the best you can be, in fact, you can forget about being at all. But throw out the mask, scrape off the wax, and what you have underneath is existence itself.

Liar Liar

Two faced is fake faced. Telling the truth frees you from the anxiety of having to hide your lies. It's not just getting something off your chest; it's being able to breathe easy and relax. Hiding requires constant pre-occupation with staying hidden. Piero Ferrucci sums this up concisely: 'Lying has a thousand faces, the truth only one.' And it's your face. If you stop pretending, all of the artifices and efforts to hold your life together fall away. It's a relief. You can chuck out your cracked, plastic masks and superglue, and stop trying to fix something that didn't exist. Best of all, you will be truly seen, unmasked for the first time since you were a child. Best of all, you can be.

The difference between authenticity and bullshit

If you got angry with someone and expressed that anger but you felt demoralized, it is because it is not authentic, honest anger. It is anger resulting from associations and thoughts, and attachments to judgements and abstractions. The reason my mother felt demoralized after getting angry with my younger brother for being slow to get out of bed in the morning or not knowing what he wants to do after he finishes school, is that it's fake anger. It's not the anger of her essence, of her being. It's the anger of a personality that her mind has created out of thinking links, a personality that 'shoulds' her to behave according to social proof and to the abstraction and association of her education of life. Quite simply, she's only angry because she's thinking about it. If, however my brother were to slap her in the face, she could get authentically angry. But in this example, it's a mask's anger. It's the anger of her ego. It's the anger of her mind. It's not the anger of her essence, which uses only senses to exist in each moment. Her ego's anger is based on principles, abstractions, generalizations and evaluations that have formed a mask, a persona, an ego of thoughts that tell her to behave a certain way. The insincerity of her ego demoralizes her because she loves my brother. She feels demoralized by the inauthenticity of her expression. True, sometimes it's hard to tell the difference between authentic anger and bullshit and that's why the following exercise is designed to help you express your resentments with integrity, and not with demoralizing bullshit.

Exercising integrity (moralive®1.3) – express yourself

(Based on exercises for Getting Into and Getting Over Anger, in *Radical Honesty*, by Brad Blanton)

1) Close your eyes for a moment, picture a person you don't like, and have an imaginary dialogue with him. Tell him what he did that you resent. Tell him your judgements about him. Then imagine his response and respond back. You may also tell him your appreciations if you have any, or if any show up after your expression of resentment. Pay attention to your body as you engage in this imaginary dialogue. Take a break from reading here and do this step now.

2) Call the person you just had an imaginary conversation with and make an appointment to tell him your resentments in person. Tell the person when you call that you want to meet him to tell him what you are mad about and get over it, and get complete with him. Ask him to meet with you as a favour to you. Persist until he agrees to meet with you.

3) Meet with your enemy. Your goal will be to forgive him not as a favour to him, but for your own selfish benefit.

4) Follow the below guidelines for communication during the meeting. These guidelines are not moral rules to be memorised and obeyed. They are rules of thumb. The purpose of these guidelines is to direct your attention to the process of learning how to express yourself in the moment so that something happens to actual feelings in your body at the level of sensation. Something will happen because of your willingness to pay attention to your experience. These guidelines will make your aware of your moment-to-moment experience of anger or of appreciation. **But beware of your mind.** The rules can be followed and still not work if you are only attending to the rules and not to your experience. The point is to be

aware of your experience while experimenting, not whether you are good at following the rules. Your goal is to be willing and to acknowledge to yourself, and to report with whom you are speaking, each new experience as it emerges, regardless of whether or not it is comfortable. You'll have no more withheld resentments or appreciations, and you'll be able to experience him newly, as he is, in that moment. When you let someone be the way they are, when you let up on your judgements of someone, there is free space in which forgiveness and love can occur. **Here are the rules of thumb for the conversation:**

I. Whenever possible, talk face-to-face to the person with whom you are angry. It is impossible to do any of this work over the phone. You need to look at each other in the eye and react to each other moment to moment.

II. Start your sentences as often as possible with the words, **'I resent you for...' or 'I appreciate you for...'** The structure of a sentence that starts with those words ensures that the anger is personal, that there is an 'I' and a 'you'. I resent you has a much stronger and more personal impact than 'I resent the fact that...'

III. Speak in the **present tense** (I resent you for ...NOT I resented you for...)

IV. **Get specific.** Even though it doesn't always feel this way, you probably resent the person for what he specifically did or said. E.g. Instead of saying: 'I resent you for acting snobbish toward me', to which he can say

'I'm not a snob', say: I resent you for turning your head and not answering me when I said hi to you.'

V. Focus as much as you can on what *did* happen instead of what didn't happen.

VI. Stay in touch with your experience as you talk. Don't rehearse a speech. Stick to expressing your feelings as they come up during the interaction. What you need to do to tell the truth and have the resentment disappear is this: first, notice the bodily sensations associated with what you have called anger (feeling constricted in your breathing, cowering, feeling tense, frowning) and state your resentment clearly. Start with, 'I resent you for saying....' When you hear yourself say whatever specifically it is you say it may end up sounding ridiculous and unfair. But note this: The unfair blaming is being done out loud. It is in the public domain where it can get cleared up, not in your secretive mind.

VII. **Stay there with the person beyond the time it takes to exchange resentments.** Keep stating your resentments as they come up, and allow the other person to resent you for resenting him, eventually you won't have anything left to resent each other for.

VIII. **After you both have fully expressed your specific resentments, state your appreciation in the same way. Say, 'I appreciate you for...' Not 'I appreciate the fact that....'** Keep checking your body to see how you feel. Are your shoulders tense? Do you feel relaxed? Do you feel like you want to get away from this situation as soon as possible? If the latter is true, there is more that you are withholding. Tell the truth of your experience even if it's: 'I still feel uncomfortable sitting here with you,' or 'I appreciate you for staying here and listening to me'. When you feel warmth in your chest and a smile on your face, express your appreciation in a clear way: 'I appreciate you for the way you look at me right now.' Some more resentments may emerge. If that happens, express those resentments and go on. Eventually you will just be sitting in a room looking at a person. You will see clearer. You be willing to live and let live. You will be grateful to him for having stuck with you through another fight.

IX. **Keep it up.** After an emotional exchange in which people tell the truth, they often retreat into superficiality. Keep up with 'I resent you for...' and 'I appreciate you for ...' as they come up. You will tend to withhold your feelings on later occasions because you have practiced that for years, but you can always clean it up with the person as soon as you realize you are withholding.

Frankness (moralive®1.4): Open sesame: the magic, transparent diary of I'm frank

The secret of the good life is not suffocating in the mind's bullshit

Brad Blanton

If you want to give your newborn son a name that's more than a name, call them Frank. If your child grows up to have the courage of their authenticity, your child can exist. Your child will be someone. Frankly, it's important so stop trying to be someone, and be. Be frank. Say what you sense with sensory descriptions, not evaluations and generalizations. By now you might be seeing a pattern emerging with honesty. Honesty is simple. And being frank is

Time to define:
Frank: Frankness is candour: The quality of being open, honest and straightforward in attitude, expression, and in speech.

uncluttered simplicity, without the Jackie O sunglasses, make-up, air-kisses, murmurs or whispers. But here's the best thing about frank: Frank is funny. There is humour in truth and comedy in errors. Think of the funniest thing you have heard. Was it based on a lie? The people that make us laugh are frank. Louis C.K was voted the funniest person alive, and if you look at his quotes, you can see they have nothing to do with lies. Take for example this quote: '*I finally have the body I want. It's easy, actually, you just have to want a really shitty body.*' No coincidence, perhaps that one of the highest rated television shows ever on the imdb database is called *Only the Truth is Funny*.

When to exercise frankness (moralive®1.4)
Every day, without exception, unless your life depends on it – but wait, your life does depend on it.

To lighten the load
What do you associate with the word candour? Frankness is the funniest part of being honest. Frank people make you laugh. Frank people may make two-faced people uncomfortable, but don't they also provide relief by saying it as it is? Frank people say someone is full of shit when no one else has the guts to. When was the last time someone

was frank with you? Did you feel you were able to resonate with what they were saying? You often experience relief that the unsaid-but-sensed is finally expressed. Having a frank conversation with someone is a simple but effective exercise for your Happiness Animal's honesty muscle.

But I don't want to offend someone by telling the truth?
If you tell someone the truth, they might be unhappy with you at first, they might authentically resent you, but at least they will know where they stand and can work out more clearly their next move. That is kinder than lying to them, and giving them false hope that can only disappoint. Doug finally chose to be frank with Mia for the sake of his wellbeing. Insincerity was making him uncomfortable, weak and awkward. True, Mia was upset and slammed a door when Doug first came clean about his feelings, but it put an end to Doug's long term suffering. The same day Doug was frank with Mia he decided to be frank with the coffee machine supplier. This opened up the business relationship again so that it became productive. The supplier would send the part Doug needed, Doug could fix the machine and they could continue to trade with each other. Frankness in business relationships is often the difference between make or break. Whether you call it frankness or candour doesn't matter. The two words are interchangeable, but the meaning is what counts. And it counts in the workplace as much as at home. Take the advice of the former CEO of General Electric, Jack Welch: 'What a huge problem it is. Lack of candour basically blocks smart ideas, fast action, and good people contributing all the stuff they've got. It's a killer. Forget outside competition when your own worst enemy is the way you communicate with one another internally. Candour works because candour unclutters.'

Say no when you mean it.

Which of the following do you prefer: 1) Genuine kindness by being ready to tell the uncomfortable truth, or, 2) the politeness of someone who avoids confrontation and says yes when they mean no? With dresses as it is with words, it is the fear of what people will say that can turn people into puppets rather than unique individuals. If your relationship is going to be real, and if it is going to belong lasting, you will be appreciated for saying no. You will be appreciated for being you and being present to the other person. It is important to say no, not save face. What face are you saving? Yes bingo, you are saving a cracked plastic mask. Tacky look.

Open sesame

Openness is magical and you see through to the magic when you are transparent. There is the enjoyment of freedom to be had in having nothing to hide. No effort needs to be made to cover anything up, to sweep something under the carpet, or behind the fridge. In the words of Piero Ferrucci: 'To be transparent is a relief. Muddy waters hide a host of unpleasant surprises.' And he goes on to explain the biological benefits of being frank: 'Because eccentrics are not subject to the stress of having to conform to other's expectations, their immune system is stronger.'

When you waste less energy repairing your mask, you have more energy in your Happiness Animal, and in your body. You're naturally a bad actor because acting is illness and you are naturally healthy. But the illness is

Time to define: mirror neuron

A **mirror neuron** is a neuron that fires both when an animal acts and when the animal observes the same action performed by another. Thus, the neuron 'mirrors' the behaviour of the other, as though the observer were itself acting. Mirror neurons have been directly observed in humans, primates and other species including birds.

contagious. Frankness is the cure to bad acting. Just like the illness, the cure is also contagious. Frankness is responded to with frankness. The internal mirror that activates with anger, also activates with frankness. The biological reason for this internal mirror is the existence of certain brain cells that you have in common with the rest of humanity, namely: mirror neurons.

It's one of the seven deadly sins for a reason

It's kryptonite to Frank and to the Happiness Animal. Nothing disturbs the harmony of social relations more than falsehood, and in its moralizing form it is one of the biggest causes of dishonesty. What I am talking about is pride. Pride needs a wall of lies to protect it, a wall of lies that hides every real thought and action that doesn't match the trophies on the wall of what you are proud of. Pride is as much about hiding the dirty laundry as it is about showing off the new suit. Frank people don't hide their problems away. Proud people rarely tell you their problems, their weaknesses, their resentments or their appreciations. Honesty expert, Brad Blanton, says withholding this kind of information is the most pernicious form of lying. Hiding does the opposite of exercising your Happiness Animal, and this is one of the reasons why pride demoralizes and weakens your Happiness Animal. There is a song I heard on the Australian radio station, TripleJ, which has the lyric 'you build a wall to protect your pride'. It's true.

Self-esteem

Don't make the common mistake of confusing pride with self-esteem, and the mistake of confusing lack of pride with low self-esteem. Pride and self-esteem are not even distant cousins: One is a creation of ego (bullshit), and the other is a truth guide. Frank people have higher self-esteem from the feeling of strength, courage, and aliveness they get from exercising frankness. Proud people often have low self-esteem, demoralized by lies. Yes truth can be embarrassing. Perhaps the truth is you didn't do any preparation for a meeting. Perhaps the truth is you have no idea what the other person is talking about. Perhaps the truth is you couldn't give a shit about what the result of the game was. Perhaps the truth is you didn't go the gym, perhaps you live in a share house, not a mansion, perhaps the truth is you blew all your cash on late night drinking, perhaps the truth is you are hung-over. The more often you tell the truth the less embarrassed you will be regardless of whatever it is you have done. If you are embarrassed, why? It's because your behaviour doesn't live up to, or is not consistent with the image (ego) of yourself that you have been presenting to the world. Embarrassment is injury to pride, and injury to ego. Can you use that embarrassment for your own development? Making yourself transparent to the world when you feel the trigger of embarrassment is an exercise in vulnerability. Exercising with vulnerability, as you will discover in the next chapter and in the chapter on courage, strengthens your Happiness Animal and boosts your self-esteem. Lying to maintain pride goes against human nature. It is a more natural to be frank than to lie to maintain the bullshit of ego. Without frankness in your honesty muscle, the SHIFT is just SHIT. So let's be frank with each other and let's start right now...

Exercising moralive®1.4 – call it bullshit.

Exercise for: washing your words

Before you next go to meet up with a friend or a family member, or go into a meeting at work, stop.

First, answer the following questions:

1. What is my intention going into this conversation?

_____

_____

_____

2. Am I operating with a second agenda?

　　YES　　　~　　NO　　(circle as appropriate)

3. What is my real motivation for this conversation?

_____

_____

_____

_____

Now, practice doing the following before your actual conversation: Get a chair and sit or stand facing it.

4. Imagine that the other person is sat in the chair. Talk out loud about what you intend to talk about during your conversation with the other person **and start every sentence with either the words 'I notice' or 'I imagine'** Restrict the use of 'I notice' to things you can physically notice right now, using your five senses. Be aware of the difference between what you can notice and what you imagine. The rule here is that unless you can actually notice something very specific e.g. you can see a specific sentence written down in front of you then you start your sentences with the words 'I imagine'.

5. Continue your practice conversation with the other person but this time instead of using the words 'I imagine', say 'I bullshit'

6. Meet up with the person. During your actual conversation, practice starting your sentences with either 'I notice' or 'I imagine' and be aware of the difference between the two.

7. Give yourself permission to speak frankly, even if it is abnormal for you to be frank. Focus simply on saying what is so and what you can notice, and the sensations you feel when talking about different topics in the conversation. e.g. 'Now we are talking about KPI8, I notice some tension in my stomach. I imagine it's because I saw...'

moralive®1.5 – Trust

Would it not be more honourable to be deceived by some than suspect all of dishonesty?

Seneca

We're never so vulnerable than when we trust someone—but paradoxically, if we cannot trust, neither can we find love or joy

Walter Anderson

I wrote in the introduction to this book that I ran an online survey to poll 700 people globally, asking them to choose the best definition of happiness from six descriptions (see p.56). The list of definitions I provided was not intended to be exhaustive, but the poll results surprised me. I had taken one of

Time to define: Trust
Firm belief in the integrity, reliability, truth, character, ability, or strength of someone or something

the definitions from an online dictionary. It was 'trust and confidence'. Trust and confidence are represented in chapter 5 (honesty) and chapter 9 (courage). What surprised me was that 'trust and confidence' were voted as the best definition of happiness by the majority of those polled. I had expected the definition 'pleasure & contentment' to be the most voted-for definition, given the majority of society's activities are dependent on consumerism – the constant striving and encouragement

to buy bigger and better things that promise pleasure, comfort, contentment, and a smiling face on our glossy screens. Yet, the more I focused on my own experience of trust and confidence, the more it made sense to me that both trust and confidence are the basic nutritional requirements for happiness. Trust and confidence are inextricably linked to each other and to the strength of the Happiness Animal. Trust is confidence, confidence in truth. And confidence, is trust in truth. You have trust in someone when you have confidence that they tell you the truth, but also, you have confidence in someone when you trust that they tell the truth. Conversely though, by showing others that you are trusting, you help to increase their confidence to tell you the truth. By being trusting, you make it possible to both trust more people and be trusted by more. The upshot is that when you feel more confident in others and yourself, you feel well. You are able to share more, exercising your kindness muscle as well as your honesty and courage muscles. You also feel free. Trust and confidence allow you to enjoy the freedom from not having to hide anything from anyone. I was fortunate enough to

Oddly Enough
When you stop trusting others you stop trusting yourself: 'Sometimes it only takes one person to determine that *nobody* is in fact trustworthy. In the process, we often lose trust in ourselves— simply because our judgement of the person or circumstance was incorrect—and we then wonder how we can believe our own judgement. As a result, we might close our hearts, repress our emotions, and walk around numb or suspicious in relationships.'
- Susanne Babbel, Psychologist.

experience a concentrated week of the joy of trust and confidence when I attended a *Radical Honesty* workshop in Greece, hosted by the author of *Radical Honesty*, Brad Blanton. On the first morning of the eight day workshop, each of us (most meeting for the first time) were asked to share a secret about our lives that we felt most uncomfortable telling anyone about, something we didn't want other people to know about us. Needless to say, this was one of the best ice-breakers I have been a part of, and it instantly created an atmosphere that it was OK to say anything to anyone in the room. We could let our guard down. We could relax with one another. And we committed to telling each other the frank truth for the next eight days. The intensive experience of group trust led to us forming lasting friendships, spending time together on the beach, in the garden, and enjoying each others company. I still have Skype calls and get-togethers with at least four of the people from the workshop to this day. And our conversations are still refreshingly frank.

When to exercise trust (moralive®1.5)

Be trustworthy by creating trustworthiness

Lying masks what we think are our weaknesses. Once hidden, we try to avoid being unmasked and this creates anxiety. But where there is trust, there is no need to wear the mask and no need to be afraid of being unmasked. Trust is the child of your honesty. And the child looks after its parent by providing the resources that grow your relationships. A relationship is only meaningful if it is trusting, and honesty is the basis not only for trust, but also for kindness. Without trust kindness cannot be kindness. It can only be the appearance of kindness. Piero Ferrucci writes: 'As long as you are not living in the truth, you cannot have trust, you cannot relate. As long as you do not call the hard realities by name, you are living in the land of dreams. There is no room for you and me there, but only for harmful illusions.

Inasmuch as we lie we have a life devoid of reality. And kindness cannot exist in a world of masks and phantoms.'

Be trusting to be trusted

Just as people are innocent until proven guilty in the United States, take the attitude that people can be trusted until they betray you. When you start with the assumption that people are naturally trustworthy, and you treat them as such, then they are more likely to be trustworthy with you. How you approach a person will effect how they respond. If you approach them with the suspicion of mistrust, they are likely to reciprocate with their mirror neurons firing all cylinders. If others see you as mistrusting, their thinking links associate you with mistrust. It's a logical deduction that if you are not a trusting person, you are also not to be trusted. Also keep an eye on your body language: Northeastern University, MIT and Cornell, in a joint study identified 4 non-verbal cues that are often interpreted as untrustworthiness by the person receiving the body language. It turns out that the following body language is also often caused by selfish and dishonest intentions towards the receiver:

- Leaning away from someone
- Crossing arms in a blocking fashion
- Touching, rubbing or grasping hands together
- Touching oneself on the face, abdomen or elsewhere.

Trust with benefits

Barbara Misztal, in her book, *Trust in Modern Societies: The Search for the Bases of Social Order*, attempts to combine all notions of trust together. She identifies three basic functions of trust: First, it makes social life predictable; second, it creates a sense of community (a sense of belonging is critical to the health of the Happiness Animal); and third, it makes it easier for people to work together. According to the World Happiness Report 2013, commissioned by the United Nations, social trust is also a strong determinant of life evaluations: 'Because trust measures have been shown to be strong supports for subjective well-being, this erosion of some key elements of institutional trust thus helps to explain the exceptionally large well-being losses in Greece.'

It doesn't matter whether you live in Greece or Guatemala, your Happiness Animal will benefit from exercising trust.

Exercising Trust (moralive® 1.5)

Exercise for: building trust in yourself and others

Part I – trust yourself (Part I is based on an exercise by psychologist Susanne Babbell)

1. Sit or lie down so that you feel comfortable.

2. Now, how can you make it even more comfortable? Get a blanket, a pillow... whatever will make you feel relaxed and content.

3. Once you are settled, ask yourself: 'How do I know this is comfortable?' This might appear to be a silly question, and perhaps even confusing. However, it is an important one in increasing your skills of building trust (using your senses, not your mind).

4. Continue to explore what sensation you feel that you recognize as comfort. For example, you might think: 'I do not feel any pain', 'I breathe easily', or 'I feel relaxed'.

5. You might be anticipating that this feeling won't last, which is true. We can't control or grasp onto this pleasurable feeling. It's only important that you are in the present moment right now, not drifting into thoughts of the future or the past. Thinking of the future can create anxiety; thinking of the past can create depression.

6. Remain aware of any sounds, the temperature, the light, and your physical sensations. Can you let yourself simply enjoy the moment?

7. You can practice this exercise for as long as you prefer and as time allows you. Just keep checking in with your level of comfort. What feelings indicate that you are comfortable? With time, you will start to trust your feelings (your senses) again.

Part II – Trust that you can trust others

8. At the next opportunity, ask a family member or a colleague if they can get you (or make you) the hot drink of your choice. And trust that they can do it for you.

9. Meet with a friend and confide in them with a secret. Even if there is a risk they could tell someone else, trust that they won't. Tell them you trust that they won't tell anyone and that you are putting your trust in them by telling them this.

10. Lend a favourite possession to a friend and trust that they will look after it and give it back to you, e.g. your favourite book, DVD, or an appliance. You could lend them your coffee machine or crêpe maker while you are on holiday.

11. Practice these trusting body language exercises: **a) eye contact** with a colleague, friend, or loved one: ask the other person to stand facing you and to stare into your eyes while you stare back for one minute; **b) eye contact with touch** – repeat step a) but this time hold hands as well; **c) proximity** – this time stand opposite the other person a comfortable distance apart, and then ask the other person to move a little closer and notice how what you feel changes as they move closer. Then increase the distance and notice how it changes how you feel.

Animal Advice

- Lying has a thousand faces, the truth only one.

- Is it better to be half you half of the time or all you all of the time?

- Your essence contains your authenticity. It is there already. You just have to rediscover it through your senses, and then give it to the world.

- Your senses channel your authenticity as the source of your creativity.

- Telling the truth frees you from the anxiety of having to hide.

- Telling the truth connects you with existence. Happiness is connecting well with existence.

- Harmony in your Happiness Animal happens when what you express resonates with what you feel.

Chapter 6

moralive®3: kindness

The spirit in which a present is given is more important than the
present itself

Seneca

There is no choice between being kind to others and being kind
to ourselves. It is the same thing

Piero Ferrucci

Animal's Anecdote

A stranger tissue

Rolf sat in his regular spot on the cushioned bench at the Don Adan café, his back against the wall. An old map of the world covered the table where he rested his laptop. Davinci's man covered the next table. Rolf's predisposition to distraction by any and everything engaged when his auto-tuner picked up a conversation an eighty-something-year-old woman was having with her daughter. Less than two metres separated Rolf from the pair, but two tables in between provided the illusion of distance. Rolf dropped his head towards his table and bent an ear towards the women:

'How is the shop?' asked the mother.

'Yeah... Alright,' said the daughter. The daughter's eyes stayed fixed on the newspaper that she pushed up against the wall to the left sliding it across the table.

'Did I tell you the neighbours are moving out?' The mother leaned forwards and tilted her forehead towards her daughter.

'No. I've got to go in a few minutes. ... I need to get something to wear for later,' said the daughter, her eyes still down refusing to budge from the newspaper.

'What do you think you will wear?' asked the mother.

'I've got to wear white,' said the daughter.

'White's a strange colour, isn't it?' said the mother.

The daughter looked past her mother and out the café window.

The mother dropped her hands to below the table. Her left hand gripped her left knee and her right hand gripped her right leg above the knee. She looked down at her lap and then looked up to her coffee cup, which she grasped and began to sip from repeatedly. As her line of vision crossed her daughter's face, she tried to catch a glimpse of her daughter's eyes.

Tension tightened Rolf's ribs. He wanted to release himself from the strain narrowing his shoulders and shortening his neck. Rolf stood up from his table and took the key to the café bathroom off the wall next to where the mother sat. He looked down and smiled at her.

'Are you a frequent drinker?' Rolf read out the words of an advertisement for the café that was on the wall, meeting with the mother's eyes as he said the word 'drinker'.

'Well I am but it doesn't sound good does it?' Rolf continued. The mother sat back quickly and jolted her eyes up at Rolf. Rolf realized that he hadn't yet connected and his eyes rushed back out onto the stage. 'You are almost as regular a drinker here as me, aren't you?' asked Rolf.

'Well…yes… yes I could be,' said the mother. Now that surprise had subsided, her face softened, and her mouth began to almost smile.

That night back at the house, Rolf described the scene to his housemate, Mia.

'I felt sorry for the mother, I had to say something to her,' Rolf said.

'But that's dangerous. You have no idea what might have happened leading up to that moment,' said Mia. She lifted her eyebrows.

'Yes that's why I didn't say anything about it to either of them…I just decided to talk to the mother so she felt more appreciated.'

Rolf could feel the buzz of thoughts that proved he was right building up into the hub of a noisy pylon in his head. It was a pylon that powered circles of electric fences around him, separating him from Mia. Each thought was an electric fence that stopped him from engaging fully in his conversation and connecting with Mia: *it was obvious the daughter was in the wrong; there was no excuse for the daughter's behaviour even if the mother had done something wrong.*

'Why would they have lunch together if the mother had done something evil?' asked Rolf, smiling, his head tilted back, as he looked down his nose at Mia. 'Some people are just assholes,' he continued. He began to feel a familiar vacuous feeling in his stomach and tension around his forehead. The next day Rolf was on a train to Central

Station in Sydney, when he felt the trickle of water-like mucus running down towards the entrance of his nostrils. It was about to break the levee – already a tickling pre-drip. Rolf had to act now. His pockets were empty. He looked around the carriage for tissue donors. Next to him was what appeared to be a mother and daughter. Unlike the two in the café, this pair were engaged in a healthy dialogue of give and take, with a warm seasoning of eye contact. He targeted the mother. 'Sorry to bother you, do you have a tissue I could borrow please?' said Rolf.

'Sorry?' she replied.

'Do you have a tissue please?' said Rolf.

A frozen expression softened to a promising look of understanding on the mother's face. Rolf felt the pull of approaching relief, but then as the mother's fumbling at the bottom of her handbag continued, the pull weakened. The drip was pooling, teasing at the tip of his nose. Rolf was now sniffing incessantly. The old woman pulled the plug on hope. 'I'm sorry, I don't have one after all. Strange. I normally carry some tissues around with me,' she said.

Rolf smiled at the lady, turned away and eyeballed disbelief. The trickle was about to reach the climax of tickle. He sniffed like a rat. The train slowed as it came into Central Station. As he got up from his seat and stepped towards the door a hand reached towards him with a fresh, folded Kleenex. He followed the hand and then arm back in the direction of its origin until he met with the nervy, wide eyes of a woman. It was the mother from the Don Adan café. She said nothing. Rolf took the tissue. His surprise took the wind out of his words. 'Thank you,' he mumbled. He blew his nose on the train, making conspicuous use of the precious gift. He stepped out onto the platform. 'Thank you,' he called out to the woman, who was now three people deep ahead of him. Unsure who the call was for, she turned around, froze eye contact for a second and then released a smile. Rolf smiled back and took a deep breath through his nose. Back at the house, Rolf found Mia in the kitchen again, as she prepared her dinner. 'You know I told you about that old woman with the rude daughter at the café yesterday?' said Rolf.

'Yes,' said Mia as she stirred the vegetables in her wok. 'Well I was on the train today and she turned up out of nowhere and gave me a tissue when my nose was running!'

'Wow, that's crazy,' said Mia , looking up from the pan to meet with Rolf's eyes.

Rolf felt the build up of verbal diarrhoea and hyperbole behind his nose. Mia was still, apart from her head that was slowly reclining as if to pull the next words from Rolf. Her eyes wide and fixed on Rolf's. Rolf sensed his pause of distraction-by-thoughts was about to be perceived as rude by Mia. *I have to switch off,* he thought. He imagined lifting a heavy sprung lever, his thought pylon's off switch. His electric fences were down and he could now reach Mia without being buzzed.

Animal Analysis

Kindness is the one virtue that unites and encompasses all others

Paul Dubois

kindness

noun: 1. The quality of being friendly, generous, and considerate

2. A kind act

Oxford Dictionary

If there is one muscle in the Happiness Animal that focuses entirely on relationships between yourself and other people, then kindness is it. Yet in all exercises of the kindness muscle, your attitude inside, is more important than your actions outside. What matters most is your intention. Exercising is made easier when you discover that there are no external constraints or conditions, and exercising is made more attractive when you experience how it benefits your Happiness Animal. It costs nothing to change your attitude. It's free, so why not change to the best attitude you can get? If I offered you a choice between wearing dirty underwear, or a clean pair, which would you choose? Changing attitudes is as easy as changing your underwear. And you don't need to wash an attitude in soap. You *are* your attitude, and your attitude *is* whatever you intend it to be. From an intention, kindness is the easiest attitude to create: Author of *The power of kindness*, Piero Ferrucci agrees, 'It [kindness] is the most economic attitude there is, because it saves us much energy that we might otherwise waste in suspicion, worry, resentment, manipulation, or unnecessary defence. It is an attitude that, by eliminating the inessential, brings us back to the simplicity of being.' In this chapter, there are five types of kindness that can be exercised: 1) Warmth; 2) Respect; 3) Recognition and Appreciation; 4) Altruism, Benefits, Consideration and Gratitude (The ABC of Gratitude); 5) Empathy and Compassion. I'm going to take you through the five kindnesses in that order. Let's get started with the first that makes the four others flow...

Warmth (moralive®2.1)

Warmth is the potential for all emotion, and therefore makes life itself possible

Piero Ferrucci

Time to define: warmth

1. The state, sensation, or quality of producing or having a moderate degree of heat: *an agreeable warmth in the house.*
2.
a. Friendliness, kindness, or affection: *human warmth.*
b. Excitement or intensity, as of love or passion; ardor.
3. The glowing effect produced by using predominantly red or yellow hues. (Source: The American Heritage® Dictionary of the English Language)

Warmth is created when energy is transferred. Warmth is fuel for all your Happiness Animal's muscles. Warmth is physical. Warmth is as much seen as it is invisible and is as much in your voice as it is in your smile. Warmth isn't only pleasurable and comforting – warmth boosts the health of all animals. A lack of warmth in childhood can also have long term health consequences: a Harvard study reports that people with cold, impatient and brutal parents are 62% more likely to develop a major disease in their lifetime. But with exercise, warmth can defrost the icy pain of your past, and improve the health of your Happiness Animal today.

When to exercise your kindness muscle with warmth (moralive®2.1)

The voice of warmth

Warmth is found in sound: a voice is physical in as much as the vibrations that start in the body of whoever is talking to you, travel, vibrating the air in between them and you, until the vibrations get into your ear, literally moving inside you. The assumption that sound only touches metaphorically is false. Sound touches you physically. Just because you cannot see sound until you turn your speakers up to maximum, does not mean that sound is not physical. Why does music move you? Why are music scores added to movies? Like music, your voice has the potential to offer warmth, or, an Antarctic freeze. More than any of the other exercises of the Happiness Animal, exercising warmth instantly spreads benefits to you and to those around you. Warmth is a human campfire, primal in nature, and an essential life force of your Happiness Animal.

Let's get physical

Warmth takes many physical forms of expression. The benefits of each vary depending on your social context. For example, an Austrian study has found that hugging your family and friends produces biological benefits, but hugging strangers does not. Hugging family and friends (for at least six seconds per hug) triggers the release of the hormone oxytocin, which boosts bonding interaction and closeness. Couples that touch are healthier and more relaxed, say researchers at the University of North Carolina: their study found that couples with more physical contact (hugs and kisses) had lower blood pressure and lower heart rate increases in response to a public speaking task compared to a group of people who didn't regularly receive physical warmth from their partner. All participants spoke for a few minutes about a recent event that made them angry or stressed, and blood pressure soared in the no-contact group. Their systolic (upper) reading jumped 24 points, more than double the rise compared with the couples who had regular physical contact. Heart rate increased 10 beats a minute for those without contact, compared with an increase of only five beats a minute for those with contact. Karen Grewen of the University of Carolina's Psychiatry department says: 'these findings suggest that affectionate relationships with a supportive partner may contribute to lower reactivity to stressful life events and may partially mediate the benefit of marital support on better cardiovascular health.' Touch is the fastest way to create and transfer warmth between two people, and the benefits are not simply emotional. As with every other exercise of the Happiness Animal, the benefits are biological. Touch increases the amount of haemoglobin in the blood. More haemoglobin means more oxygen in the body, which means more oxygen to the heart and to the brain. An increased supply of haemoglobin helps the body to heal faster from illness, but also prevents depression. Studies have shown that eight hugs a day provide mental stability, and twelve hugs a day aid psychological development: 'We need four hugs a day for survival. We need eight hugs a day for maintenance. We need twelve hugs a day for growth,' says author and psychotherapist, Virginia Satir, who is widely regarded as the mother of family therapy. As well as releasing oxytocin, hugging a loved one triggers the release of the hormones serotonin and dopamine, hormones that are chemically linked to feelings of happiness.

Mata Amritanandmayi or 'Amma', has become known as the 'Hugging Saint', for the reason that she has embraced more than 32 million people around the world. Amma believes that the warmth of individual hugs spreads both within and beyond the countries of those individuals: 'The fight in individual minds is responsible for wars. So if you can touch people, you can touch the world.' There is biology that supports Amma's philosophy that hugs diminish animosity and the fight in individual minds: hugging triggers activity in the cerebellar brain system, and it is this brain activity that produces the emotions of trust and affection. During the writing of this book I started out single, living on my own, and now I find myself in an affectionate relationship, that involves regular hugs, almost every day. I do feel more relaxed than I did living alone and find it easier to make contact with new potential collaborators. I can't attribute my calmness directly to the daily hugs, and my work on *The Happiness Animal* in general has had a profound effect on the strength of my own Happiness Animal, but the hugs undoubtedly make their own contribution. I have started to pay more attention to how I feel before and after hugs and I can honestly say regular hugs do help me to relax and to 'let go' of potential sources of frustration. Of course, you don't need to be dating someone to obtain these benefits, but it does highlight the importance of paying attention to the relationships in our lives. If you don't have a partner, consider meeting up with a close friend more often, and hugging when you meet. Hugging family offers the same Happiness Animal benefits. And if you live in a share house, hug your housemate every day.

I'm starting with the man in the mirror
True it would be odd at best and uncomfortable at worst to shake hands with a complete stranger, let alone hug them, but warmth doesn't have to involve bodily contact. The person who smiles at you can give you warmth without laying a finger on you. When someone smiles at you, their smile often activates your mirror neurons triggering you to smile. The next time you're out walking around, give a stranger a smile or a nod. Research published by Livescience reveals that smiles, and other tiny gestures, make people feel more connected. According to a study by the Society for the Study of Motivation, people who have been acknowledged by a stranger feel more connected to others immediately after an encounter than people who have been ignored. 'Ostracism is painful,' says study researcher Eric Wesselmann, a social psychologist at Purdue University in Indiana. Warmth, can be considered the opposite of ostracism and has many reciprocal benefits, the most contagious being cheerfulness. Cheerfulness is an internal attitude but

is often the first sign of warmth: the smile, the whistle, the relaxed yet energised posture, the body language that benefits both the creator and the observer. And from the warmth of cheerfulness, friendliness is a natural bi-product. Warm people are friendly. Friendly people make friends. They make friends in a way that has nothing to do with the politeness and 'how are you?' of meet and greet small talk, but in a way that has everything to do with authentic curiosity for the wellbeing and ideas of others. Friendliness, warmth and cheerfulness come as a package. Your voice is the sound of the warmth of cheerfulness. Your eyes and your smile are its light.

But how can I be cheerful when I'm the one that needs cheering up?

What happens when you say cheers to someone? You meet another glass with your own. If you don't offer your glass, you don't get cheers. Take doesn't cheer. Take demoralizes. Cheer can only be given and it starts with an intention to cheer up someone else. Oddly enough, cheering someone else up not only cheers you up but also increases your self-esteem. You feel useful to someone. By focusing only on what you can do for yourself, you take heat from the fire without adding any wood. The fire

DEFINE

Time to define: friendliness
A feeling of liking for another person; enjoyment in their company.

soon goes out and leaves you cold. But feed the fire in others first and you will make it warmer in the room for yourself. Start out with small tinder: offer smiles, cups of tea, a hug. Move onto the longer lasting logs: offer to help with something that's on their mind. Perhaps they are stuck on something at work and you can brainstorm some ideas together. Perhaps they are caught in thoughts of indecision around an important life move. Asking a few questions may help them to untangle themself from their mind, freeing their arms to give you a warm hug.

4 smiles, 4 hugs and a cup of tea: exercising warmth (moralive®2.1)

Exercise for when you are feeling lonely, cold, or isolated. This is an exercise that warms up your daily routine.

Instructions

Hugs: Offer to give someone you know (or someone you don't know but would be comfortable hugging) a hug: 1) in the morning 2) at lunch 3) in the afternoon 4) in the evening. Ask as many different people as you feel comfortable hugging.

Smiles: On the way to work (in the car, while walking, on the bus) smile at least one person. Do the same on your lunch break, and again on the way home from work.

Cup of tea: In the office, or at home: If someone seems stressed, upset or just tired, tell them you are making a cup of tea for yourself and them and ask what kind of tea they drink. Go get it and bring it back to them. Alternatively if you happen to see someone crying out on the street, at the bus stop or train station (and you feel comfortable talking to them), approach them and ask them what the matter is. Offer them a hug and a 'let's get you a cup of tea'. Buy them a cup, and then say goodbye with a smile.

Respect (moralive®2.2)

Without respect kindness is blind

Piero Ferrucci

Find out what it means to me

Respect is paying attention. And not just to a warning sign in a street. Respect is reverence for every living being. It is an appreciation of the miracle of existence of every animal, insect, woman, man, plant and child. It is seeing value in every form of life, whether we eat it, protect it, live next to it, or fall in love with it. Respect is acknowledgement of existence of the beings we come into contact with.

When to exercise your kindness muscle with respect (moralive®2.2)

Respect my space

Respect of someone's physical and mental space is one of the easiest ways to open up a relationship, letting someone be who they are without surrounding them with our thoughts and ideas, judgement and advice. Respect happens when you become aware of and then release all pressure that you apply to the thoughts of others by expressing judgments and hopes that others should be or behave in a certain way (normally the same way you do). Instead of telling your friends that they should be a certain way or should do something, you communicate that you trust them to make their own best choices. It will go a long way for your friendship if you can exercise respect for your friend's ability to work things out on their own without pressuring them when they haven't asked you for your opinion. If you communicate a judgement before allowing the other to explore, you are applying pressure to their space. That's forcing them into a smaller space. Your offering of a judgement is linked to your desire to control others and things. When you don't give your judgement, you give others freedom. This doesn't mean you can't offer your opinion when others ask you for it and it does not mean you can't discuss ideas with curiosity and give your tolerance muscle a workout. But the trust that comes from you noticing, accepting and releasing – rather than speaking – your judgement will be noticed by your friend, and it goes without saying that a more trusting relationship is a happier relationship. If, however, you outpour your ego's views of how your friend should behave, you suffocate them and your kindness. Kinder than the gift of advice, you can give others the space for their ideas to breathe. Imagine the respect that you want to receive for your own ideas. When can you offer the same respect to your friends and family?

Respect should be seen and be heard

Respect is listening to how, not just what, is being said. When you listen, you are taking your blinders off and your earplugs out. Listening benefits you by allowing you to hear and then see more of the orchestra of life. If you present only your own stories you are restricting your view to one miniscule, fixed window on the world. This is the barred window of a prison cell. When you listen to others, you escape your cell and discover new rooms with new windows, each window holding a unique piece of an infinite panorama. The more windows you look through, the more the windows disappear altogether and the more you become part of the infinite view itself. Your ears become your doors, best left open. 'The ear is the image of our openness to the world,' says author of *The power of kindness*, Piero Ferrucci. The key to good listening, to ensure you get the best view, is to stop multi-tasking. Imagine trying to review your to-do list while standing at a lookout over the Grand Canyon. Will you enjoy or appreciate the view?

Phone a friend

When you next have a conversation with someone, ask yourself what thoughts are competing for your attention. What are the competing sounds, sights, smells, pains and worries, all doing their best to distract you from what the person is trying to tell you. Your mind is doing its best to distract you. Your distraction, if seen, is disrespect of the other person. Respect is not only allowing the other person to speak uninterrupted, but also, allowing yourself to listen to the other person uninterrupted by your thoughts. Just like Rolph with Mia, learn to move your thoughts switch to off so you can drop the buzz of electric fences that separate you from the person who is talking to you. It is this kind of respect that is necessary for you to be able to relate to other people, to feel a connection to other people, and to feel a sense of belonging with other people.

If you are finding it hard to give someone who is speaking to you your full attention, because you are distracted by your own thoughts, try making a game of looking at the speaker's body language and become aware of – by noticing – shifts in their body language that correspond to shifts in what they are talking about or the energy of their voice. Do they clench their fist? Touch their face? What type of talk triggers what type of language? If you are distracted by your own thoughts, notice how your own body feels. Where is there tension? Start of the top of your body and relax each body part one by one until you reach your feet. Often by relaxing the tension in your shoulders, then noticing the feeling of your breathing going in and out of your body will be enough to bring you to being present with the person who is speaking. Don't make an effort to breathe. Just notice three of your breaths in and out. Notice the pauses in between breaths, and the feeling as the air rushes inside you. And if you are still having a hard time listening, try the exercise at the end of this section.

The listener: Co-creator of authenticity

Even people who appear so dull that they couldn't possibly have anything interesting to say, do have something interesting to say. Guaranteed. But first, you have to take a look through their window to see it. Ever had a first impression of someone along these lines: tiring, monotonous voice, dull? Ever been surprised by the insights on life that later bubbled out of their barely moving lips? Did you pause your thoughts to see the view from their window? When you do, you become a co-creator of their authenticity. When you focus your attention completely on what is being said, others feel comfortable enough to be themselves authentically. Every individual has the capacity to be authentic and respect encourages it. Respect is not easy given the number of distractions there are around you all the time but the more you exercise listening, the stronger you will get at it. Indeed, your Happiness Animal benefits instantly from every workout. The irony is that the introduction of new communication technologies has turned us into terrible listeners. Every smart phone, tablet, and messaging App is a distraction away from listening to the person who is standing or sitting right in front of us.

Reverence – a higher state of respect

Respect applies to more than human beings. You don't just meet people every day, you also eat living things whether it's plants or animals. You also encounter bugs, bees, pets and crawlies. When was the last time you stopped for a minute and looked at what these 'things' are? Can you see that it is not a thing, but a living being? When did you last look closely at an ant and watch it moving all its legs or watch it picking something up? Why have most of us been conditioned to dismiss this creature as a thing of no value, something we can squash without hesitation? Look closely at it through a magnifying glass or your camera's macro zoom. All these creatures, whether they be cockroaches, ants, spiders or mice are all creatures because they are the result of an act of creation. Human beings have that much in common with ants – we are both creatures. Our tiny relatives deserve a little more respect, and reverence is the basic respect for all living things, not just human beings. And reverence doesn't mean you can't eat animals. I am not a vegetarian and my body has the ability to absorb nutrients from meat. But I have learned to appreciate that whatever I eat is absorbed by me. If you eat a steak, appreciate that it came from a bull. If you are eating a chicken appreciate the creature you are absorbing into your body. It is natural for animals to absorb other animals and that is how we transfer energy from creature to creature. But to kill an insect for the sake of killing it or because you are afraid, is not respectful of life. It will demoralize you. If you killed something recently that posed no threat to your existence, how did you feel after you killed it? The next time you are about to kill one, pause. Get as close to the creature as you can. Look at its eyes, its legs, and its body. What do you imagine it's doing? Of course, in the rare instances when you are under attack, you need to instinctively defend yourself.

Perhaps a mosquito is sucking your blood and you swat instinctively without remorse, but how often do you experience a genuine attack from your creature cousins?

Exercising respect (moralive®2.2): hear me now

Exercise for any face to face conversation. This is an exercise in active listening and giving your full attention. It is an exercise in not disagreeing out loud if your first reaction is to disagree with what's being said. It is an exercise in respecting that this is simply what the other person is saying. It is impossible to disagree that someone is saying the words they are saying to you. If, during this exercise you find yourself tempted to disagree with the person you are listening to, simply repeat back what the other says: if your child says, 'I don't want to go to school today', you say to your child, 'you don't want to go to school today' (instead of the common response: 'of course you do') . In Gretchen Rubin's *The Happiness Project*, she describes this as 'Acknowledge the reality of people's feelings'. Gretchen's strategies for acknowledging the reality of people's feelings are: 1) write down what the other person says to you; 2) don't feel as if you have to say anything; 3) don't say 'no' or 'stop'; 4) admit that tasks that the other person says they are finding it hard to do, are difficult (by replying to them with comments like 'yes it is not easy to do that'). Try and make use of these four strategies in the following exercise:

Instructions
1. Before you start listening, imagine your head full of the thoughts you have right now.
2. Imagine that you are starting to pull the huge lever for your thoughts to the off position. As you get closer to off, it will spring to that position with force on its own. Imagine the noise of the power springing to off.

3. Now you have switched off, you are ready to receive power from the other person. Now you are ready to begin to notice things that are not your own thoughts or ideas.

   TIP: If you find thoughts creeping back in – acknowledge them and accept them. To bring your presence back, notice the feeling of your breath going in and out of your body. Relax your shoulders. This will be enough to bring you into being present with the person who is speaking. Don't make an effort to breath. Just notice three of your breaths in and out, the pauses in between, and the feeling as the air rushes inside.

4. Notice which parts of the speaker's body are moving as you listen to them. Notice their hands, their ears, their jaw, their cheeks, their eyebrows. Pay attention to all their movements and acknowledge them to yourself. Watch for eye movements as the other person talks to you.

5. Paraphrase back what the other person has just said to you every time they pause.

6. Regularly ask a question that takes the form of repeating back what the person just said to you that shows your understanding. Try opening your question with 'So you ....' and ending your question with a smile and a 'Is that right?'

Recognition and Appreciation (moralive®2.3)

To love is to recognize yourself in another

Eckhart Tolle

It takes a nod, a smile or a comment & the ripples are huge. You feel better & the recipient will think of that moment for the rest of the day.

I challenge you to do it and not smile

Time to define: appreciation
n.
Recognition of the quality, value, significance, or magnitude of people and things. (The Free Dictionary)

Martin Pratley

Recognition is not politeness. Recognition is not categorizing. Recognition is not pigeonholing. Recognition and appreciation involve not just seeing, but also acknowledging someone's presence and in so doing, appreciating both their uniqueness, and their intentions. The Latin word for respect, 'respicere', means to see truly, or in the words of Piero Ferrucci; 'to look into the soul's deepest and most beautiful kernel.' If your true self is not seen when someone looks at you, you are hurt. When you sense that someone really sees you, and sees your intentions, not just your role or job title, you feel recognition and appreciation. You feel connection with existence.

When to exercise your kindness muscle with recognition and appreciation (moralive®2.3)

I have spent over nine years away from my family in England living in Germany, India, Australia, and more recently, the USA. As a child, my grandparents, who lived within a very short distance of my teenage

Oddly enough: appreciation aphrodisiac

Appreciation helps your Happiness Animal have a healthier sex life. Appreciation promotes activity in the **parasympathetic** nervous system, which as well a lowering your blood pressure also improves the healthy stimulation of erectile tissue in both men and women. The parasympathetic nervous system differs from the **sympathetic** nervous system, which triggers all animal's 'flight or fight' response by releasing the stress hormone and adrenalin.

The more stressed (sympathetic nervous system) you are the higher the chance of low libido and of premature ejaculation (the sympathetic nervous system activates ejaculation in the male). The more parasympathetic you are the more easily you will be turned on by your partner and the longer your sex will last.

parents, spent days and nights looking after me. I formed a close bond with them. But now that I only visit England once or twice a year those close bonds sometimes seem to have been broken, and the relationship can turn polite. This afternoon I drove my grandparents, now in their early nineties, to do some grocery shopping at the local supermarket. When we got back to their house, we sat around the kitchen table for a cup of tea and a bun. Conscious of how much they had aged, I sprung my thoughts lever to off. I paused to notice their facial expressions. They sensed that I was present with them. For the first time since I was a child, my grandfather and then my grandmother started to tell me stories about their siblings and parents, and of losing them. My grandmother told me that her sister had died when they were both children, and her mother had written a song for her lost child. My grandmother read a line from the song, titled 'Stay Awhile and Listen'. The line described how her mother had been able to listen to her lost child in the stillness of the night. It struck a chord in me, and I resonated with my grandmother again. Really looking at someone is an act of reciprocal warmth, just like a smile. How you look at someone determines how that person is in your world. If we see people as interesting and special, our world becomes more interesting and special.

You recognize intention when you notice what people are doing. Recognition of intention often leads to appreciation of intention. In the café, Rolf recognized and appreciated the mother's intention of warmth towards her daughter that her daughter could not see. He recognized the tension in the mother's face and body. By addressing the mother, Rolf showed her that he recognized her existence, and that his intentions towards her were friendly. Because he had already appreciated the mother's intention of warmth, he reciprocated warmth, easing the mother's tension, with humour. Appreciation benefits both the appreciator and the appreciated. As appreciator you feel freer, your blood pressure reduces, and your parasympathetic activity increases. Parasympathetic activity is considered protective of the body as it helps the body rest and digest, and maintain a regular heartbeat. Studies by Rollin McCraty, Barrios-Choplin, Rozman, Atkinson, and Watkins show that when you appreciate, the increase in your parasympathetic activity improves your hormonal balance and reduces the production of the stress hormone, cortisol, as well as increasing the production of DHEA, the 'anti-aging hormone'. A less stressed Happiness Animal is a stronger, more youthful, Happiness Animal. So let's exercise some recognition and appreciation right now...

Exercising recognition and appreciation (moralive®2.3): I appreciate you

Exercise for: Anytime you are around other people (strangers, family or friends)

1. Identify an individual. It could be someone you are talking with, or a complete stranger.
2. List 3 body movements you notice in the individual. **Tip: look at their hands, feet, eyebrows, jaw, shoulders, neck, mouth.**

1)_____

_____

2)_____

_____

3)

_____

_____

3. List one of the body movements or positions you also notice as similar in yourself. If you can't notice something similar, write how you differ in one of the body movements.

    _____

    _____

4. List one description – physical, verbal, or behavioural – of the individual that you appreciate them for e.g. (their eyes, smile, hand position, posture)
    I appreciate their

    _____

5. Make eye contact with the person, smile and tell them what you appreciate them for. Start your sentence with 'I appreciate your_____' or 'I appreciate you for _____. **Note:** If you feel too awkward to give verbal appreciation to a stranger, simply acknowledge the other person with a smile or a nod when you make eye contact with them.

moralive®2.4 The ABC (Altruism, Benefits, Consideration) of Gratitude

The best thing of all is to anticipate a person's wishes; the next to follow them. The better course is to be beforehand with our friends by giving them what they want before they ask us for it

Seneca

Of all five types of kindness in this chapter, moralive®2.4 is the kindness most commonly and immediately associated with giving. But for a gift to be kind, it must first be based on your consideration of the other person. The most important consideration is this: is the gift beneficial to the person who receives it? A gift is only kind if a gift is given with an intention of kindness that recognizes and appreciates the circumstances of the person you are giving to. You only know what will be kind once you have recognized and appreciated the person's intention and their circumstances. Only then can you anticipate which gift will be a benefit.

When to exercise your kindness muscle with the ABC of Gratitude (moralive®2.4)

If you recognize someone has tried to avoid physical affection from you, and that their intentions towards you are not romantic, a diamond necklace will be of no benefit. If you recognize they are looking for a job, offering to review their CV or sharing recruitment contacts with them will be a benefit. If your friends or parents say they

Oddly enough Seneca dedicated more time than anyone else in history to the discussion of benefits, writing an entire book on the subject: *On Benefits*

are trying to get rid of some furniture, taking them out for a meal will not be as great a benefit as helping to move their furniture or selling their furniture for them on eBay. If they complain they are too busy to do anything, doing some of their chores for them around the house will be of more benefit than a dinner invitation or spending money on them.

Helper's High (and low blood pressure)

In 1979, psychologists first coined the term called 'helper's high' when they discovered volunteers were happier than non-volunteers, and that your brain produces more dopamine (the high) when you are involved in altruistic actions. If you are anything like me, your first reaction to the idea of being a 'volunteer' may be to walk away and pretend you never had that idea. Well, here's the good news: you can feel the helper's high just by being considerate in everyday interactions. Exercise with everyday interactions is enough to rapidly build up the strength of your kindness muscle. The author of *Why Kindness is Good For You*, Dr David Hamilton, explains why: 'If you do an act of kindness face-to-face with someone – for instance you help someone carry their shopping – you create an emotional bond. The body produces oxytocin, the bonding hormone. It binds to the lining of our blood vessels and causes the dilation of the arteries. The side effect of all that is a reduction of blood pressure. Oxytocin is a cardio-protective hormone.'

Exercising your kindness muscle is literally exercising and protecting your heart. But the benefits don't stop with the heart: 'the longest nerve in the human body is the vagus nerve, which controls inflammation in the body. It plays a role in keeping your cardiovascular system healthy. Studies show that people who practice considerate altruism have a more active vagus nerve.' Dr Hamilton adds that you don't have to do anything drastic to exercise your kindness muscle and practising considerate altruism can be with a matter of very small, easily achievable things, like helping someone to get off the bus with a pram, making a cup of tea for someone, paying a stranger a compliment. It's not only an apple, but also an act of kindness a day that keeps the doctor away.

Consider this: the unkind gift of expected reciprocation

You can tell an inconsiderate gift from a considerate gift in that the inconsiderate gift applies pressure to the receiver, whereas a considerate gift relieves pressure. Some gifts imply expectation of reciprocation. And reciprocation, 'the golden rule', has been exploited by sellers since civilisation began, whether it be by offering free samples, wine tastings, or dinners. When implied reciprocation enters the domain of romance, it is known as 'supplication'. If a man gives a woman he is attracted to but not in a relationship with, a diamond necklace, the woman may feel like he's trying to put down a relationship deposit, and maybe she's not ready, or not that into him. This was the case in Chapter 2 when Ko paid for an expensive hotel room and dinner for Charlotte in the expectation of intimate reciprocation. Often pressure to reciprocate pushes the receiver away from any idea of romance with the 'giver'.

Sen Says:
He who gives too much acts as wrongly as he who gives too little. First let us give what is necessary, second what is useful and thirdly what is pleasant.

Giving someone a tissue can be more generous than giving them a diamond necklace: if you, a stranger, give a tissue to someone with a runny nose and no tissues, like Rolf on the train. If you gave Rolf anything other than a tissue at the point of a tickling, dripping nose, it would more likely be a cause of frustration, than a cause of gratitude. Giving what is needed is appreciated with more gratitude than giving what is not. Being inappropriately generous with gifts can be a good indicator of: a weakness of a person's kindness muscle; a weakness in a person's courage muscle (courage to present yourself without embellishment of gifts); a weakness in a person's awareness muscle (knowing what is enough and what is too much); a weakness in the person's honesty muscle (representing yourself with a mask of gifts); and a weakness in a person's tolerance muscle (unable to deal with and curiously explore the other's needs). In fact, being excessive with gifts is a good indicator of the poor health of a person's Happiness Animal.

Consideration is anticipation

Piero Ferrucci writes 'true generosity is guided by awareness of what people really need for their next step forward'. Gifts where the giver gives from their own values or beliefs, like giving someone your Scientology book, a Bible, or the Quran, apply pressure (to read it and reciprocate) and show a lack of respect for the receiver's ability to have their own value system, but giving Rolf a tissue allowed him to step out off the train without mucosal incident. There was no expectation of reciprocation, but reciprocation was a natural bi-product when he offered his gratitude back to the giver.

Consideration for others doesn't stop with the considering. It means giving help where you see help will be a benefit, without necessarily being asked to help. Consideration leads to anticipation, which leads to benefits being offered and received: considering Rolf's failed request to the old lady on the train for a tissue, the bystander anticipated that Rolf would need a tissue, and so she was

Sen Says (on benefits)

That which is given is the same but the manner in which it is given makes the difference. We prize much more what comes from a willing hand, than what comes from a full one.

To remind people of the benefits we have given them is to ask them to return them.

A benefit is only a benefit if the intention was there.

A man may be grateful in intention even though he may not be able to lift a hand to prove his gratitude.
A benefit is an evil plight if we cannot be grateful for it even when we are empty handed.

He who receives it with good will returns a benefit.

ready to hand him one. The giver exercises kindness and the receiver reciprocates the kindness by offering gratitude in return. Both people strengthen their Happiness Animal in tandem.   Given there are numerous daily opportunities for considering others, try working out with your regular casual relationships that maybe you have just seen as transactional, like the guy in the café that makes your coffee. Offer some warmth where there is cold. Try asking a friendly question like: You know what, you don't look your normal upbeat self today. Are you OK? Just by offering a smile with this question, you have given them the gift of your warmth.

Generous with benefits

Generosity generates freedom in the giver. It frees you from being possessed by possessions. After all, you only really own something when you have the power to give it away. If you don't have the power to give something away, how can you really own it? It is healthy for your Happiness Animal not to confuse your identity with your belongings and not to let your belongings have more power over you than you do over them. But being generous doesn't just relate to giving things that cost money, or 'precious' possessions. You will feel a lot freer by being generous with how much of yourself you give to others: share your stories of what

Oddly Enough
In his book, *The power of kindness,* Piero Ferrucci documents several studies that support the correlation between generosity and self esteem.

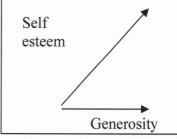

Self esteem

Generosity

you delight in, not your observations on the weather that anybody can see for themselves. Share your piece of the puzzle and share like no one's watching. It is possible to be generous with your attention, by supplying others with little known or precious information. Are you generous enough to take the trouble to tell someone where the toilet is if you can see they are looking? Or if someone has lost their sunglasses and you can see where their sunglasses are? Your altruism is your unique gift to the world, and the more you exercise it, the more of a sense of belonging you will feel. When you help someone, you open up another connection to the world. The more connections you open, the more you increase your bandwidth of belonging to the world. Whether you recognize proactively that someone needs help, or someone asks you for help, you can act authentically in response, and feel the Happiness Animal health benefits immediately. It's an increase in blood flow to your muscles. The alternative is demoralizing and unhealthy. When you don't respond to a request, you are likely to feel ill at ease. Avoiding the request disturbs your peace of mind. Your mind can't avoid a request that it knows about, no matter how hard it tries, and the harder your mind tries to avoid the request, the more attention the request gets in your mind. It is healthier for your Happiness Animal to accept that the request for help exists, and to do something about it, even if that means saying: 'no, I can't help you this time.'

The Freedom of Being Generous

Sometimes to offer a service, we must improve ourselves in order to do what needs to be done. You can be generous in the service you provide at work by doing more than you have been asked to do. This allows you to break free of the limitations of your role, increasing your career path options within the company. If you give more freedom at work, you get more freedom at work. It is also possible to be generous in the capacity of a hiring manager: if you know someone has a criminal record, you can be generous by continuing to review their

Time to define: altruism
It's called altruism for a reason. It's all true, and all includes you. Altruism benefits you as well as the person you help. Altruism is giving something to someone without any expected return: the reward you get for altruism is the exercise of your kindness muscles that you feel strengthening your Happiness Animal.

application on its own merits, and appreciating that person in the present moment. Outside of the workplace, generosity loosens our grip on possessions and allows us to let go of their imagined value and importance. Generosity, my precious, stops you from being Gollum. Piero Ferrucci advocates the giving away of possessions as a cure to mental illness that is as common as a cold: 'if we hold our possessions back from others, it's because we are both afraid, and feel too self important. The reality is that our most precious material belongings are just like sand castles, which eventually will decay and be washed away. Generosity is liberating in that it allows us to stop clinging to sand castles. Generosity may make us poorer materially and financially, but it makes us feel richer, freer and kinder.'

Time to define: benefits
A benefit is simply a loan of good feeling. A benefit is the spirit in which something is done or given, not the thing itself. (Seneca)

The benefits of withholding

If you give cigarettes to a smoker, or a bottle of whisky to an alcoholic, it does them harm, regardless of what they want and regardless of whether or not they appreciate your gift. For the purposes of exercising your Happiness Animal with benefits, what it comes down to is your intention. If your intention is to be kind, it doesn't matter whether you give or you take away. Sometimes you could do nothing and still be kind, as long as you were doing nothing out of an intention of kindness: not passing judgement when your friend makes a drunken mistake; not doing the dishes so you can spend more time entertaining when your family or friends are over for a meal; not asking a non-urgent work question of a colleague who appears stressed or busy. In these cases it is your non-action that benefits others.

The efficiency gain of gratitude

Gratitude is the easiest way to be happy

Piero Ferrucci

Gratitude can make you at least 25% happier

Dr David Hamilton

As a rule of thumb, what is good for your Happiness Animal is also good for your physical health, and gratitude is no exception. In a recent study gratitude was shown to boost not just health, but also efficiency. How could gratitude do this? Because it makes us feel more complete. Gratitude allows us to let go of the idea that we are complete as individuals, and to acknowledge that we need the help of other people to exist as human beings. The more you acknowledge when you need help, the easier it is to be efficient in what you do. You do not get held up in trying to do something when you don't have the skills, talent or ability. The prouder you are, the harder it is for you to acknowledge a need for help, and

Oddly Enough: Gratitude with benefits. The saying that it is better to give than it is to receive is not true. Neither is better than the other. Receiving with gratitude does wonders for the health of your Happiness Animal. The documented benefits of exercising gratitude include:

- Prevention of anxiety and depression (Wood, 2008, Journal of Research in Personality)
- Feeling of being present, increased joy from moments (Robert Emmons, 2003)
- Happiness (Overwalle, Mervielde, & DeSchuyter, 1995)
- Rejuvenation after negative life events, and in response to stress (Tugade & Fredrickson, 2005)
- Increased social integration, life satisfaction, and academic achievement. (Froh, Emmons, Card, Bono, & Wilson, 2009)
- Decreased depression, materialism, and envy. (Froh, Emmons, Card, Bono, & Wilson, 2009)
- Increase in healthy social and psychological functioning, and stronger relationships (Emmons & McCollough, 2004)

the harder it is for you to be grateful for help when it is offered. Yet there are no downsides to freeing yourself from pride. Letting go of pride has nothing to do with letting go of self-esteem, courage, or self-confidence. Paradoxically, pride weakens your courage, confidence and self-esteem. Pride is protection of a self-image, an image that is nothing more than an ego-mask. If you protect the false, you weaken the truth. You weaken your courage, your self-esteem, and you weaken your Happiness Animal. Pride is an obstacle to truth, whereas self-esteem, courage and confidence align with truth: a proud person is often dishonest about their failings, their resentments or their gratitude, in order to keep their ego-mask intact. Pride demoralizes, whereas

exercising gratitude strengthens your relationships and your Happiness Animal. Rolf's gratitude for the tissue relaxed him and opened him, freeing his breath. A proud person may have refused to ask for, or accept the tissue, instead preferring to hide their problem or to try and wipe it away with their hand.

Time to define: pride
noun 1.a high or inordinate opinion of one's own dignity, importance, merit, or superiority.

Choosing gratitude or choosing selfishness
Without gratitude you are reduced to your inner monologue, and a monologue can only be by definition, selfish. Selfishness is demoralizing and is linked to depression. But when you are able to feel gratitude in everyday scenarios, like someone holding a door open for you while you carry a box into the post office, you end your demoralizing monologue and create an unselfish connection, increasing your bandwidth of belonging to the world. Sonja Lyubomirsky Ph.D., a professor in the Department of Psychology at University of California, has completed extensive gratitude research, which appears in her book, *The How of Happiness*. She says people who write down five things they're grateful for once

each week, are happier, more optimistic and more connected to others. Here are Lyubomirsky's top two tips for expressing gratitude:

1. Write a gratitude letter. It doesn't matter whether you send it. Lyubomirsky says this activity makes you feel content and improves your mood because it can help you appreciate your relationships.

2. Keep a gratitude journal.

The founder of positive psychology, Martin Seligman also recommends writing down three things that went well for you each day in a 'what went well diary'. I personally find this a quick and effective method for giving my Happiness Animal a boost. I have also noticed a recent Facebook trend to 'nominate' friends to do a daily post,

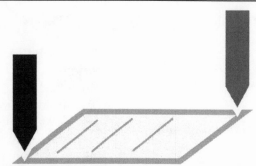

Pens with benefits
Write down the name of someone to whom you are grateful, and what you are grateful for. Think of the main people in your life. It could be your parents. You may resent some of the things they have done so bracket that resentment, and express it with the exercise of moralive®1.3 either before or after this exercise. An appreciation mixed with resentment is not an appreciation at all. Here just focus on expressing your appreciation.

Name:

What I am grateful for:

containing a list of things they are grateful for. There are plenty of options for exercising gratitude so go with whatever method attracts you the most.

Gratitude: a Happiness Animal health barometer

Piero Ferrucci believes that how much gratitude a person shows is a sign of how well they are. If you are able to show a healthy amount of gratitude, it means that you are neither overestimating yourself (that you need no one else), nor are you underestimating yourself (which would make you feel that you were undeserving of anyone's gifts and that your gratitude had no value by which to repay that gift). To be grateful is to let yourself be known: when you are grateful, you drop your defences and your pretences and you show yourself authentically. The next time you feel someone's gratitude, look at their facial expression. Listen to their tone and observe how freely they speak, and whether their body language is more relaxed after they express their gratitude. Do you get more or less of them when they express gratitude? The experience of gratitude can be liberating for your Happiness Animal, your spirit, your being, so liberating in fact that it can often lead to tears of joy.

A tissue! Exercising kindness with the ABC of Gratitude (moralive®2.4)

Exercise for on a train, on the beach, in the café, in the supermarket, in the queue, or at home. You will need a pack of tissues for this exercise.

Instructions:
1. Watch for anyone who could use a tissue (someone spilling something on themselves, sniffing their runny nose, sneezing, suffering from hay fever, or crying).
2. Take your pack of tissues out so it is clearly visible in your hand.

3. Notice any tension areas in your body and relax those areas. Imagine your shoulder blades dropping gently down your back, and that all your joints are loose. Smile.

4. Approach the person with a smile, make eye contact, and ask them 'would you like a tissue?' Offer the pack of tissues towards them.

5. If they take the tissue and thank you, notice how you feel. If they don't, start again from step 1.

Note: If you don't have any tissues with you, you can exercise by simply anticipating and then offering assistance e.g. if you are in a café and someone with a laptop is looking around the café, you can tell them what the wifi code is. Or if you see someone coming to your building with a lot of bags or boxes, offer to help them carry their things, or if you anticipate that they will need help getting in, hold the doors open for them. If you are in the supermarket and someone seems fidgety or anxious in the queue, perhaps looking at their watch, offer to let them go ahead of you. It doesn't matter what you exercise with, the key is how you exercise: anticipate and then offer help.

Empathy & Compassion (moralive®2.5)

Phone a Friend
Call the person, you named in the pens with benefits on page 142. Tell them you are calling them to exercise your gratitude to them. Tell them what you wrote above. Even better, meet with the person face to face.

If you want others to be happy, practice compassion. If you want to be happy practice compassion

Dalai Lama

You know that feeling you get when you lean back too far on a chair and almost fall? How about that feeling you get when you realize you have just stood on a snail? Or that feeling you get when you get in a bath and realize the water is too hot? The feeling you get when you are walking back to your car and you see a parking ticket stuck to the window? If you can relate to any of these feelings, it is because you can empathize. But how does empathy boost the health of your Happiness Animal? It does so by removing demoralizing self-attention. Empathy frees you from your ego, your self (and selfishness) and connects you to others. Every social encounter is an opportunity to see another soul. Human beings can only thrive in community and with empathy, you sense a belonging to that community. As a human being with empathy, you connect to an infinite whole of humanity. As you connect to the infinite whole, you transcend your existence to a higher level, a level where your Happiness Animal roams freely.

When to exercise your kindness muscle with empathy and compassion (moralive®2.5)

Let's resonate

Music is what feelings sound like. When we empathize, we enter into a state of resonance with the music of another person. To resonate is to first allow yourself to feel the sounds of another, and then to harmonize, to play along to their tune. A cut crystal glass vibrates when a door slams. The seats and windows on a bus vibrate when the engine hits certain revolutions per minute. But for your Happiness Animal strings to vibrate to the tune, tone, and frequency of another, you need to remove all obstacles from touching the strings of your inner violin. If the strings of your inner violin are pressed against the plastic mask of your ego, they will be muffled, or silent. The way to unmuffling your strings is to move your attention away from yourself and to focus attention on the person you are with. If you are paying attention to the other person, your auto-tuner will soon find the chords of their feelings and you will feel the vibrations in your inner strings. You will tune into the other person. If you have ever been in a group of musicians, you will have experienced how when one musician starts jamming the sounds of their new creation, another musician with no prior knowledge of what the other is playing, is able to provide accompaniment in tune and contribute harmoniously to the music. Two words ring the bells of empathy: 'me too'.

Why resonate?

Empathy is a pre-requisite for successful communication, collaboration, and social cohesion. If we annul empathy we return to savagery or cease to exist

Piero Ferrucci

If you don't empathize, you create a clash of sounds, a conflict of feelings, a din. Without empathy, you act without considering the feelings of others. And it is easy to clash sounds instead of resonating. When two individuals are not paying attention to each other in a marriage, or in an everyday encounter, you can hear the two voices as noise that is the disharmony of a relationship. But when two people are listening to each other, noticing each other's body language as they talk, mirroring postures, they are resonating with each other. Disharmony is

Oddly Enough: Music's First Aid Kit
You can't tune a violin in a nightclub. Yet one of the easiest ways to practice resonating is with music. If you are finding it hard to empathize, try listening to your favourite tunes. What song makes your hair stand on end and tingles your spine? What makes you want to party? What makes you cry? Music can change your mood, and it does so by resonating your inner violin. It resonates to a feeling in you. The talent, the gift of the musician is to resonate in many. While writing this book, I discovered a Swedish band called First Aid Kit. Whenever their song comes on the radio, it soothes me, and I feel instantly calm. Musical resonance can be a First Aid Kit for the soul.

interference. Empathy is stereo, tuned into the Happiness Animal's favourite station.

'She says there's no success like failure, but that failure's no success at all'

Bob Dylan's words ring true. Empathy has more to do with failure than success, more to do with suffering than with joy. But with empathy, the area of pain, of suffering and of trauma becomes the area of service, and of success. Your own suffering can unlock your ability to empathize. The greatest empathy is often towards those whose suffering is closest to yours. Maybe you've already been through a divorce, maybe you were fired, maybe you had a serious accident, maybe your heart was broken. You can relate to that. But you don't need to suffer to empathize. The easiest way to empathy is not through suffering, not through pain, but through acknowledging the other persons feelings. Simply by stating back to the other person what they have said (changing the 'I' in what they said to the 'You' in what you say. You can also use your imagination as a tool for empathy: imagination can be a curse when it is used unconsciously as a zoom lens, creating stories in your mind, but with empathy, imagination is used consciously as a tool to exercise your kindness muscle. Imagination is the pain-free route to empathy. Instead of experiencing pain, you only have to imagine the type of feeling the other person is having given what has happened to them or what they have done. Although you may not have been through the exact same, specific experience as the other person, you will be able to acknowledge and relate to the base feeling associated with that experience. Whether their feeling is shame, sorrow, or fear, you can relate to the feeling through your own experiences of shame, sorrow or fear. And that means you can relate to life in the other person's shoes. Once the other person feels their pain is recognized, and acknowledged, they feel connected to you and, by association, to other human beings. At the same time, your Happiness Animal's music grows stronger by harmonizing with another. The unfinished symphony that is your life is the creation of harmony within your orchestra that grows in number of musicians every time you empathize. As cultures come together, the more potential you have to grow your orchestra and its repertoire of harmonies. An orchestra with healthy empathy is in very little need of anything else. It is an orchestra of authenticity that resonates only in honesty, playing three instruments: attention, awareness, and curiosity.

The curious case of empathy

Now it's time for you to exercise three of your Happiness Animal's muscles at once: your curiosity (tolerance) muscle, your honesty muscle, and your kindness muscle. The result is empathy. Set yourself the challenge of asking one person a day how they are feeling. Radical empathy requires radical listening. Focus your attention on every word the other person uses. Watch and notice any movements in the other person's body. Pay extra attention to the person's body language when they are talking about a specific subject. Do they look away when you mention a specific word? Are their hands moving? How? Do their shoulders or facial expression tense up when you ask a question? Does a part of their body look more or less comfortable when you move from one subject to the next? Imagine how they are feeling when their body moves in a particular way when they say certain things. You can consciously mirror their body language so you physically feel some of the same sensations that they are feeling. Regularly acknowledge and

Oddly Enough: Experiential Empathy When another person's life becomes a best-seller.

In 1920s Britain, the author, George Orwell wanted to discover what life was like for those living on the social margins. So he dressed up as a tramp, and lived with beggars on the streets of East London. Orwell not only realized that homeless people are not 'drunken scoundrels,' he also developed new friendships, had the greatest travel experience of his life, and it was an experience that led to a best-selling book: *Down and Out in Paris and London*.

paraphrase back what the other person has said to check your understanding. When you express what the other person is saying out loud, as well as feeling their body language, it will accelerate your passage to empathy. And it will show the other person that you not only listen, but also, understand them.

Compassion – the gift of taking

If you are looking for the ultimate considerate gift, choose compassion. It is a gift that gives by taking. Compassion gives freedom as it takes suffering. Compassion goes beyond empathy: with empathy, you resonate with another person's suffering or with their joy. With compassion, you not only resonate with another person's suffering, but also, you suffer with them and share the burden of the pain. You take suffering away, and you give freedom back. Kindness expert, Piero Ferrucci defines compassion as relation in its pure state. Relation in its pure state is relation without the screens or defences that prevent you from resonating to the tune of another. It is relation free from the harms of competitiveness, jealousy, grudges, spite, envy, and seeing people as a means to an end.

Time to define: compassion.
Participating in the suffering of other human beings with sincere and intense identification.

'Compassion is the final and noblest result of empathy.' (Piero Ferrucci)

Just as music is a natural way to empathy, music can also be a way to open you to compassion. Have you ever felt your inner strings being tugged when a musical score is introduced at a critical point in a movie, depicting the suffering of someone else? Charities do well when they are able to shortcut to our compassion with the right music in their advertisements. They do well by getting you to resonate to their tune, and then ask you to own their problems with them. And you also do well if you do resonate and own their problem with them, because the biggest winner of all is your Happiness Animal: Dr. James Doty, a Clinical Professor of Neurosurgery at Stanford University and Director of The Centre for Compassion and Altruism Research and Education, found in his research that compassion is a key to personal, social and global happiness. He says that compassion, not science, will be the influence that will lead humanity to the peak of its potential. Dr Doty believes that all crises – personal catastrophe, ecological catastrophe, global warming, poverty, war – are problems of the human heart, and that the way to resolve these crises is to stop treating them as external to ourselves, and to start treating them as problems that can be resolved more by our own compassion, than by science:

'the reality is that while science and technology have the potential to offer incredible benefit, it is the simple interventions known to us for thousands of years that can have a profound effect on the lives of individuals and society,' says Doty. Social Scientist, Dacher Keltner, says evolution of human beings no longer adheres to Darwinism and the survival of the fittest. Keltner believes it is the survival of the kindest that now determines how human beings next evolve. Our evolution now hinges on your compassion.

So how do you practice compassion?

Compassion has one pre-requisite: honesty. Honesty communicates that you are open enough to be vulnerable, and that you are vulnerable enough to share in someone's suffering. Vulnerability is no weakness. It is the strength in your kindness muscle. It is your capacity to alleviate suffering. It is your capacity for compassion. Your friend or family member will be more willing to share with you if you are open and vulnerable, than if you are hiding behind ego and defenses, reluctant to disclose your own failings and feelings. Before you can exercise compassion, you need to lower your defenses, drop your shields, and take off your uniform. Show the courage to let your guard down and you are more likely to inspire that courage in others. Did Gandhi touch the hearts of millions through the pride of protecting his ego, or through his vulnerability? OK so you are not Gandhi. A good way to show your vulnerability to the person you want to exercise compassion with is to talk about your feelings and your greatest fears. If you know what the other person's suffering relates to, talk about feelings and fears you have that relate to that suffering. If the person you are talking to has recently had a relationship break up, and you also happen to live on your own, you might have genuine feelings you can share such as: 'I feel so alone at the weekends when I have the house to myself. I worry I will be alone for the rest of my life'. But before you attempt to exercise with compassion, it is key that your Happiness Animal's honesty muscle is in good shape. Once you have given your honesty muscle a workout, you can exercise empathy, and then, you are ready for compassion.

Exercising empathy (moralive®2.5): musical chairs

Exercise for empathy: You can do this exercise to empathize with anyone, and it works well if you have had a difficulty with someone important in your life, such as an argument with your significant other, or parents.

Instructions
1. Arrange two chairs facing each other.
2. Sit in one chair. This is your chair. Imagine the other person you want to exercise empathy with is sat opposite you.
3. What do you want to say to the other person you want to empathize with? Say it to them now, as if they were there. Stay honest, and make your comments as specific as possible. (If you have anger or resentment you want to express, use the language from the exercise in moralive®1.3).
4. Focus your attention on the other chair imagining the other person is sat there right now as you talk to them. You may feel silly at first, but feeling silly is your trigger to drop your

protective ego. If you feel silly, it is because you are not dropping your guard enough to empathize yet. Talk like no one's watching (in this case no one is watching!).

5. Now, get up and sit in the other chair. Imagine you are the other person and respond back to the other chair. Focus your attention as you talk on the other chair imagining that you (as seen through the eyes of the other person) are sitting there.

6. Repeat steps 3 & 4 until you have said everything you'd like to say to the other person, and have responded back as the other person from the other chair. Every time you respond in step 5, you are empathising with the other person, imagining what they would be thinking and feeling and what they would say to you.

When I do this exercise I often feel an emotional wave coming over me when I respond as the other. It's the warmth of empathy of understanding another person. This exercise is also great for exercising tolerance of others and gives your Happiness Animal's tolerance, kindness and honesty muscles a workout all at the same time.

Additional steps for exercising compassion:
Continue with the use of the two chairs placed opposite each other.

1. Sit in 'your' chair and imagine the suffering of anyone you know. If the person is different to the person you exercised empathy with, complete the empathy steps (above) for the new person first.

2. Now, get up and sit in the other chair. Imagine that you are the one suffering.

3. Reflect on how much you would like your suffering to end.

4. Now imagine the person in the chair opposite would like your suffering to end. What would you like for that person to do to end your suffering?

5. Switch chairs. You are you again. Focus on the chair opposite, imagining the other (suffering) person sat there. Imagine what you would like to do for the other person's suffering to end. Imagine doing something to help ease their suffering. If you want to, talk to the other chair as you did in the empathy steps. If you feel even a little that you'd want their suffering to end, reflect on that feeling. With exercise and experiencing the warmth of this feeling, your kindness muscle, and your Happiness Animal will flourish.

6. Once you get good at step 5, practice doing something small each day to help end the suffering of others, by imagining what it's like living in their body, and what they would want someone else to do to help. It could be as simple as picking up some groceries, getting their lunch, or giving them a lift home from work.

Animal Advice

- Your attitude and intention inside are more important than your actions outside.

- Starting with a cheering up intention towards someone else, not only cheers you up but also increases your self-esteem.

- Smile at strangers; hug your friends and family.

- When you help someone, you open up another connection to the world.

- Pride weakens your courage and self-esteem. Pride is protection of a self-image, an ego mask.

- If you don't empathize in relationships, you create a clash of sounds, a conflict of feelings, a din.

- Without gratitude you are reduced to your inner monologue. Monologues are by definition, selfish. Selfishness demoralizes.

- Even people who appear so dull that they couldn't possibly have anything interesting to say, do have something interesting to say. Guaranteed.

Coming up next...
Now you've warmed up your honesty and kindness muscles, it's time to exercise with the weights of all things that frustrate you. It's time your tolerance muscle got a workout.

<u>Chapter 7</u>

moralive®3: tolerance

Nothing need arouse one's irritation so long as one doesn't make it
bigger than it is by getting irritated

Seneca

Mood goes up mostly with increased tolerance in the nation

Martin Seligman

To understand all is to forgive all

F. Lacordaire

The happiest states of the US are the most tolerant

Livescience

Tolerance is a virtue because it takes human beings very seriously,
recognising that without the freedom to err people can never acquire
the freedom to discover truths

Frank Furedi

Animal's Anecdote

Peak Power

Bang! The light bulb above Pengelly's desk exploded showering him with glass. His hi-fi silenced cutting off Lana Del Rey mid *Diet Mountain Dew*. Pengelly walked out of his room and saw through his housemate Mishka's open room door, him kneeling on the floor, unplugging his fan heater. 'I'll go and switch the power back on,' said Pengelly.

'Thanks man,' said Mishka, picking up his longneck of Coopers red beer from the floor and taking a swig.

Pengelly went down to the fuse box by the kitchen door, and sure enough, the switch had been tripped. He went back upstairs and looked at the calendar on his bedroom door. It was the fifteenth of October. He knew the electricity meter would be read on the seventeenth and the bill would soon follow. Pengelly's breath quickened. He felt his lungs closing, reducing in size, losing capacity. His two body balloons were trapped in a vice, and no matter how long he tried to make his breaths, he couldn't prise the vice apart. He couldn't work out how much electricity he and his three housemates had used since the last, mammoth bill but when he had called the electricity company midway through the quarter, they had told him that the total usage was already double what it had been for the first bill of the year.

I wish Belle hadn't asked me to look after the electricity for the house, they'll blame me, thought Pengelly. His eyebrows tightened and thickened. Pengelly imagined his housemates' reactions to the bill. He visualized their faces of few words and few facial movements above rigid bodies that would march down the wooden floors from the kitchen to their rooms, closing their doors with the calculated force that would mask a fully expressed slam. These thoughts slipped his lungs further into the vice, up to his collar bone. *What if Belle refuses to pay me?* thought Pengelly. *I have two thousand dollars coming off my credit card in November, and I don't have any money left..., I really don't know what I am going to do.* Since Pengelly had looked at the calendar, he had forgotten about his plans for going kayaking that day, forgotten about the coffee machines he had sold and needed to take to the post office. Pengelly's thoughts began to grasp for potential ways to explain the high bill to help him justify it to his housemates. *I'll never be able to prove it was their heaters that caused it, and they will blame me because I'm the only one at home in the daytime. I don't know how to stop the next bill from being high either, I can't do this,* thought Pengelly.

Pengelly looked at his to do list, and felt the panic of being stuck in a pit with a truck over head burying him with cement. 'The customer is still waiting for me to post the coffee machine. Oh shit,' said Pengelly. He started boxing up a coffee machine when he felt a pulse of pain behind his ear above the back his jaw. Pain spasmed again and raced, twinging to the back his head. He winced. He wondered if he could feel pressure behind his eyeballs. He pushed his fingers into his face below his eye socket, closed his eyes, and then palmed his eyeballs, waiting for any deeper pain to emerge. 'Has my headache stopped now?' he asked. 'I can't feel it now can I? Wait, there it is again. Damn it, do I have any painkillers?'

A week later, Pengelly's headaches had subsided, as had his questioning of whether or not he was getting abnormal sensations of pressure behind his eyeballs. On his phone he could see he had received an email from Dodo with the latest electricity bill attached, but decided to wait until after lunch to look at it. He opened the attachment, and saw the figure was even higher than the previous bill, which had taken everyone by surprise: this time it was one thousand, one hundred and twenty dollars of doom.

'Shit, I need to get the money off Belle and Mishka before that gets taken off my credit card. I need to get the message out now,' Pengelly said. Pengelly walked downstairs, confirmed that no one else was in the house and thumb-typed a group text message on the keyboard of his BlackBerry with the amount and his bank details. Then he ran out of the house to the bus stop and boarded the first bus to the city.

Pengelly's phone vibrated against the bus seat. As he opened the text from Belle he felt an ice rod pierce his solar plexus. Before he had read a word, he could feel his heart palpitating in his temples. His beats per minute were rising, pumping the pace of his blood-flow. Pengelly opened the text message. Key words and phrases flashed at him from a blur of screen: *can't understand why it's so high*; *can't afford it; we need to switch provider*; *other provider was cheaper*; *it's because we are on peak now*. Pengelly knew that the last of these statements was false. He felt like he'd had a triple latte and it pumped fresh muscle into his mind. Here was his chance to prove he was right. He started typing on the phone at a rate that would meet minimum words per minute requirements for a typist on a full keyboard. Anger, adrenalin, this was flight or fight. He punched these words back at Belle: *We've always been on a single tariff rate. We still have the same old meter we've always had.* Belle replied within a minute: *Well I used to work at Ausgrid and I phoned them up. They said we were on peak so you can see why I'd think that.*

Pengelly's forehead tightened around the edges and pushed up a mound above his nose. His fingers snapped into reply: *The first bill we got from Dodo was cheaper than the old provider.* Then he napalm texted a triple bombardment to finish the job: *I spent several days researching the rates and Dodo is the cheapest. The reason for the high bill is we've been using more electricity. There can't be any doubt that it's because of the fan heater in Mishka's room.*

Pengelly got back from the city at around 9pm. He was about to plate up his dinner when Mishka arrived and lent his bicycle against the wall outside the kitchen. Mishka took off his helmet to reveal the redness of his forehead and hair dampened down with sweat. He walked into the kitchen where Pengelly, body frozen, greeted him with a bug eyed half-grin that said 'well…'

'Just so I understand, or well help me to understand, I'm just getting really frustrated by this whole electricity thing. Can we just break the contract and switch to another provider? We never had any of this shit with the previous provider,' said Mishka

Pengelly received a full-face injection of red heat righteousness, pressure came in a tsunami behind his lips that could hold it for only seconds before bursting.

'You're frustrated by the electricity? I have the triple fucking frustration of dealing with all this bullshit and coordinating with everyone else in the house. It's bloody ridiculous, if you want to switch provider, there is a fee to break the contract, but if you want to switch provider, go ahead, just the new contract will need to be in your name,' said Pengelly, his voice uncharacteristically raised. He looked at his hands trying to gauge whether or not Mishka would notice them trembling.   Mishka walked upstairs to his room, closing the door behind him, leaving Pengelly shaking in the kitchen, his heart pounding. He had lost control of his body.

Pengelly ate, and chewing gave him warm sedation. His shaking subsided, but as the bolus of food started to move deeper down into his guts, he felt a familiar rotting feeling emerge low in his belly, and at the back of his throat. He felt like he was losing meat from his gums. Belle's cat startled him as it scratched the kitchen window, and when Pengelly turned to look through the glass back at the cat, it was staring directly into his eyes. 'Maybe from Belle's point of view I would have said the same thing. I just need to show them that so they can see it for themselves,' he muttered. He went up to his desk, and searched through the second drawer down through the previous electricity bills. He found the bill for the same time last year for the quarter ending October. *Total due $1,160.* 'What the fuck. We paid *more* last year'.

Pengelly half-knocked on Mishka's door. 'Yeah,' he heard from behind the closed door. He opened it slowly, sending out words in advance to defend and shield his presence: 'Sorry man, we all want the same thing here, to pay the least amount possible for our electricity bill. I've got the bills together from the previous provider and we'll go through it tomorrow ok? The bill for the same time last year is more than the one we just got. Sorry man, I just want to get this sorted as much as you do, we're all coming from the same angle, all in the same boat with this one…I just…yeah..'

'Ok its fine. If you can get the old bills it would be good,' said Mishka. His eyes did not move from the television. Pengelly turned to exit and in his peripheral view spotted Mishka's balcony door was wide open, letting in the cool evening air. Directly in front of the open door, Mihska's 2400- watt fan heater was on full blast pumping dry heat into the room. It had been a warm day. Pengelly had no heater, but he had also closed his bedroom's balcony door after the sun had gone down. Pengelly bit his tongue, let it go, and walked out of the room with a smile that was teased up by new confidence. Electricity was old news.

Animal Analysis

For most people, tolerance is a weak link in their Happiness Animal. I ran a global online poll and forty-eight percent of those polled said tolerance was the weakest of their five Happiness Animal muscles, and the muscle most in need of exercise. There are five different types of tolerance that can be exercised: Tolerance towards fear, tolerance towards pain, tolerance towards others, tolerance towards events, and tolerance towards self. Think of using your fpoes card (fear, pain, others, events, self) with unlimited withdrawals. Let's start using it.

Tolerance towards fear (moralive®3.1)

There is a difference between exercising tolerance towards fear and exercising courage. Fear can be tolerated in so much as it can be tested as to whether or not it is justified, whereas courage is the opposite of fear. Tolerance towards fear precedes the chapter on courage in this book for a reason: you don't need courage for fear you can tolerate. Exercising courage with fear you can tolerate is like exercising your calf muscles by paddling a kayak. With fear, there are more opportunities for you to walk, than there are for you to kayak. And walking towards fear has its benefits: Twenty-three percent of those

> **Threats with no benefits**
> Your imagination & your senses have a negativity bias. Jonathan Haidt explains that it's linked to nature's way of protecting us from real threats: 'If you were designing the mind of a fish, would you have it respond as strongly to opportunities as to threats? No way. Responses to threats and unpleasantness are faster, stronger, and harder to inhibit than responses to opportunities and pleasures.'
> People with anxiety are like fish, but with an imagination, caught in a feedback loop in which distorted thoughts from imagination cause real negative feelings which then distort thinking further. 'A big part of cognitive therapy is training clients to catch their thoughts, write them down, name the distortions and then find alternative and more accurate ways of thinking,' says Haidt.

polled in an online survey I ran, said exercising tolerance with fear had made more of a difference to their happiness than exercising tolerance with anything else.

When to exercise your tolerance muscle with fear (moralive®3.1)

Imagination is magnification: Tolerance uses the most common type of fear as its exercise equipment: real fear, of an unreal future. As we saw in chapter 2, human beings are notoriously bad at making accurate predictions of their futures, and notoriously bad at predicting how they will feel when they get to those futures. It turns out that you are not only inept at predicting what you will want in the future, but you are also inept at predicting how frightening your future will be. We rarely test out our fears against our past experience or against the evidence of our current reality, and then we are surprised when our future does not turn out to be as frightening as we predicted. Unfortunately for you, every thought you have about that future fear, draws a circle around the fear, zooming its importance in your mind to 2x or 3x magnification. Pengelly's imagination's zoom lens saw angry faces in the future, that would later turn out, in the reality of the present moment, to be one frustrated face, and he saw himself not being paid in the future, that would later turn out, in reality, to be him being paid. My own imagination used to zoom in on fears of not being able to say the 'right things'

Time to define: Reality testing

The human being's capacity to distinguish what is occurring in one's own mind from what is occurring in the external world. It is perhaps the single most important function because it is necessary for negotiating with the outside world. One must be able to perceive and understand stimuli accurately. Reality testing is often subject to temporary, mild distortion or deterioration under stressful conditions. Such impairment can result in temporary delusions and hallucination.

in meetings, not being able to present presentations. It was my zoom lens zooming in on the fear of being seen as a failure at work. Once I learned to reality test and zoom out, my fear began to disappear.

Reality testing

There are questions that you can ask yourself to free yourself from the zoom lens of fear, the kind of questions that can erase all circles around the fear, and leave more space in your mind for more wellbeing-promoting ideas. These are the reality testing questions that you can pose to any fear caused by your imagination:

1. What is the worst that can happen?
2. How likely is it, on a scale of 1-10, that the worst will happen? (based on previous experience with 10 being absolute certainty that it will occur)
3. What can I do to reduce the likelihood of this happening?
4. Can I survive the worst and live with it if it does happen?

Try the exercise of recognising the distortions between your reality and your imagination by asking yourself the four reality testing questions whenever you feel fear or anxiety.

Exercising tolerance with fear (moralive®3.1): Life through a lens. From telephoto to wide angle

Phone a friend
Ask a friend what they are worried about at the moment. Then ask them the following, in order:

1. What is the worst that can happen?
2. How likely is it, on a scale of 1-10, that the worst will happen?
3. What can you do to reduce the likelihood of this happening?
4. Can you survive it and live with it if it does happen?

Exercise for when you are trigger-happy with your zoom button, and would benefit from switching to a wide angle lens. Instead of zooming in on one fear, you can see what's in the bigger picture: your lifescape. Human beings have a tendency to be trigger-happy and over-zoom, so this exercise helps you to zoom out your magnification back to the natural 1x of your senses.

Instructions:

1. Write down a current fear or anxiety in the middle of a blank sheet of paper.

2. Using a pencil, draw one circle at a time around your fear.

3. Notice how your circles are forced to get bigger each time you draw another circle around the previous one. This is exactly what happens in your mind: The more attention, questions, thoughts, associations, and links you give a problem, the more space the problem takes up in your mind, the more the problem dominates your being.

4. Erase the circles one by one starting with the largest circle, until you are left only with the word that's been causing your fear.

5. Using the free space on the paper that was previously taken up by your unnecessary circles, write down the name of someone whose company you value.

6. Write down the name of something you would enjoy doing for that person.

7. Write down when you can do it.

8. Using more of the newly freed-up space, write down the name of an interest you enjoy and feel drawn to finding out more about.

9. Look back at the fear that you have written down. What was more detrimental to you, the fear or your circles of zoom around the fear?

10. Were the circles of zoom unnecessary?

11. Were the circles not leaving much space for the good things in your life?

12. Laugh at yourself. Laugh at yourself for drawing unnecessary circles around something that just is.

13. Laugh. No seriously, laugh. Laughter has been clinically proven to reduce the stress hormones cortisol and adrenaline, hormones linked to medical problems such as adrenal fatigue, high blood pressure, and depression. Laughter relaxes blood pressure and increases immune system activity by increasing the release of interferon.

Still suffering with thoughts of fear and anxiety? Reality test your fear and anxiety:

1. What is the worst that can happen?

_____

_____

_____

2. How likely is it, that the worst will happen, based on my experience on a scale of one to ten, with ten being most likely?

    1   2   3   4   5   6   7   8   9   10

3. What can I do to reduce the likelihood of this happening?

_____

_____

4. Can I survive the worst and live with it if it does happen?

> Yes I can survive this   No I won't survive

5. If you said no to question four, have you ever not survived anything in the past?

> Yes   No

6. If you said no to question five, what makes you think you won't survive something this time?

_____

_____

_____

7. Laugh at yourself. Laugh at yourself for giving so much attention to one piece of your life that represents infinitely less than a dot in the universe. Good, now you're not feeling as anxious, it's a great time to talk about one of the most frequent sources of human anxiety and fear: Pain.

Tolerance towards pain (moralive®3.2)

Pain can be tolerated in so much as it can be tested. The test is: Does the pain justify its expression? You can test pain with the same reality testing questions that were used for testing fear, but pain that remains is the hardest thing to tolerate. It is precisely because pain gives you one of the hardest tests of your tolerance, that it provides the potential for the most exercise of the tolerance muscle, and for the greatest gain in strength to your Happiness Animal. Tolerance of Pain, maximum gain: That's the sentiment echoed by the overwhelming majority, or sixty-three percent of those polled in an online survey for this book, who said that exercising tolerance of pain had made more of a difference to their happiness than exercising tolerance of anything else.

When to exercise your tolerance muscle with pain (moralive®3.2)

Pain often starts out in your mind as a distraction. Like an itch you keep probing at it until it goes from vague sensation to noticeable all the time. The drawing of circles that happens around a source of fear also happens around a source of pain. Each of Pengelly's questions about his first sensations of pain, amplify his pain. Each question creates another ripple that runs pain onto the banks of his imagination: Was it coffee? Was the pain getting worse? How should I treat it? Do I need painkillers? What type of painkillers? When is this pain going to stop? Each question raises uncertainty, allowing imagination to reply by applying the zoom lens, increasing how much pain you create in your mind. The more pain in your mind, the more likely you are to feel it, and the more you feel it, the more painful it becomes. It doesn't matter if this pain is physical, or psychological (such as sorrow, loss or longing), or if it is a pain that's in between. Nor does it matter if it's just an unpleasant sensation, such as tiredness. The more attention it gets, the more you feel it.

Building resilience (toughness)

Before we get to the exercising tolerance of pain you can feel, there are ways you can build resilience (or toughness) when you are not feeling any pain so that you are better prepared for future pain when or if it does eventually strike. For tips on building toughness and tolerance of pain, I went to someone for whom pain is part the job: a boxer. In *Got Fight?: The 50 Zen Principles of Hand to Face Combat,* boxer (and

New York Times bestselling author) Forrest Griffin describes how he strengthens his tolerance muscle with pain:

'How do you build this kind of toughness? The answer is simple – do things that make your body and mind scream at you to quit, but don't. Personally, I use the treadmill to accomplish this. Every other day, I'll rev that sucker up to twelve miles an hour and do three five-minute intervals. Running at that speed for that duration doesn't come naturally to anyone – it's hideous, absolutely horrible. But by pushing past the pain, you become progressively tougher. You prove to yourself that your pain is just that, pain. You can walk away from it afterward knowing that you surpassed a barrier that makes most humans curl into the fetal position and weep for Jesus. If you're not in good shape, you don't have to run at twelve miles an hour. You could run at eight miles an hour, but it is

Oddly enough
Exercise in general will increase your tolerance of pain. University of Heidelberg researchers led by Jonas Tesarz reviewed 15 studies that compared pain threshold tolerance in athletes vs. moderately active people. They tested 568 male and female athletes from endurance and strength sports & 331 normally active control participants. Amongst athletes a significantly higher percentage of those tested could tolerate higher levels of pain than could the group of moderately active people.

important to set goals for yourself. If eight miles an hour becomes too easy, push it up to nine miles an hour. The most important part is setting a pace that is more than you think you can achieve. It is also important not to do exercises where the pace isn't set. I choose the treadmill over running outside because when I'm on the track, my body naturally slows down as the pain sets in. On a treadmill, you don't have that option.'

Of course, what Forrest Griffin is advocating isn't going to be of much use to you if you are already suffering from pain, but if you work on strengthening your toughness when you are pain free, it will increase your capacity to tolerate future pain.

The similarities between pain and fear are physiological: Fear and pain activate the same parts of the brain. Both pain and fear lead to elevated adrenaline release in the body, higher blood pressure, increased heart rate, shifts in circulation, and greater muscle tension. Both pain and fear cause reactions in the central nervous system including visual disturbances, decreased fine motor control (such as the ability to use your hands for delicate work), and decreased ability to perform normal thinking tasks like writing an email to a work colleague. Studies have shown that tolerance to both pain and fear increases when you go from being alone, to being in the presence of another human being. Given the similarities between pain and fear, it follows that the exercise you used for building tolerance of fear can also be used for building tolerance of pain, and although the following exercise is designed for use with pain, it can also be used with fear:

Exercising tolerance with pain (moralive®3.2)

Exercise for when you are finding it hard to think about anything other than how much pain you are feeling.

Deep Breathing: Breathing is the bedrock of yoga. Yoga has been around for three thousand years. And it's never been more popular than today. But I also know that amongst my readers there are likely to be more than just a handful of yoga sceptics, dismissing yoga as wishy washy or hokus pokus, aka non-scientific bullshit. But yoga can be analysed scientifically, more specifically in terms of its biological benefits. Google it. It has been around for three millennia so you'd kind of expect some criticism, but there is also scientific validation. So back to my point: you don't have to believe in yoga to benefit from this book, but this is the one exercise in the book that uses principles from yoga to take your attention and focus away from pain. If you are not in pain, you can use discomfort of any kind, or bookmark this exercise as a tool you can use like a first aid kit.

Pre-exercise: If I didn't feel pain, what feeling would I be left with right now? Write your answer below:

_____

_____

_____

_____

WARNING! Physical pain also occurs when your body is telling you something is wrong. If pain persists, make an appointment with your doctor who can help you eliminate as much uncertainty as possible. But remember to switch off your imagination, which is a zoom lens to pain. And stop Googling your symptoms already! Googling symptoms sends your imagination zoom lens into paparazzi-on-steroids mode.

Oddly enough: Breath is the natural pain reliever. I remember being given oxygen by ambulance crew when I broke my leg and ribs while trying to kite-buggy in a field. At the time, I thought that the oxygen the crew gave me was to help me breathe. Then I started feeling happier and I forgot the pain.

Breathing more deeply enables more lung exposure to oxygen. Dennis Lewis explains: 'When we breathe fully and deeply, the diaphragm moves further down into the abdomen, and our lungs are able to expand more completely into the chest cavity. This means that more oxygen is taken in and more carbon dioxide is released with each breath. Deep breathing takes advantage of the fact that the lungs are larger towards the bottom than the top.'

A study by the Department of Psychology at Arizona State University, analyzed the pain responses of 52 similarly aged women. Half (27), suffered from chronic pain, the remaining 25 were in good health. Both groups of women were exposed to low and moderate levels of pain, delivered by pulses from a heat probe on their palm.

The results showed that slow, yogic breathing reduced the experience of pain intensity and unpleasantness in both groups of women. As the degree of pain increased, the women experienced increasingly significant reductions in intensity and unpleasantness by yogic, diaphragmatic, breathing. The study reveals that how we breathe does alter our perceptions of and responses to pain. According to the study's lead researcher, Dr. Alex Zautra, slow, diaphragmatic breathing may combat pain through establishing a better balance between the sympathetic and parasympathetic nervous systems. The sympathetic nervous system, or "fight-or-flight" response, is triggered by stress and causes an increase in heart rate, blood pressure, and sweating. The parasympathetic nervous system, known as the "resting-and-digesting" response, allows the body to rejuvenate and heal itself.

Exercise Instructions (adapted from: *The Science of Breath*)

1. Sit upright, in an easy posture, being sure to hold the chest, neck and head in a straight a line as possible, with shoulders slightly back and hands resting easily on the lap. In this position the weight of the body is largely supported by the ribs and the position may be easily maintained. Yoga instructors have found that you cannot get the best effect of rhythmic breathing with the chest drawn in and the abdomen protruding.

2. Breathing through the nostrils (it is important to keep your nostrils clear all the time and breath through them as much of the time as possible), inhale steadily, first filling the lower part of the lungs, pushing out the lower ribs, breast bone and chest. Then fill the highest portion of the lungs, protruding the upper chest, thus lifting up the chest, including the upper six or seven pairs of ribs. In the final movement, the lower part of the abdomen will be slightly drawn in, which movement gives the lungs a support and also helps to fill the highest part of the lungs. The inhalation is continuous, the entire chest cavity from the lowered diaphragm to the highest point of the chest in the region of the collar bone, being expanded with a uniform movement. Avoid a jerky series of inhalations, and strive to attain a steady, continuous action. Practice will soon overcome the tendency to divide the inhalation into three movements, and will result in a uniform continuous breath. You will be able to complete the inhalation in a couple of seconds after a little practice.

3. Retain the breath for a few seconds.

4. Exhale quite slowly, holding the chest in a firm position, and drawing the abdomen in a little and lifting it upward slowly as the air leaves the lungs. When the air is entirely exhaled, relax the chest and abdomen. A little practice will make this part of

the exercise easy, and the movement once acquired will later be performed almost automatically.

5. Steps 1-4 are called a 'Complete Breath' in Yoga. Now we make it rhythmical. Repeat step 2 again, but this time as you inhale count six beats of your pulse. Then retain the breath for three beats of your pulse.

6. Exhale slowly through the nostrils over a period of six beats of your pulse.

7. Count three pulse beats between breaths.

8. Repeat steps 5-7 a number of times, but avoid tiring yourself out.

9. Once you have established a rhythm, feel an intention inside you (if you believe in will power, this is the time to use it – if you don't, just be aware of yourself having an intention to follow the next instruction. Use your will power or intention to carry this thought: Each inhalation is drawing an increased supply of energy from not just the oxygen, but all the other stuff you are breathing in. It is a fact of physics, that there is energy in the air you breath because atoms in the air you breath are vibrating. Vibrations are energy. This is literally, not metaphorically, energy of the universe (universal energy), which is taken up by your nervous system.

10. On the exhalation, will the thought, or be aware of your intention, to send the universal energy you have inhaled to the painful part of your body, to re-establish the circulation and nerve current.

11. Inhale more of the universal energy for the purpose of driving out the painful condition, then exhale, holding the thought that you are driving out the pain.

12. Alternate between the two mental commands with each exhalation: on the first exhalation, re-establish the circulation and nerve current; on the next exhalation, drive out the pain.

13. Repeat step 12 for seven breaths.

14. On the next inhalation, retain the air for a few seconds. Then pucker up your lips as if you were going to whistle (but do not puff out the cheeks), then exhale a little air through the opening with short, sharp force. Stop exhaling for a moment, retaining the air, and then exhale a little more air. Repeat this stop-start exhalation until the air is completely exhaled. Remember to use considerable vigour, exhaling through the puckered opening of the lips. Yoga instructors call this step the cleansing breath.

15. Rest for a minute.

16. Repeat steps 11 and 12 and this time continue until pain relief comes, which will be before long. Many pains will be relieved before seven breaths are finished. If the hand is placed over the painful part, you may get quicker results. Send the current of universal energy you have inhaled down the arm and into the painful part through your hand.

Oddly Enough – Different nostrils, different sides of the brain?

If you feel tired, close your left nostril and breathe through your right nostril for five minutes, Closing your left nostril and breathing through your right nostril has the effect of waking you up whereas closing your right nostril and breathing through your left nostril relaxes you and provides pain relief, especially from tension headaches. Each nostril corresponds to the opposite side in the brain (right nostril – left side of the brain, left nostril – right side of the brain).

Tolerance towards others (moralive®3.3)

Walk a mile in another man's moccasins before you criticize him

(Native American proverb)

True tolerance, is not putting up with, and being put up with. Tolerance is calmly questioning and submitting differences in opinion, belief, and behaviour to the judge of your being. The judge's role is to find out why there are differences in opinion, belief, and behaviour, and to do so in a way that recognizes the other person's right to be authentic. The judge of your inner reasoning can both present his or her own authenticity, and appreciate others' authenticity with passion. Differences in opinion create new choices for your judge, and are essential for challenging your judge's beliefs, to prevent your judge's ignorance, and to develop your judge's perception of what is truth. By nature, you as a human being are a very curious judge indeed. Curiosity is critical to your evaluations and to growing the knowledge base of humankind. Two opinions are greater than the sum of their parts and from the clash of opinion, truth can be glimpsed. An opinion on its own is a monologue cloud that has the potential to rain, but to create power it needs to touch another. When you exercise tolerance of another person, you rub your cloud with theirs, and create lightning that can supercharge both your Happiness Animals.

When to exercise your tolerance muscle with others (moralive®3.3)

Anger: the ultimate sign of intolerance. M-m-m-m-m madness. Think about why we use the words angry and mad interchangeably. Then think about the real meaning of mad. Mad is insane. Anger is a demoralizing mental raving that affects both your happiness, and your

Sen Says:
Anger begets madness

sanity. Anger is also a demoralizing mental raving that is hard to avoid. One of the most common anger traps you encounter is the reflex reaction trap: the trap that auto-activates your mirror neurons and bounces anger straight back in the direction where it came from.

Before you know it someone else's anger has become your anger, and it can explode. It's your 'fight' response. Pengelly didn't just mirror Mishka's frustration about the electricity bill. He sent it back at triple strength. Yet he didn't express his resentment towards Mishka in a way which exercised his honesty muscle. Instead, his imagination and thinking links caused his resentment to balloon into generalized, abstracted anger.

Lost your cool and then cried?
Do you remember an incident where you or a family member or friend got caught in the reflex reaction trap, auto-activated the anger mirror, and then, after the argument was over, burst into tears? Had anger demoralized and weakened, or had anger strengthened the Happiness Animal? Whether it's you or your family member who is angry, you are not alone. According to the Raymond W. Novaco, a social behaviour professor at the University of California, Americans report losing their temper on average three to four times a week. Novaco invented anger management, so you'd expect him to have some tips on how to exercise the tolerance muscle. One such tip is: Call it anger: 'The minute you feel your temperature rise, tell yourself, I'm bothered, and that may blur my judgment.' By being aware of and accepting your anger you can begin to detach from it and then release it. Two thousand years before Novaco, Marcus Aurelius offered some wisdom to humanity that still helps me exercise tolerance in the heat of the moment: 'Our anger and annoyance are more detrimental to us than the things themselves which anger or annoy us.' That's a good incentive to let things be. With anger as it is with pain and fear: don't draw circles around what is. Anger's circles are bands of microwaves that quickly cook the space inside your mind. Limit anger to the specific thing you are angry about, and how that physically makes you feel. For example, do you feel tension in your neck and shoulders? Is it making you frown with a tight forehead? Concentrate on the specific bodily sensations of the experience of being angry. If you allow

yourself to experience the physical sensations, it will allow you to detach and release the anger. If resentment remains, state to the other person the specific thing they have done to make you angry. Avoid drawing circles of generalizations and abstractions around the specifics. Expressing abstract terms like 'always' and 'never' is not expressing the resentment. Resentment is only authentic if it applies to something specific that somebody has done on a specific day. **Tip: If you need to express resentment, exercise moralive 1.3.**

Prevention is better than a cure, but sometimes you need a reliever
Anger is like asthma, if you exercise your tolerance muscle enough you won't need to vent(olin). But no one is immune. There are times when there's so much dust flying around that something sneaks into your lungs, surprises you, and you are victim to a reaction. Shit happens. If you resent someone, you need to be specific about what you resent them for, and you need to exhale and express it completely honestly to get the resentment out of you. Psychologist and bestselling author of *Radical Honesty*, Brad Blanton explains: 'What you need to do to tell the truth and have the resentment disappear is this: first, notice the bodily sensation associated with what you have *called* anger (feeling constricted in your breathing, cowering, feeling tense, frowning) and state your resentment clearly. Start with, "I resent you for saying ..." For example, I resent you for saying, "Did you remember to get something for Grandma for her birthday?"
"I resent you for your innocent, phony tone of voice". "I resent you for your tone of voice when you asked me that question" (more specific); "I resent you for looking at me now"; "I resent you for frowning". This may sound ridiculous and unfair. But note this: the unfair blaming is being done out loud. It is in the public domain where it can get cleared up, not in your secretive mind.'

Judgmental behaviour

There is generally much to learn before any judgement can be
pronounced with certainty on another's doings

Marcus Aurelius

Tolerance is just as good an exercise for avoiding premature and negatively biased (unnatural) judgement, as it is for exercising good judgement. Exercising good judgement has nothing to do with being judgemental: Good judgement prevents you from using ignorance or doubt to dismiss others' ideas, beliefs or behaviours. Using your senses, rather than your judgemental imagination, good judgement empowers your Happiness Animal with reason, enquiry and curiosity. Instead of taking the shortcuts of your own learned evaluations, associations and abstractions of mind to dismiss others and their ideas, you challenge what you sense with curiosity and questions. You apply this curious and questioning approach when you meet with newness and diversity. And exercising tolerance is important because newness and diversity challenge the sameness of what you are used to: For example, you are starting to work together on a project with a new colleague who speaks openly about their religion. If you decide to treat them with curiosity rather than suspicion, once you identify mutual benefits, your differences will disappear in the pursuit of common goals and in pursuit of the overall project's success. It also helps you exercise your tolerance muscle when you remember that both you and your colleague have got to this exact moment from your own very different and unique paths of education, attraction and thinking links. Your colleague talks to you with the brains, thinking links, and tools that they possess and not the brains, thinking links, and tools that you possess.

Determined to determine

Determinism is the force behind thinking links. Determinism is also the force behind attraction, association and education. And yes, it is attraction and association, education and thinking links, which lead people to doing things that make you angry. Awareness of determinism is the number one cure for intolerance. It makes tolerance of others easy, because it makes it obvious that someone doesn't just do something. A baby doesn't get up on the delivery table, perform a gymnastics routine, and score a perfect 10. The baby doesn't take her first look at her mother and tell

Time to define:

Determinism is a philosophy stating that for everything that happens there are conditions such that, given those conditions, nothing else could happen. (Wikipedia)

her she looks hideous in that dress. A lot needs to happen first. Only when you have awareness, can you see why you picked up this book and began reading it. Only when you have awareness of determinism are you no longer caught up in the chains of thinking links.

Given the thoughts, thinking links, education, attraction and association available to them at an instant in time a criminal didn't have a choice to act in any other way at the moment of the crime. In Albert Camus' book, 'The Stranger', the hero of the book has no choice but to fire the gun at the climax of the story. Do you think a criminal is aware of the determinism of her thoughts when he or she is holding up the post office? Do you think your family are aware of the determinism of their thoughts when they annoy you? Do you think you are aware of the determinism of your thoughts when they annoy you? There's an instant miracle cure. As soon as you start asking yourself, are they, am I, aware of what's making me have this thought, you break the shackles that determinism holds over you. This could have helped Pengelly to avoid demoralizing himself if he had applied some awareness of the determinism of his thoughts when texting his housemate Belle. Belle had worked for Ausgrid, the electricity network provider. Her education and thinking links created her association between electricity and Ausgrid, hence why, when she was looking for an explanation for a high electricity bill, she called Ausgrid. An Ausgrid customer support representative told her that the house Pengelly and Belle shared was on peak rate. A new thinking link between a high electricity bill and a peak rate determined her focus of thoughts on a peak rate. Pengelly's focus was on Mishka's heater. Ignorant of what was determining their associations and thinking links on different causes to the same problem, Pengelly became frustrated with Belle. He associated her behaviour with an idea that she wanted to be difficult and spontaneously pulled her opinion from thin air to undermine him. If, however, he had remembered that Belle's opinion, in the moment of the text message, was the cumulative result of the determinism of her thinking links, her education, her attraction and her association, he would have avoided his frustration with her altogether.

Immunity

Awareness of determinism's puppet strings grants you immunity from social proof. Instead of being carried away by the crowd, you look at the whole crowd from a balcony, just like the Pope or the Queen of England. But you are also able to read a story about the crowd from that balcony. A story

Phone a friend
Get a notepad and pen. Even better record your next conversation with a friend. Write down the subjects as they come up in natural dialogue. Write what links one subject to the next. Each link you can write down is a an example of your awareness of determinism of attraction and association at play with your and the other person's thoughts. **Note:** Just because you can't remember or identify what the thinking link was, doesn't mean there wasn't one. Often, the link is an interruption by an external noise or a person. These interruptions force themselves into your existing links, thus changing your attraction and associations.

that makes it clear that everyone looks at one event from a different position on the ground, and that no two people have exactly the same point of view, however large or small that difference in point of view may be. And it's because everyone has had different amounts and combinations of exposure to beliefs, cultures, family values, and living conditions. The more time they've lived in the sun, the more suntanned or sunburnt they will be. When you ask why there are differences, you create awareness. The more awareness you have, the more gradients of skin colour you see. The more gradients of colour you can see, the richer your experience of awareness. The more points of view you are able to see, the less likely you are to be socially swayed to accept one group's beliefs or values, without submitting them to your own, well-reflected judgement first. Awareness is your immunity against social proof, and with awareness of determinism, you see that people do not buy Coca-Cola for the taste.

Pass the photo album

Belle and Mishka were unaware of a critical piece of information held by Pengelly, namely that the electricity bill for the same quarter in the previous year totalled more than the electricity bill this year. Pengelly could have facilitated a mutual understanding if he had shared all the information he had rather than focusing on the gaps between views. The more photographs you have, the more depth you give your picture of a person, place or event. It's exactly the same with information. A photo of Rome at night doesn't show you what it's like in the day, a photo on a cloudy day, doesn't show you what it's like on a sunny day. The sharing of information, like the sharing of photographs, increases the amount of mutual information that can be seen from everyone's individual angle. Pengelly knew that Belle and Mishka hadn't seen more than a couple of pages of the electricity bill's photo album, and he used his larger portfolio of pictures against them, withholding information to support his authoritarian approach to winning the argument and to validate his viewpoint over theirs. His deck was loaded, theirs was empty. Nobody won. Pengelly became angry and frustrated, demoralized. He didn't know that exercising tolerance would have strengthened his Happiness Animal, and he didn't know that he could have exercised that tolerance by seeing Mishka and Belle's ignorance for what ignorance really is: a missing piece of education; an opportunity to educate by sharing a free copy of a piece of the infinite jigsaw puzzle. Recognize the gap and then share the information. It is against human nature not to share information. Why do people gossip, write songs, write books, paint, photograph, film? Why do children trade the collector cards they have duplicates of in the playground? Are adults as smart and as open as children when it comes to trading knowledge? Trading truth costs nothing but makes everyone richer, and it exercises the tolerance muscle, strengthening the Happiness Animal. Remember Brad Blanton's words: 'withholding is the most pernicious form of lying'. Withholding demoralizes your Happiness Animal. Closing others down by limiting and withholding your flow of information to them, makes the other person angry, and you then reciprocate with your own anger and frustration at the others' 'ignorance'. If that sounds familiar, don't worry. Tolerance of others has its own ER (Emergency Room) that can be accessed regardless of what you or they have done, and it's an ER called Forgiveness.

Oddly Enough
Forgiveness makes you happy. Conversely, not exercising with forgiveness has disastrous consequences for the Happiness Animal: Professor of Sociology, Wes Perkins provides the statistics: 'the risk (of being really unhappy) more than doubles for those who can't forgive.' And in a study of those who forgive quickly only 4% say they are unhappy.

Forgiveness is....tolerance after intolerance.

If you couldn't stop yourself from being intolerant of someone's bad behaviour (again), whether their bad behaviour was calling you an idiot, showing up late for a date, cheating on you with someone from work, punching a hole in your favourite painting, smashing your guitar, or just telling you to 'go fuck yourself,' then it's time to play your get-out-of-intolerance free card: That's the card that has forgiveness written all over it. Forgiving frees you from the problems of others and it frees you from your own bitterness. It frees you to feel your kindness, courage, awareness and honesty muscles again. Forgiving frees you from demoralizing slavery to the thinking links of your mind. And it doesn't mean staying with your cheating partner. Sounds easy, right, but a lot of the time it isn't. If you are anything like the majority, you find it hard to forgive, at least some of the time. In a study of US graduates only 25% said they forgive easily. So how can the other 75% learn how to forgive? By putting on their glasses. The same glasses that work for exercising tolerance at the time of seeing the 'bad' behaviour, are also the best glasses for exercising forgiveness for the 'bad' behaviour: Determinism glasses. When you look through them, you see the reasons for 'bad' behaviour that are blowing in the wind. The determinism glasses always ask what could have happened to make that person think and behave that way. They ask what was the person doing that day before they said or did what they did, and what is going on in the rest of that person's life at the moment. The determinism glasses also ask one other very important question: Does the person understand how determinism is determining their current behaviour? Once you accept that the answer to this question is almost always no, it is much easier to 'forgive them, for they know not what they do'. When your partner forgets to pick up the groceries, when they are late for a date, when they don't wish you good luck before you go out the door to a job interview, or when they suddenly shout at you, ask what thinking links could have determined them to behave that way.

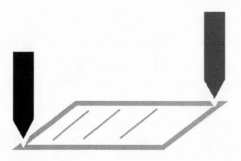

Pens with benefits – And you behaved perfectly?

Your benefit: You avoid damage to your most valuable relationships. Finding fault with yourself by identifying your weaknesses is also a key to overcoming anger. If you eliminate any possible hypocrisy and judgmentalism from your behaviour, you can avoid damage to your most valuable relationships:

1. What was a recent conflict you had with someone else, where you didn't do anything wrong but the other person undoubtedly acted in a morally wrong way towards you?

_____

_____

_____

_____

2. Imagine yourself in that conflict and picture the scene. What was one way in that scene in which you could have responded better to the abusive/intolerant/angry/offensive/cruel/selfish behaviour from other person?

_____

_____

_____

_____

3. Can you acknowledge this one way where you could have responded better as a weakness, however small, where with a little exercise, you could improve your behaviour?

Don't rush your answer to this question, but consider how the possibilities could improve your life. As Jonathan Haidt writes in *The Happiness Hypothesis*: 'When you first catch sight of a fault in yourself it will hurt briefly, but if you keep going and acknowledge the fault you are likely to be rewarded with a flash of pleasure. It is the pleasure of taking responsibility of your own behaviour. It is the feeling of honour.'

4. During the conflict you had with the other person, would you have rather been in their shoes or in yours?

_____

5. Do you feel relief that you don't have the other person's issues yourself?

_____

6. Do you feel sorry for them?

_____

7. Can you forgive them?

_____

8. If not, why not?

_____

_____

_____

_____

9. If you answered no to question 7, reread your answer to question eight. Do those reasons make it 100% impossible for you to forgive?

_____

10. If you answered no to question 7, is not forgiving tugging at your inner peace of mind, and irritating you, maybe even prompting some anger in you?

11. If you answered no to question 7, go back to page 151, and do the exercise for empathy (moralive 2.5). Then, redo this exercise from step 1.

What to do if you still can't forgive

If you have done the exercise for empathy on p.151 and the pens with benefits exercise on the previous pages, and you still can't forgive, then you need to express your resentments. The below are Brad Blanton's six minimal requirements for forgiveness. He says you cannot skip any of the below.

1. You have to tell the truth about what specific behaviour you resent to the person, face to face (see exercise for expressing resentment (moralive 1.3))
2. You have to be verbally and vocally unrestrained with regard to volume and propriety
3. You have to pay attention to the feelings and sensations in your body and to the other person as you speak
4. You have to express any appreciations for the person that come up in the process, with the same attention to your feelings and to the other person as when you are expressing resentments (see also exercise of moralive®1.3)
5. You have to stay with any feelings that emerge in the process, like tears or laughter, regardless of any evaluations you have about how it makes you look
6. You have to stay with the discussion until you no longer feel resentment of the other person. That means no one walks out of the room until every resentment has been expressed.

The patronizer of false respect

Does it mean something negative if you tolerate someone?

Does it mean that you're putting up with their shit, begrudgingly at best, and really, their habits annoy the crap out of you?

Is it a forced, false feeling of being obliged to put up with someone?

Do you patronise someone when you tolerate them?

Do you take the attitude of not caring what they do?

If you answered yes to any of the above, then it's an indicator of tolerance that's doing more to demoralize, than to exercise your Happiness Animal. And you're not alone. Instead of questioning difference, there is an increasingly global, social trend of apathy towards accepting difference and diversity, or accepting diversity begrudgingly, and patronisingly. Companies say: 'We embrace diversity', but then don't explore the differences diversity provides. Difference is 'respected' and 'embraced'. Or at least that's what the statement says. But what does it really mean? Diversity in itself has no more value than sameness, and accepting differences and diversity unquestioningly out of political correctness, is accepting ignorance. That is no more respect of diversity, than it is ignoring someone when they are talking to you. Yet diversity can provide infinite opportunities for respectful learning and mutual benefits, especially when the challenge is to do what has never been done, for example when a new country is being formed, or when a new technology is being developed.

Fake plastic diversity

Are we all different? Are you a part of the diversity of society, or are you separate from it? Strange, don't you think, that we often see diversity as something separate to ourselves? Have you ever waited at a company's reception desk, and seen a message on a plaque that says 'we respect diversity?' Or is it part of your employee code of conduct to respect diversity? But who is the 'we' who is respecting the diversity? Who or what is the diversity? In the statement: 'we respect diversity,' diversity is a separate object to the subject (subject: we; verb: respect; object: diversity). The truth is we are diversity. There is not one human being who is exactly the same as another. If there was, they'd be a clone. But if you are a part of diversity, why do you sometimes feel separate or isolated from diversity? How does feeling separate or isolated feel? Is it a feeling that strengthens your Happiness Animal? Is it a feeling you want to hold onto? So how do you stop feeling separate or isolated? By exercising your tolerance muscle. When you exercise your tolerance muscle, you reengage with the whole that is diversity.

Imagine you are joining a new company. Do you think you will do better in the company if you:

a) Find out who does what in the company, how your work feeds into theirs, and how what they do affects your workflow?

b) Accept that everyone does something different and it's better not to ask why?

Employees that answer and act on a) do well when they exercise curiosity, and seek out information about the company and the roles and responsibilities within that company. According to a study by Saks, A.M and Ashforth, published in the Journal of Vocational Behaviour, employees with curiosity adjust to an organisation more quickly. But for the majority of employees, curiosity is limited to questions about the company's roles and responsibilities. Regardless of who does well in the company, almost all employees, top and bottom performers, practice more blanket (apathetic) acceptance of diversity, than exercise curiosity towards diversity.

Liberal apathy

Is it possible that an increase in blanket acceptance of diversity without curiosity, and the social proof influence of 'we respect and we embrace diversity' statements are linked to an increasingly underused, and therefore increasingly weaker tolerance muscle? Is it possible that through inactivity the tolerance muscle has been weakened by the disease of apathy? Apathy leads to atrophy. The irony of a more liberal society is that after a founding period of tolerance and understanding, the lasting effects, if that society does not actively continue to exercise tolerance with curiosity, can be intolerance to questioning that society. Is it because diversity is glossed over, with a 'we respect and we embrace diversity' statement, that it is separating and isolating the people who have not exercised enough curiosity to penetrate the gloss? It is a paradox that the less you question the diversity of others in society, the less freedom you have to be authentically you within that society. 'Stay hungry, stay foolish,' was the advice of Thoreau and Steve Jobs. If you can't present your honest perceptions the way you see them, and curiously seek out information to build your own picture of diversity, then you are not free to be foolish and not free to be truly you.

This is where diversity becomes depressing. It's a demoralizing realisation that there are hundreds of beautiful places to visit around your city but there is a power preventing you from leaving your house: The demoralizing power of apathy. Apathy is kryptonite to your Happiness Animal. The more you accept diversity with apathy, the more separated from diversity you become, the more isolated you become, the more lonely you become. Ten times more people suffer from major depression now than in 1945. How many companies had a 'we embrace diversity' plaque at their reception desk in 1945? Was there a stronger sense of belonging in 1945 or now? Was there a stronger sense of community in 1945 or now? Are people living more as isolated individuals in 1945 or now? Today, we might be more politically correct, but is PC good for strengthening your Happiness Animal? Was it politicians who fought the most since 1945 for equality and civil rights, for an end to racism? Or was it the people, united by their diversity who were not afraid to ask: What are the differences in our points of view and why? It is against human nature not to share information, but it is also against human nature not to curiously seek it out. Everyone sees the world from a unique perspective, everyone has a piece of the infinite jigsaw puzzle of life that can be shared, when it is sought. It is when you begin to question difference that you begin to sense what every human being has in common. The 'Humans Of New York' facebook page is particularly effective at presenting diversity in universal human truths. If you haven't yet explored that page I'd encourage you to take a look at the diversity of photographs of New Yorkers combined with the vivid instances of their story, which accompany each photograph. But differences that are more accepted at face value, than curiously explored, make questions unusual. If you accept something, you don't question it. How often have you been questioned about something personal or unique to you, either socially or in the workplace and when you questioned, you took it as a personal insult, and responded defensively? False tolerance has made it socially unsafe to challenge people's opinions and beliefs, even if you do so in the pursuit of truth. False tolerance has created intolerance, intolerance to curiosity, and apathy towards pursuing the truth. The good news is that's not the kind of tolerance you will exercise in this chapter. So how can you exercise your tolerance muscle with curiosity, without being offensive? By remaining honest about how you feel and sticking to the specifics that you can notice, and by not creating any stories or generalizations or abstract opinions. And if something someone does or says makes you resent them for it, tell them you resent them for it.

Exercising tolerance of others (moralive®3.3): all in the same boat
Exercise for tolerating other people

Instructions
Do this exercise if your first reaction is one of disdain or dismissal towards anyone. For example it could be a reaction in your self of disgust towards a shaved haircut, a beard, a tattoo, a loud voice or colored hair.

1. Look at the person. Notice your reaction. Notice the physical sensations in your body of that reaction and stay with those sensations for 30 seconds (or until they disappear).

2. With your attention geared to the other person, tell yourself the following in this order (from 'Just Like Me' by Harry Palmer):

    a. 'Just like me, this person is seeking happiness in his/her life.'

    b. 'Just like me, this person is trying to avoid suffering in his/her life.'

    c. 'Just like me, this person has known sadness, loneliness and despair.'

    d. 'Just like me, this person is seeking to fill his/her needs.'

    e. 'Just like me, this person is learning about life.'

3. Look back at the person. Notice any movements they make. Start at their feet and check each body part. Notice any movements in different parts of their body. What are they doing with their hands? Their fingers? Their shoulders? What internal feelings do you think those bodily movements relate to? Do you notice any movements in them that you recognize in yourself?

4. Notice your own body. How have the sensations changed from your first reaction (in step 1).

Tolerance towards timing and events (moralive®3.4)

Patience is the best remedy for every trouble

Titus Maccius Plautu

If ever we can be free of the need to get there first, do more, earn more, then other people will no longer appear as obstacles to our urgency

Piero Ferrucci

If I have made any valuable discoveries, it has been owing more to patient attention than to any other talent

Sir Isaac Newton

Have patience with all things, but chiefly have patience with yourself. Do not lose courage in considering your own imperfections but instantly set about remedying them – every day begin the task anew

St. Francis de Sales

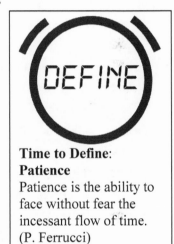

You may be wondering why you are reading so many quotes before you get to the start of this section. So tell me, what kind of tolerance helps you to tolerate unplanned quotations, events, traffic jams, a queue at the café or at the airport, a late bus, waiting for someone to show up, or someone taking too long to tell a story or explain something you know already? And what kind of tolerance helps you avoid demoralizing frustration, anxiety and panic?

Time to Define:
Patience
Patience is the ability to face without fear the incessant flow of time. (P. Ferrucci)

Slowing down does. Taking it easy does. Patience does. Patience is a virtue, possess it if you can. I don't see many who can when I watch people on their way home from work, using alien intensity to create a this-is-my-space tunnel of power walk on the pavements of Sydney and London: Bodies that become fighter drones until they reach their destination of urgency. The irony is the destination of urgency is often relaxation. It's a rush to relax, but does that rush give you more time to relax? What if getting home five minutes later didn't matter to you? What if the entire journey, and not just the time at destination was relaxed?

When to exercise your tolerance muscle with situations and events (moralive®3.4)

Pengelly panicked when he realized what date it was on his calendar, even though it was still days before the electricity meter had been read, before the bill had arrived. He responded instantly to every text message he received from Belle. Could he have responded better if he had paused, slowed down before he sent each reply? What would he have done for the rest of the day if he hadn't noticed what date it was on his calendar? But he applied magnified urgency to the date, and the associated electricity bill. Pengelly spent more time in the present worrying about the future, than he spent time living in the present. When the bill arrived, he zoomed to urgency to get

Oddly enough

The flow of time is an illusion. There is no need to be in a panic of hurry, because now is not running away from you. Now doesn't run away. This extract of an article taken from the Scientific American explains why: 'As you read this sentence, you probably think that this moment—right now—is what is happening. The present moment feels special. It is real. However much you may remember the past or anticipate the future, you live in the present. Of course, the moment during which you read that sentence is no longer happening. This one is. In other words, it feels as though time flows, in the sense that the present is constantly updating itself. We have a deep intuition that the future is open until it becomes present and that the past is fixed. As time flows, this structure of fixed past, immediate present and open future gets carried forward in time. This structure is built into our language, thought and behavior. How we live our lives hangs on it.Yet as natural as this way of thinking is, you will not find it reflected in science. The equations of physics do not tell us which events are occurring right now—they are like a map without the "you are here" symbol. The present moment does not exist in them, and therefore neither does the flow of time. Additionally, Albert Einstein's theories of relativity suggest not only that there is no single special present but also that all moments are equally real. Fundamentally the future is no more open than the past. [See "That Mysterious Flow," by Paul Davies; *Scientific American*, September 2002].

the money off his housemates now, today, even though his credit card wouldn't be charged for another month. He couldn't tolerate the future timing of events in the present because he was looking through an imaginary zoom lens at events in the future.

When you're up against your own emotions of impatience, frustration, and resistance towards a change of plan, the reality test helps you again. Reality test the importance of being on time. Reality test the importance of 'the plan'.

You can ask yourself these same four questions every time you feel the zoom lens of urgency and when you feel impatient, frustrated, or resistant to a change to the plan:

1. What is the worst that can happen?
2. How likely is this to happen based on actual experience (on a scale of one to ten, with ten being most likely)?
3. What can I do to reduce the likelihood of this happening?
4. Can I survive this worst case scenario and live with it if it does happen?

Your life will never go exactly 'to plan'. We already know that because we know we are notoriously bad at predicting the future. The best plan is to assume that the plan will change along the way.

Stress is selfish

'People who know how to transform stress into an enjoyable challenge spend very little time thinking about themselves,' says author of *Flow*, Mihaly Csikzentmihalyi. By focusing your attention on noticing what is happening around you, it empowers you to adapt to the real world that exists, rather than being stuck, clinging to the idea of an imaginary world that your ego wants. When things aren't going to schedule, remember that the planned or expected schedule is a creation of ego (your mind's associations of thinking links of how you *imagine* things 'should' be). Any frustration or stress that results from things not going to plan is a frustration of your ego caused by things not going the way the ego wants them to. What the ego wants comes from your imagination, not from reality, which you can notice right now in this moment with your senses. Your ego doesn't want to let go of the ideas of how things 'should' be. But when you notice what is going on around you, you feel more connected to the world around you: 'When attention is focused away from the self, frustration of one's desires have less of a chance to disrupt consciousness. To experience psychic entropy one must concentrate on the internal disorder' says Csikzentmihalyi.

By not paying attention to your ideas of how things 'should' be and your frustrations inside, but instead paying attention to – noticing – what is happening around you, you exercise tolerance of things not going to plan. When you choose the intention of using your senses over your ego's attachment to ideas, you release your ego's psychic entropy and you release your ego's stress. I was looking at my phone while I was waiting for a bus and didn't

Time to define:
Psychic entropy
is information that conflicts with existing intentions or that distracts people from carrying out intentions. Whenever information disrupts consciousness by threatening its goals we have a condition of inner disorder, a disorganisation of the self that impairs its effectiveness. (Csikszentmihalyi)

notice the bus was coming, so I didn't hail it down for it to stop. When I looked up I saw the bus had just gone past and I ran after it. It stopped at the traffic lights just up ahead. The driver refused to open the door and drove off without me. The next bus wasn't for another hour and it was already 10pm at night. My old habit of frustration almost kicked in, my ego was ready to keep thinking about the fact that I'd missed that bus, about why the driver didn't stop, about how I shouldn't have been looking at my phone, and every thought that could attach itself to how this missed bus had ruined the plan for the rest of the night. Instead I noticed I was hungry, and walked down the street. I noticed I had 50 minutes before the next bus, which gave me 50 minutes to get something to eat. I saw a Turkish restaurant and I smelled the aromas of food coming out the door that made me salivate.

I decided to go in and get a meal and use my remaining 45 minutes. I noticed the restaurant had a wifi sticker on the window, so I asked the waiter for the code. While I waited for the meal I replied to a couple of important emails I had received on my BlackBerry, and uploaded a video for this book's facebook page to YouTube. I then ate and tasted a delicious meal that I wouldn't have tried if I hadn't missed the bus, and went home feeling satisfied and relaxed. If I had stayed at the bus stop, I can imagine my ruminating on the missed bus and how if only I hadn't looked at my phone, that I 'should' have been home by now, that everything had gone to shit and so on and so on, would have made for an entirely more stressful experience.

TTYL

Rushed conversations are often incoherent conversations. Incoherence causes misunderstandings in relationships, and incoherence demoralizes relationships. Yet you have conversations while rushing to a meeting, or you take a phone call when you are busting to go to the toilet? How much do you remember from those conversations? You are better understood, respected, and more likely to be creative without damaging but adding value to your relationships, if you can slow down. Pause, and come back after you've been for a number one or two. That also goes for text messages. Think of the damage to Pengelly's relationship with Belle, caused by his triple bombardment of napalm texting. Exercising patience, by contrast, gave Pengelly's tolerance muscle a work-out, burning off incoherence, and building coherence. When Pengelly saw Mishka had put his heater back on, he was able to pause, bite his tongue, and let it go. After a week of leaving electricity be, perceived problem circles around electricity began to disappear circle by circle. Pengelly's patience enabled him to zoom

Sen says:
What is waited for sinks in more readily. I am telling you to be a slow speaking person.

out to see his life through a wide angled lens. The more often you exercise your patience with lights and heaters left on, the more you will be able to exercise patience with disruptions to your plans, and the more you will build strength in your tolerance muscle and your Happiness Animal. Pause, and zoom out. Get the wide angle of your entire life, and you will have more control over that life. You'll never have the future, never have the past, but you've always got now. You won't worry about the days, minutes and hours when you're having the time of your life.

Exercising patience (moralive®3.4): a plant, a jug, five mugs and a teaspoon

Patience can't be acquired overnight. It is just like building up a muscle. Every day you need to work on it

Eknath Easwaran

Oddly enough, the exercises for tolerance of pain and tolerance of fear also work for exercising

Phone a friend. Or try this in your next interaction with a work colleague...

- **Be slow to speak:** enunciating words and making sure every syllable is clearly articulated ensures clear speech.
- **Be quick to listen**
- **Shut up** until they are done talking. Don't interrupt when they are telling you something. Let them speak without criticism, comment, or correction.
- **Notice movements** in expression (both sound and visual movements of the speaker).
- **Talk in questions:** Statements are one way streets, and you can't have a one way relationship. You might as well talk to yourself.
- **Talk to prompt:** View your speech as the prompts to get as much valuable information from your speaking partner as possible.

patience at the time you are feeling impatient. Practice using those exercises as tools whenever you are already feeling the impatience. To use an asthma analogy, the exercises for tolerance of pain and fear are the Vent(olin) relievers for feelings of pain, fear and impatience. The following is more a preventative exercise for impatience, the brown steroid inhaler or Becotide, that works best when you are not already feeling impatient but will prepare you and increase your resilience to future impatience triggers. This exercise is based on a Tibetan Buddhist meditation ritual. You can try the original ritual but you will need to find five hundred tiny bottles first. Given I don't know anyone who keeps five hundred empty bottles around their house, I have adapted this exercise.

You will need: a large plant, a jug, five mugs and a teaspoon. If you don't have a plant to water, use the nearest tree or lawn.

Instructions:
1) Fill five mugs to the brim with water.
2) Carry the full mugs one at a time over to where the plant is and put them down slowly. Imagine you are doing it as calmly as you possibly can, making sure you are breathing easily through your nose, while you focus on not spilling any water.
3) Pick up the teaspoon and the first of the five mugs.
4) Take one teaspoon of water at a time out of the mug and feed it to the plant, lawn or tree. Focus entirely on the spoon and the water (and not spilling the water). Continue spooning until the mug is empty.
5) Put down the empty mug and pick up the next mug and repeat step 4.
6) Repeat step 4 and 5 until all mugs are empty.

Exercising tolerance towards yourself (moralive®3.5)

Finish each day and be done with it. You have done what you could. Some blunders and absurdities no doubt crept in; forget them as soon as you can. Tomorrow is a new day; begin it well and serenely and with too high a spirit to be encumbered with your old nonsense. This day is all that is good and fair. It is too dear, with its hopes and invitations, to waste a moment on yesterdays.

Ralph Waldo Emerson

Other people, yes, other things, sure, but tolerance of myself? How can I be tolerant of myself? There is an ancient Indian saying: you are your own friend and enemy. If that's true, I'd like to add the following to the end of the saying: and your friend can exercise tolerance of your enemy. You've exercised with the equipment for tolerance of other people. Exercising tolerance of yourself is like upping the weights as you get stronger. The heaviest weights to exercise with are feelings of guilt, remorse, regret, low self –esteem, and shame. But once you are able to exercise with these heavy weights, it will also make the weights of forgiving and tolerating others easier to lift. Alexandra Asseily, a prominent psychotherapist and founder of The Garden of Forgiveness in Beirut, agrees that forgiving yourself first, makes the weight of forgiving others easier to lift: 'If we all just remember that if we forgive ourselves, it's a wonderful beginning to forgiveness. Because if we really forgive ourselves for all the wickedness we think we have inside or all the things we think are wrong with ourselves, we would then be so much more compassionate with others. And I think it's our lack of compassion with ourselves that makes us so upset with others'.

Oddly enough
'The capacity for getting along with our neighbor depends to a large extent on the capacity for getting along with ourselves. The self-respecting individual will try to be as tolerant of his neighbor's shortcomings as he is of his own.' – Eric Hoffer

Forgiving yourself is as critical to the strength of your Happiness Animal as forgiving others. Holding back forgiveness of yourself is holding kryptonite against your Happiness Animal. Often it's the accumulation of small daily 'unforgivings' of yourself that create a pile of kryptonite dust around your Happiness Animal. Exercising tolerance of yourself is making peace with your today by forgiving yourself your daily blunders, vacuuming up the dust of small 'unforgivings', and it's also about finally blasting those boulders of kryptonite that have been blocking the path of your Happiness Animal for years. It's time you got out the vacuum and the dynamite.

When to exercise with tolerance of self (moralive®3.5)

Shame: The secret epidemic

So you messed up. Be honest about it. You are a human being and you are vulnerable to messing up. When your existence is dominated by your mind that is full of unnatural distractions and associations, and all the bullshit fed to you incessantly at work, on television, on the street, from the mouths of masks of other people, you will be attracted to making mistakes and doing things that are sometimes what your mind tells you are bad. It is your vulnerability to do bad things as well as good things that makes you a human being. You are not some all-powerful, perfect creature – no one is – and so it's ok to be honest about that. It's more important to be yourself than to be strangled by your own self-righteousness. But here's why not just being tolerant of the bad things you have done, but embracing being vulnerable to doing the wrong thing, could save your life: When you pretend you don't do 'bad' things and feel secret, silent shame about those 'bad' things, you don't get a chance to do the good things that you would do if you were truly you. You don't get to live your life. If you allow shame to dominate your existence through the tyranny of your ego and your mind, you are not being you to those around you. You are a faker. People aren't getting the real you, and the real, authentic you is just what they want, warts and all. There's enough bullshit in the world already. As clinical psychologist, Neil Fiore, writes: 'It's tremendously liberating to simply state: "So I'm not perfect. So What? I'm only human. But I'm still here and worthy of life." There's no shame in admitting our human vulnerability and imperfection. Quite the opposite. It's the denial of humanness and the attempt to be perfect and invulnerable that causes us pain and shame. I'd like to speak up for letting go of trying to be perfect and invulnerable and to compassionately embracing our human imperfection.'

Embracing imperfection and vulnerability and letting go of shame doesn't give you the right to go do bad things. Because you are not distracted by thinking about the bad things you have done, you are more likely to do the good things that are true to who you are. But you are more likely to continue to do things that make you feel shame if you keep thinking about your shame, because when you try to be someone you are not, you are perverting who you are.

Remorse as a teacher, but a teacher who should not outstay their welcome

> Remorse is the sheep dog biting the strayed sheep; he must not
> continue to bite when the sheep only wishes to do right
> Paul Dubois

Remorse's purpose is as a means to your regeneration. The intensity of your remorse reminds you of the extent of your morality. Just as your body will tell you that off prawns are not good for you by giving you a stinking feeling, your body releases remorse to tell you something is bad for your Happiness Animal. But once remorse has taught you to

Oddly enough: There's no such thing as perfect so why do we pretend to be? Below is an abridged version of an article by the world's leading shame expert, Brené Brown. The article makes one point crystal clear: that we are more worthy now than we will ever be by pretending to be perfect: 'Why, when we know that there's no such thing as perfect, do most of us spend an incredible amount of time and energy trying to be everything to everyone? Is it that we really admire perfection? No -- the truth is that we are actually drawn to people who are real and down-to-earth. We love authenticity and we know that life is messy and imperfect. We get sucked into perfection for one very simple reason: We believe perfection will protect us. Perfectionism is the belief that if we live perfect, look perfect, and act perfect, we can minimize or avoid the pain of blame, judgment, and shame. Perfectionism is a 20-ton shield that we lug around thinking it will protect us when, in fact, it's the thing that's really preventing us from being seen and taking flight. What's the greater risk? Letting go of what people think -- or letting go of how I feel, what I believe, and who I am? We're all so afraid to let our true selves be seen and known. Why are we so paralyzed by what other people think? The greatest challenge for most of us is believing that we are worthy now, right this minute. Worthiness doesn't have prerequisites. Here's what is truly at the heart of whole-heartedness: Worthy now. Not if. Not when. We are worthy of love and belonging now. Right this minute. As is.

Letting go of our prerequisites for worthiness means making the long walk from "What will people think?" to "I am enough." But, like all great journeys, this walk starts with one step, and the first step in the wholehearted journey is practicing courage. I think we've lost touch with the idea that speaking honestly and openly about who we are, about what we're feeling, and about our experiences (good and bad) is the definition of courage. Courage is about putting our vulnerability on the line. If we want to live and love with our whole hearts and engage in the world from a place of worthiness, our first step is practicing the courage it takes to own our stories and tell the truth about who we are. It doesn't get braver than that.'

stop doing something, remorse has no other purpose. If you hold onto remorse, you are continuing to sniff at stinky prawns. If you sniff at those prawns long enough, happiness eating parasites will jump prawns, into you, infect you, and rob you of your health and vitality. Pengelly's remorse started as a rotting feeling at the back of his throat, a draining feeling, and a feeling of losing flesh from his gums. In his case he chucked out his stinky prawns by apologising to Mishka, but how often do you hold onto your stinky prawns until the parasites get you? Bag them up and put them out with this week's rubbish. If you can't see the bin, you might need to put your glasses on again. Just as putting on your determinism glasses helps with forgiving others, it also helps with forgiving yourself. In fact your determinism glasses work just as well on yourself. That's because they enable to see your thinking links that led to the action that has caused your body to release remorse. The role of remorse is education, and when you wear your determinism glasses to your lesson of remorse, your Happiness Animal goes straight to the top of the class. Don't get me wrong here. I am not saying that having a pair of

Oddly Enough: tolerance towards yourself *is* a laughing matter. Laughter reduces cortisol and adrenaline, which are stress hormones linked to medical problems. Laughing also relaxes blood pressure and increases immune system activity by increasing the body's release of interferon. Laughing 100 (ha-ha) times a day also gives the same cardiac workout as 10 minutes of aerobic exercise. Maciej Buchowski, a researcher with Vanderbilt University, conducted a study that proved 10-15 minutes of concentrated laughter burned 50 calories.

Do try this at home
This exercise promotes blood flow to the thyroid gland, exercises the face and neck muscles and definitely inspires more laughter: Stand with your feet shoulder width apart. Raise your hands like paws. Open your mouth as wide as you can, stick your tongue out as far as it will go and open your eyes as wide as you can. Now laugh as hard as you can. Walk around laughing like this and move your body like a lion for about a minute, then relax your face. (Source: Tina Gallagher)

glasses and a good dose of remorse is an excuse to go do evil. Not at all. Determinism authorizes no future bad deeds, but it does provide awareness of likely new determining influences you will encounter in the future. Wearing determinism glasses when you feel remorse strengthens the vision of your Happiness Animal. Your vision allows you to turn over a new leaf, retaining the lesson learned of what thoughts led to the action that made you feel remorse, but free from any bitterness of the memory of what you did. Pengelly's remorse determined Pengelly's next action to apologise to Mishka about his outburst, it determined that he didn't repeat an outburst when he saw Mishka had put his heater back on with an open door, and it determined a different approach to his interaction with his housemates: an interaction of increased, open communication.

Exercising tolerance of self (moralive 3.5): Curiosity and self-forgiveness

Exercise for challenging limiting beliefs about you, and for forgiving you.

Instructions

Part I – Noticing the difference between what you can notice and what you imagine about yourself

1. Write down five sentences that begin with the words '**I notice…**' Whatever you notice must be something you can physically notice **about yourself** with your senses (vision, hearing, taste, smell or touch, right now in this present moment). You can't notice something that happened in the past or in the future. Write these sentences down below.

    e.g. I notice an itch on my inner thigh

1.

_____

_____

2.

_____

_____

3.

_____

_____

4.

_____

_____

5.

_____

_____

2. Now write down five sentences starting with the words 'I imagine'. Each sentence is about one thing you **imagine about yourself**.

> e.g. I imagine I am a bad in bed with my girlfriend; I imagine I am a loser; I imagine I won't get the job; I imagine I am a failure.

1.

_____

_____

2.

_____

_____

3.

_____

_____

4.

_____

_____

5.

_____

_____

3. How many of the negative things or limiting beliefs you have written about yourself are things you imagine vs. things you can actually notice in this moment?

_____things I notice about myself, _____ I imagine about myself are negative.

Part II - Optional additional exercise for self forgiveness

Exercise for when you can't forgive yourself for something. Adapted from an exercise by Jonathan Haidt in *The Happiness Hypothesis.*

It's important to go into this exercise with an awareness that you don't have to show what you write to anyone, so there is no need to be afraid of what you are writing. Brené Brown says that shame needs three things to grow exponentially: Secrecy, silence, and judgement. If you put these three ingredients into a Petri dish, they will grow shame. This is an exercise to break your secrecy, silence and judgement, which are making it impossible for you to forgive yourself. If you hate to write, talk into an audio recording device. The crucial thing is to get your thoughts and feelings out in words without imposing any order on them, but in such a way that after a few days some order is likely to emerge on its own.

Instructions

1. Take a blank piece of paper and write the words: 'I can't forgive myself for....' at the top of one of the pages.
2. Choose one thing you are struggling to forgive yourself for. It could be something minor in the context of your whole life or it could be something you are ashamed of that happened today, or it could be a deep regret from your past. Preferably choose an experience you have not talked about with other people.
3. Finish the sentence 'I can't forgive myself for....' by adding a brief summary of what you can't forgive yourself for.
4. Take up to five minutes to write, freely, without pausing to edit what you write, about what reasons may have led to you doing the thing you can't forgive yourself for. Try and remember what you had been doing prior to the thing you are trying to forgive yourself for. What was going on in your life around that time? Try and identify at least one reason why you would have done what you did.
5. Now write freely about the reasons you have for not forgiving yourself. What is preventing you from forgiving yourself now?
6. Write about what good you can derive from what you did, about any feelings you have about what you did, and write in any order as the thoughts come to you.
7. Repeat steps 4-6 of writing continuously for up to five minutes a day for several days. Don't edit or censor yourself. Don't worry about grammar or sentence structure; just keep writing.

Write about what happened, how you feel about it, and why you feel that way, and in whatever order you like.

8. Before you conclude your last day of writing (you will know it's your last day when you have nothing more to write about it) be sure you have done your best to answer these two questions: Why did this happen? What good might I derive from it?

9. If you still feel guilty, check to see if you still are imagining anger from the person you offended. Check to see if this anger you imagine they have towards you, is actually the anger you feel towards them. Often the source of guilt is anger you feel but have not expressed towards someone else. Brad Blanton explains that often mistakes are made out of anger and that people who are perennial screw ups are usually angry people.

10. Now think about a friend (imaginary or real) who is unconditionally loving, accepting, kind and compassionate. Imagine that this friend can see all your strengths and all your weaknesses, including the details of yourself you have just been writing about. Reflect upon what this friend feels towards you, and how you are loved and accepted exactly as you are, with all your very human imperfections. This friend recognizes the limits of human nature, and is kind and forgiving towards you. In his or her great wisdom this friend understands your life history and the millions of things that have happened in your life to create you as you are in this moment. Your particular inadequacy is connected to so many things you didn't necessarily choose: your genes, your family history, life circumstances – things that were outside of your control.

11. Write a letter to yourself from the perspective of this friend – focusing on the perceived inadequacy you tend to judge yourself for. If it helps, do this using the model of the musical chairs exercise you used for empathy, and actually get up and

switch chairs when you go to write the letter. What would this friend say to you about your "flaw" from the perspective of unlimited compassion? How would this friend convey the deep compassion he or she feels for you, for the pain you feel when you judge yourself so harshly? What would this friend write in order to remind you that you are only human, that all people have both strengths and weaknesses?

12. Add to the letter any suggestions for possible changes, and as you write from the perspective of this friend, be aware of how these suggestions would embody feelings of unconditional understanding and compassion. Try to infuse the letter with a strong sense of acceptance, kindness, caring, and desire of your friend for your health and happiness.

13. After writing the letter, put it down and leave it alone for a few hours or days. Then come back and read it again, really letting the words sink in. Feel the compassion as it pours into you, soothing and comforting you like a hot drink on a cold day. Love, connection and acceptance are your birthright. To claim them you need only look within yourself.

14. Finally, ask yourself: Am I more valuable to others as a vulnerable human being, who is still willing to step into the arena, who is willing to dare to do better but who admits to making mistakes, or as someone who hides secrets and poisons themselves with their own self-judgement and shame?

15. Share your story. People like to know they are not alone in not being perfect. Vulnerability is the strength of a human being who knows they are not perfect but dares greatly nonetheless. Showing vulnerability to the world, as Brené Brown says, is the most accurate measure of courage.

Animal Advice

- To understand all is to forgive all.

- Imagination is a zoom lens better at imagining risks and threats, than imagining peace and quiet. Your senses are your wide angle lens. Use them.

- Breathing brings you back. Breath is a natural pain reliever.

- Laugh. Laugh longer. Laugh at yourself. Stop taking yourself so seriously.

- 'Stay hungry, stay foolish,' but most of all, stay curious.

- Imagination is magnification. Most fears are based on imagined, unreal futures.

- An opinion on its own is a monologue cloud that has the potential to rain, but to create power it needs to touch another.

- Anger begets madness. Limit anger to the specific thing you resent, and how that physically makes you feel.

- Exercising good judgement of what you can notice with your senses, is not the same as being judgemental.

- Whether you believe in free will or not, awareness exists.

- We are diversity.

- Reality test the importance of being on time, and the importance of 'the plan'.

- Embrace your human vulnerability as your potential for courage, and dare greatly.

<u>Chapter 8</u>

moralive®4: awareness

It is not that we have a short time to live but that we waste a lot of it

They achieve what they want laboriously; they possess what they have achieved anxiously; and meanwhile they take no account of time that will never more return.
It is a small part of life that we really live.
Until we have begun to go without certain things, we fail to realize how unnecessary many things are. We have been using them not because we needed them but because we had them

Seneca

If you wish to enrich Pythocles, do not add to his riches, but lessen his desires

Epicurus

Animal's Anecdote
Jekyll and Hyde

Two policemen leapt from their car and sprung Ko's arms behind his back, hand-cuffing him in one movement. The police drove him to the Drunk Tank. At the admission desk, Ko blew a blood alcohol reading of .28. One of the policemen took the handcuffs off Ko, and then a nurse walked him into a white walled, white-floored dorm. The security doors locked behind them as the nurse showed him to his vinyl mattress. Ko passed out.

Three days prior, New Year's Eve, Ko was in Juliette's kitchen as Juliette was sitting on the sofa, catching up on some work.
'Baby, I'm going to cook you something special for lunch. You keep working and I'll have it ready for 1,' said Ko.
'Thanks babe, you are so sweet,' said Juliette.
Ko opened the fridge door, took out the lobster tails he'd bought earlier that morning, along with some fresh garlic and a pack of butter, and grabbed a roll of foil out the drawer. He took the Moet out of the fridge and put it in the freezer to chill further for another half an hour. As the lobster cooked in the oven, Ko went into Juliette's bedroom, and made the bed. Then he showered, shaved and put on his best cologne and a freshly dry-cleaned, pink shirt. He pulled out a bunch of a dozen roses he'd been hiding in the closet since that morning.
'Lunch is ready baby,' said Ko to Juliette.
'Perfect timing. I've just got to save this and I'm done,' said Juliette.
Ko gave Juliette the flowers and she got up and wrapped her arms around him. They kissed and Juliette's hands moved downs Ko's back, then her right hand moved around and down to Ko's fly where her fingers unfastened the first button.
'Hey baby, lunch is ready! Let's eat first and have a special siesta after we're done eating'.

'Fine,' said Juliette. She slapped Ko's butt. Ko put the plates of lobster on the table and then went to the freezer. As he pulled out the bottle of Moet, he knocked a bottle of vodka over onto its side. He picked it up and looked at it for a second before putting it back in the freezer.

'But I'm the only one drinking. You're spoiling me. Don't you want to have a glass of champagne with me seeing as it's New Year's Eve?' asked Juliette.

Ko paused with the bottle of Moet in his hand after he'd poured Juliette's glass. 'No I'm good baby thanks. I just can't drink anymore'

'More for me then,' laughed Juliette.

Ko woke and saw the white clock on the wall behind the staff desk, and the twelve rows of filled dorm beds in between him and the wall. The black clock hands marked 4 am. Ko began to notice the sounds of wailings and mumblings. He looked around chasing the sounds and saw the deformed faces of alcoholics. He began to notice the stench of stale bodily fluid drying in the grime of their clothing. A man opposite Ko's bed with an elongated face and inflated skin was telling Ko, or whoever was listening, that he'd written a book. The man's eyes bulged towards the ceiling as he spoke. Ko felt himself sticking to the vinyl mattress where the sheet had come away from the edge. He had to stand up. He began pacing the floor. His face shrivelled as his eyes squinted. His chest was compressed. He was having a panic attack. His brain felt paralysed and he shivered despite the heating. Something was confusing his body. Perhaps it was the cigarettes he had chain smoked when he had been drinking. His eyes watered and his skin felt like it was being pricked from the inside. His pores were pouring out toxicity, wide open, burning open. His body was aching and his mind was craving. He thought that one cigarette would cure his pain. Ko felt a dull, vague ache in his lower back, and his throat so dry that he hadn't been able to speak audibly to the two only sane looking inmates of the dorm. The other thirty inmates appeared to be drifting in and out of consciousness, emitting sudden outbursts amongst their mumblings. Ko's eyes burned, his tongue was swollen, covered in a white-greyish fur that would have been at home in a Petri dish. His tongue was desperate for icy hydration.

'Am I dying? What if I can't breathe?' thought Ko

'Excuse me when can I leave please?' Ko asked. The overweight receptionist raised his eyebrows and then looked at the sheet of paper on his clipboard. 'It says here you will be sober at 1:30 pm. That's your release time,' said the receptionist.

It was 4.01 am. The last minute had consisted of slow-motion, whole, seconds.

'How can this be happening? Jesus, I need to get out of here and get back to Juliette.'

Ko had begun the path to imprisonment three days ago, on New Year's Eve at Juliette's friend's party. *Everyone's going to get drunk and have fun. I'm missing out*, thought Ko. 'I won't be able to have as much fun'. Ko didn't normally drink at all since he had been hypnotised to stop the habit a couple of years ago. 'I'm just going to try having one glass of wine so I can relax and enjoy the party with everyone,' said Ko.

'You know I won't stop you,' said Juliette. She smiled and kissed Ko. Juliette had never seen alcohol as a problem for Ko, but they had only met six months ago. As the group gathered around at midnight, Ko snuck up the steps into the kitchen and poured himself another full beaker of wine. When Ko and Juliette got home around 3 am, Juliette undressed and got into bed. Ko lay next to her until he was sure that she was sleeping. He felt the thump of his heartbeat in his temples and he felt the heat of his blood. The alcohol was in him and it was squeezing a band around his forehead. Ko had adopted a habit of not tolerating anything other than pure sobriety or pure drunkenness. He couldn't stand the uncertainty of the feelings in between. He didn't like the feeling of fuzz in his blood. He got up, closed the bedroom door behind him and went to the kitchen. He took an almost full bottle of red and he poured himself a glass. He took the wine over to the table by the window where his laptop was plugged in and opened facebook. He sipped quickly on the wine as he browsed friends. He noticed an attractive photo of a girl he had only spoken to for less than five minutes, an air hostess he had met on a flight from Singapore to London almost six months ago. The wine began to warm Ko's body. Drunken voices started to echo in his mind as the alcohol oozed through his veins. He walked to the kitchen and emptied the remainder of the bottle into his glass, and carried the glass over to his laptop.

I've been thinking about you a lot, typed Ko.

Really? I've been thinking about you a lot too, replied the air hostess.

The wine felt warm in Ko's temples and he was now swaying a little in the chair.

I have been having fantasies about you, typed Ko. He couldn't remember ever having a fantasy about this woman, but he wanted to push the conversation. How far would this stranger go for him?

The messages back and forth continued until 6 am when Ko slid his heavy body into bed and fell asleep with his shirt still on. At 10 am on New Year's Day Juliette woke and stirred Ko by sliding her hand along his leg.

'Why is your shirt still on?' asked Juliette.

'Oh, I wanted to sleep with it on. I do that sometimes,' said Ko, realising he hadn't taken it off. Ko felt heat in his body. The heat of a foreign substance. Ko had a low tolerance for discomfort. He wanted to numb it now. A quick fix. He had no time for the feelings in between purity of health and discomfort. He was good or he was bad.

'Let me cook you some bacon for breakfast,' said Ko. He put a half packet of bacon into Juliette's frying pan and as it began to heat he opened the fridge door and pulled out a bottle of white wine. He kept the wine below the countertop. Juliette was sitting on the couch with the television on. Ko turned on the tap and while the water ran into the sink he poured himself a mug of wine and began to swig. By the time the bacon was cooked he had downed two thirds of a bottle. 'You seem a little strange. What do you smell of? Do you have a new body wash?' asked Juliette as they ate. When they were done, Ko took the breakfast plates over to the kitchen and put them in the dishwasher. He ran the tap again and poured himself the remainder of the bottle of wine. The prickling in his veins from when he woke up this morning had been numbed by the fluid warmth of wine running through his body. His facial muscles relaxed and a slow smile emerged on his face.

'I'm not going to do any work today. Let's just sit and watch movies together on the couch all day and cuddle,' said Ko.

'That's fine with me. I love you,' said Juliette.

'I love you too,' said Ko. He hugged her and kissed her on the forehead.

Ko was still in disbelief that his relationship with her was real. She was too perfect to be real. And so he felt he had to pretend to be perfect too. Ko walked over and sat down at the table where his laptop still stood, with Facebook open on the screen. He saw that Charlotte was online. 'Hey come and have a look at this, this is my opera singer friend. She's feeling depressed because she can't talk to her boyfriend. What advice shall I give her?' asked Ko. Juliette got up and walked over to stand behind Ko, looking at his screen. At that moment, a new message popped up from the air hostess: *It was like for those 3.5 hours you and I had a secret relationship that no-one else knew about.*

'Who is that?' asked Juliette

'Oh no-one'

'Let me see the messages from her'. Juliette took her arms off Ko.

Ko quickly tried to delete the drunken conversation but it all came back up again. Juliette read everything. She began to cry. 'I'm going out, I can't deal with this now,' she said. She grabbed her handbag, make-up and some clothes, and left her apartment.

Through the warm ooze, Ko felt tension spring back into his chest and across his forehead. He opened the freezer and took out the bottle of vodka. He mixed the vodka with some more white wine and drank it until the tension began to subside. He drank more, and then he crawled his way to Juliette's bed. And passed out.

Ko drifted in and out of consciousness until around 10am the next day. His forehead throbbed, anxiety tingled his spine and his guts. 'What the fuck have I done,' he said. He walked to the kitchen and downed the last of the vodka. Then he went back to Facebook. He found the last of Juliette's wine but by noon, he had run out of alcohol. He put his shoes on and left the apartment. He crossed the street to the sports bar.

'What beers have you got?' grinned Ko at the waitress.

'Would you like to try a sample of this one? It's very hoppy.'

Ko felt energy in the front of his forehead and across his temples. It pushed lightly inside his head, he wanted to remove it but he didn't know how. *I know that feeling,* he thought. *This is what makes me want to drink. Every time I want a drink I feel it in the front of my head. Go on drink, it will make the feeling go away. But it never does. It makes it worse. Go on just one more drink.*

Ko ordered a burger and a beer. Then a Tequila shot. Then some wings. And then he asked a CEO who was home for the holidays to play table tennis with him.

By 5 pm Ko had downed three shots with the CEO and had sipped away six beers.

Are you planning on coming back anytime soon? read Juliette's message on his phone.

'You'd better go back and see your girlfriend. Good luck,' said the CEO.

In a cloud of alcohol vapour that both anaesthetised Ko and followed him across the street, he swayed his way back to Juliette's apartment.

He unlocked the door and saw a face he recognized from Juliette's facebook photos. It was Meredith, Juliette's best friend.

'Hi,' smiled Ko as he opened the door.

'Have you been drinking again?' asked Juliette.

'I just had a couple in the sports bar,' said Ko.

'I can't believe you,' said Juliette.

'I can't believe you are still pissed off at me about messaging that girl. It meant nothing. Nothing,' slurred Ko.

'Give me back the keys to my apartment and get out,' said Juliette. Ko felt warm ooze in his body contract to a hot pumping to his brain. 'I hate you. Bitch.' Ko threw his phone onto the floor by Juliette's feet. Then picked it up. Then threw it again. And again. Then he stood swaying with his arms across the doorway.

'Get out of here or we're calling the cops,' said Juliette's friend, Meredith. She walked right up to Ko's face and stood directly facing him in the doorway. Ko was intimidated by this tall stranger. He turned and walked away.

'Wait,' shouted Juliette. 'I have called a taxi and told the driver to take you to a hotel so you can sober up. I will talk to you when you are sober.' Juliette and Meredith waited with Ko in the lobby until the taxi showed up. 'Take him to the Holiday Inn,' said Juliette. The cab pulled away. 'Take me to the nearest bar downtown,' said Ko.

After six more drinks at the bar, the bartender looked at Ko's head drooping towards the bar and shook his head. 'I can't serve you any more, you will have to leave,' said the bartender. Ko staggered out onto the street.

'Only real men where a fucking pink shirt,' Ko shouted at two men who were laughing at him outside the bar.

'If you don't get out of here we're calling the cops' said one of the men. Ko stared at the man's effeminate haircut, shiny grey office suit, and well-groomed facial hair. *This man is violating all men. He's a fake, plastic imitation, and a bad actor, full of metrosexual conformity,* thought Ko.

'Fuck your corporate bullshit,' shouted Ko.

The men stopped smiling. 'Get out of here,' said one of the men.

'No you get out of here,' said Ko.

In the cold winter haze of a downtown street, Ko felt his neck muscles flexing and his chest expanding with a deep inhalation, flaring his nostrils as he did so, his jellied eyes blearing at the men.

'OK we're going to call the cops on you.' said one of the men.

'Go on then,' Ko laughed, shaking his head. Minutes later he was cuffed.

Ko's phone had been confiscated along with all other personal belongings on admission to the drunk tank. 'Juliette is going to be so worried. I have fucked up so bad this time,' said Ko to Mark, who seemed the most lucid and approachable inmate Ko had been able to identify in his current prison. 'I need to wake up. I only started drinking because I wanted to fit in with her friends, and then I kept on drinking because I refused to put up with the feelings of a hangover. It's so stupid'. Ko turned and began pacing the floor. Each step was a pace in the nothingness of the white walled, white-floored room for hours of minutes of frozen seconds. Finally the coma passed. 1:15 pm came and a nurse asked Ko to go into a counselling room. The nurse rapid fired questions about how much and how often Ko drank. The nurse walked him to a locker, and handed back his belongings. The security door opened; he walked through and was left at the reception desk. 'If you pay today it's half price,' said the receptionist. Ko handed over his credit card and paid. Ko tried to switch on his phone to message Juliette but the battery was dead. 'Would you like to charge your phone here so you can call someone?'

'No it's ok,' said Ko. He wanted to leave. Thoughts of Juliette were haunting him and the tension between waiting to charge the phone to call or just getting to a computer to message her was tearing his brain in half. He knew she'd be panicking that she hadn't heard from him and be thinking the worst had happened to him.

He walked outside and ambled from cross street to cross street looking for a taxi to hail. A run-down Ford with two twenty-something year old men inside pulled up next to Ko. The subwoofer speaker vibrated the cars windows to the sounds of drum and bass 'You looking for a cab? I'm a cab,' said the driver, waving his arms. Anxiety pressed on Ko's temples. 'I'm ok, thanks,' said Ko.

'No C'mon get in, you look like you need a ride, where you headed?'

'Mosman' replied Ko. He blinked trying to clear his eyes.

'Yeah we're headed that way now'.

Ko opened the back door and got in. 'Thanks a lot,' he said as he shuffled a couple of four packs of beers across so he could put his seat belt clasp in it's socket.

'Yeah grab me a beer,' said the passenger in the front. 'We're still going from New Year's. You look like you've had a rough night. Drink a beer; it'll calm your nerves.' 'Yeah man, grab a beer and chill yourself,' said the driver.

Ko took one of the beers out of the plastic sleeve and handed it to the passenger at the front of the car.

'Dude! Happy new fucking year! Where's your beer?' said the passenger. Ko noticed the passenger's eyes bulging. He recognized lust in the passenger's eyes before he took a sip of the beer. *The beer is controlling him*, thought Ko.

Ko picked up a can. *Go on have one. It will help you calm down before you see Juliette. Just one,* Ko heard his thoughts. *Wait what is this. This is the same argument that said I'd feel better last time and this feeling in the front of my head didn't go anywhere. What is this fucking feeling in the front of my head? It's just a little pressure. It doesn't hurt. Stop being a pussy and just accept it. Come on, how bad can this feeling get. Bring it on.*

'Drink up dude,' said the passenger.

'No, I've got to get out' I think I'm going to be sick,' said Ko.

'Dude pull over,' said the passenger.

Ko got out of the car and starting running. He felt his blood pumping in his body again and some warmth coming back to his cold, sickly limbs.

By the time Ko made it back to the lobby of Juliette's apartment building it was 3:20 pm. He pulled up a chair at the building's cyber lounge in the lobby, logged into facebook and saw Juliette's messages:

Worrying about you is making me physically ill. Please contact me or somebody. You aren't answering your phone and I know you have your charger. I don't understand how this happened, I thought we were doing so well. I am so worried and upset and angry I don't know what to do. Please let me know that you're ok. I'm home today, you can come back. I am so worried about you, this is killing me.

I am so sorry. Are you at home? replied Ko.

Yes, where are you?

Downstairs

Are you sober?

Yes. Totally. I detoxed.

I have been so worried about you, messaged Juliette.

I have no idea how I came to lose my shit. I love you so much. I can't believe how I could be so stupid. I am scared, typed Ko.

I'm scared too.

Can we talk?

Ko took the lift upstairs and knocked on Juliette's door. She opened the door. They hugged. They'd always been perfect together. To be honest about his excess and cravings would mean that he – and their relationship – was no longer perfect. But the truth was no one was perfect. So they talked. Ko told Juliette about all his insecurities, about not wanting to feel the discomfort of the pressure at the front of his head, and how he thought one drink would ease it, and he told her he'd been focusing too much on one thing at a time. He told her that the pressure at the front of his head came up when he spent too much time on one thing or another, of if he made himself too busy. It happened because he'd been working from waking till sleeping every day, including week-ends. He told Juliette about his wanting to be a 'perfect boyfriend' and a 'perfect artist', and that he had been withholding his insecurities from her. And that his withholding of his insecurities triggered the pressure at the front of his head. He'd pay more attention to the pressure if it started again. He'd tell Juliette if he felt uncomfortable around people or if he felt like he was missing out by not drinking. From now on, they swore they would tell each other everything. Ko would start taking the week-ends off work. He told Juliette that he would do more little things every day rather than focusing everything he had on one project, and that he'd notice and tell her how he was feeling, so he wouldn't get to this build up to breaking point again. But if that feeling came back, he'd recognize it for what it was, and he'd know what arguments his thoughts would make to try and get him to drink again.

Animal Analysis

What's your first thought when I mention the word moderation? What words do you associate with it? Many of you think of moderation as being a restriction. But what if what you needed to moderate was restriction itself? What if you moderated the moralizing about what limits you should be placing on yourself? What you should or shouldn't do. Psychotherapist, Brad Blanton says that 'when you should, you shit on yourself.' The type of moderation I talk about in this chapter does the opposite of restrict you, and helps prevent you from shitting on yourself. The biggest 'should' of all is that we should be doing something. That we should be busy. Yet this misses a universal truth: We are created to be us. Our purpose is to be us well. Busy doing is not busy being. Busy doing is not being enough. How do you know when you have done enough? By exercising awareness. By knowing you are not straining yourself, but are strengthening yourself. By not going too far. By knowing what is enough to satisfy your wants. Exercising moderation isn't against your interests: awareness ensures there is enough energy left for you to have authentic interests and enough energy for you to authentically create. In fact, it is critical to your existence to exercise moderation in everything, with the exception of one thing alone: truth. Truth in the way you see, smell,

Time to define: moderation
Moderating, exercising moderation – what does it really mean? It means to oversee and be aware of. It means to choose what is good for your Happiness Animal based on what you are consciously aware of. A moderator in an exam oversees. Moderator is defined in my dictionary as: 'an arbitrator or mediator'. When you exercise your awareness muscle, you become the overseer, the arbitrator and the mediator of your own life. Moderation gives control of your life back to your being, and away from the demoralizing limits of your ego.

hear, touch and taste. The way to truth is to notice what is – what exists – using your senses. If Ko had exercised awareness, not just with working hours, but with alcohol, as well as the self imposed restrictions when it came to Juliette, he would have felt a much healthier Happiness Animal. While awareness automatically occurs when exercising the other four muscles in the Happiness Animal, awareness is also a muscle that you can exercise proactively. Exercising awareness is noticing what is good for the health of your Happiness Animal, and what has a negative impact on the health of your Happiness Animal. Exercising awareness is overseeing your health. It is being aware of what you are doing before, and while you are doing it. It is asking the question: what is my intention right now?

What is the difference between moderation and restraint? Moderation in this chapter does not involve restraint. The handcuffs are off. Exercising the Happiness Animal with moderation is exercising the Happiness Animal with awareness. It is exercising the use of instincts to empower you to follow your gut more often. Self-imposed restraint is not healthy for your Happiness Animal, nor is moralizing. Both restraint and moralizing lead to madness from the denial of what you want. When your madness finds resistance against your denial, it often results in rebellion with a splurge of excess and cover-ups, and demoralizing dishonesty.

Oddly Enough moderation isn't something that prevents you from enjoying yourself. Moderation encourages you to have a good time, and to have enough. Enough of everything. One benefit of moderation is it improves health by preventing you from being too anything: too fat, too drunk, too hungover, too tired, too passionate, too sleazy, too touchy, too sensitive, too emotional, too busy.

You cannot deny desire. Desire is like fear in that it can only be dissipated by facing it head-on, accepting it acknowledging it, being honest about it. First, you have to see it for what it is. The best part of exercising awareness is you get to notice the difference between what you desire and what you instinctually want. It turns out that the exercise of following your gut is a lot of fun.

Exercising awareness with the FAD of excess (moralive®4.1)

Private possessions are the greatest source of human misery....how much lighter is the pain of not having money than of losing it...the less poverty has to lose the less agony it can cause us

...

The free man is the one over whom Fortune has no hold at all

Seneca

What is excess?
Too much is enough of a description of excess.

When to exercise with moralive®4.1

We are living in a material world.
Remember Animal's myth no. 2: Material things will make you happy. When I asked 6213 people what one thing would make them happier, 3110 people said: more money. What is the main use of money? To buy things. Studies show that an increase in material wealth and goods in America has had no effect on the wellbeing and happiness of its people. Here's an extract from the United Nations World Happiness Report, 2013: 'The psychological burdens of hedonism have been grimly exposed, especially in the United States, the most hyper-commercial society. Study after study confirms the ancient wisdom that an exaggerated desire for wealth and consumption leads to

personal unhappiness, addictions, ill health, and other psychological, social, and physical burdens. Relentless advertising and media imagery greatly amplify these problems.' When your consciousness is not taken up by things, forms, labels, and comparisons, it allows you to exist. 'True happiness is created by the least thing,' says Eckhart Tolle. This is the state where your Happiness Animal thrives – an atmosphere of be more, do less, create more, buy less, notice more, think less. 'It is from inner space, the unconditioned consciousness itself, that true happiness, the joy of being emanates,' says Tolle. If you can minimise how many things take up your attention and create space for noticing with your senses, for being you, then you are well on your way to a healthier Happiness Animal.

Food, Alcohol, and other Drugs (FAD)

Your senses tell you what is right for you to consume. If something smells good, you want to eat it. If you notice your stomach rumbling or feeling empty, you know you are hungry. If your mouth feels dry, you know you are thirsty. For anything else the best test of whether you should consume something is to ask yourself the following: Will it do me any good? Is it good for my health? Is it good for my happiness? Both your body and your Happiness Animal become unhealthy when you don't exercise awareness with consumption. In fact, millions of human beings die every year because of consuming too much of some kind of substance.

Animal's Alcohol myth

There is no link between alcohol and happiness, but there is a link between alcohol and depression. Many of us know Coca-Cola is not good for us, and doesn't even taste that great. But many of us are aware of how strong a brand Coca-Cola is without falling victim to it. Alcohol has many brands, but it also has the most powerful marketing tool of all in its favour: word of mouth. Not just word of mouth. It's in most of our mouths. It has become the norm to drink alcohol at almost every social occasion in the Western World. Ko's binge drinking initiated from a desire to have 'one drink' to fit in. But when did this start? When did the pressure to 'drink to belong' begin? In 1990 only 56% of Americans drank alcohol. By 2010, that number had increased to 67%. 18-20 year olds experienced a 56% increase in binge drinking between 1993 and 2001. The most recent estimates of alcohol-related deaths suggest that about 2.5 million deaths each year are directly attributable to alcohol, with the highest percentage of alcohol-related deaths among people between 15 and 29 years old (alcohol is responsible for nearly 1 out of 10 deaths in this age group worldwide). But it's not just your health and your life that is at stake. I can say with full experience, that the health of your Happiness Animal will increase if you exercise alcohol awareness. Ko realized that he was drinking not for pleasure, but to numb the tension in his head. I want you to notice and be aware in the moment of how much enjoyment you get from each alcoholic drink every time you have a drink. Also notice how you feel a couple of hours later, and the next day. I know you probably won't believe me if I tell you drinking doesn't make you happier. Most people who drink believe that they enjoy

Oddly Enough
Alcohol is social medicine that makes you antisocially depressed. Numerous studies have proven the link between drinking alcohol and depression. The more you drink, the more you increase your risk of depression. Alcohol has been proven to be more dangerous than Crack, LSD and ecstasy. According to the Net Pleasure Index, alcohol doesn't provide a lot of actual pleasure, and even if it did, if you have got to here in the book, you know that pleasure is not the same as happiness.

drinking. So let's agree that we don't agree. But try this experiment and make sure you take regular observations.

Pens with benefits – wine tasting

Do this the next time you are at home alone with a bottle of wine:

1. Before you take your first sip – write down how your body is feeling and how relaxed you are feeling. How happy you are right now on a scale to 1-10?

_____

_____

_____

_____

2. After your first two sips what has changed from your first answer. Are you feeling more or less relaxed? How happy are you right now on a scale of 1-10?

_____

_____

_____

_____

3. After your first drink /two drinks what has changed from your first answer. Are you feeling more or less relaxed? How happy are you right now on a scale of 1-10?

_____

_____

_____

Alcohol is a pain-killer. It numbs your mind so you feel like you have less worries, but it also numbs your senses. You may feel like you experience more pleasure just as you would experience more pleasure at a game if you took painkillers to get rid of your headache first. The problem is that as well as being toxic for your body, alcohol also numbs your Happiness Animal. It's liquid kryptonite, liquid poison for your Happiness Animal. Unfortunately, social proof has made alcohol as common as breathing. And in the social setting of the bar we rarely talk about the toxic effects alcohol has on our body, and on our happiness. Yet we can all recognize it when someone has a drinking problem: they start taking days off work, and are always the first to get wasted at the office functions. Sometimes, like Ko, they get into an altercation and get locked up in the drunk tank, or worse. Alcohol consumption is the highest it has ever been in history. The cigarette had its heyday, when almost everyone smoked.

Sen Says

Drunkenness is nothing other than a state of self induced insanity. Add to this the drunkard's ignorance to his situation. No amount of fluid will ever satisfy one whose craving arises not from a lack of water but from burning internal fever, for that is not a thirst but is a disease. Nor is this true only of money or food: the same feature is found in every desire which arises not from a lack but from a vice.

Then the dangers became more widely known and accepted. Now alcohol is having its heyday and although the dangers are known in the medical community, very little is discussed publicly with regards to the dangers of alcohol. The notable exception was the discussion initiated by UK government advisor, Dr. David Nutt who stated publicly that alcohol was more dangerous than several illegal drugs, and was fired for doing so. Very few people believe that drinking alcohol is equally as harmful as smoking crack, yet which drug causes the most social and individual harm? Without exercise of their awareness muscle, drinkers become unhealthy, lesser versions of themselves. Drunks are not enough of themselves. Drunks are not being, let alone not being happy. You are who you are through your senses and when your senses are tampered with or numbed, they are no longer your authentic senses and you are no longer authentic.

Time to define: Drug
Noun
A substance that has a physiological effect when ingested or otherwise introduced into the body.

Verb
Administer a drug to (someone) in order to induce stupor or insensibility.

During the marriage in a state of want and selfish, demoralizing thinking Ko and Rachelle suffered from indecision. Ko started using alcohol daily to try and avoid and numb the thoughts of his indecision. Ko became more and more a schizophrenic as his drunk self and sober self manifested more and more as opposing personalities. In Ko's moralizing attitude towards himself and the moralized attitude he presented to Juliette, pride forced him to lie to maintain his ego's existence. If, instead he had asked himself what were the real benefits of drinking, and how much he noticed himself enjoying drinking, then he may not have wanted to drink. It's true that not everyone drinks to excess. One glass with a meal is often the norm when you go out on a date. But what does that glass of wine really do for you on that date? Does it make you better in bed? If you believe the advice of the author of *The Happiness Hypothesis,* Jonathan Haidt, it may encourage you to do things you will end up regretting: 'alcohol has the effect of dulling the intellectual operations and moral instincts: seeming to pervert and destroy all that is pure in man, while it robs him of his highest attribute – reason.'

Dutch Discourage

Discouragement is a beverage both bitter and poisoned – two very powerful reasons for avoiding it. Drinking alcohol is the consumption equivalent of consuming discouragement. Isn't it ironic that it's called Dutch courage? The biggest reason why people started drinking, and then continued to drink is social proof. Drinking went viral. One giant crowd singing, come drink with me! I sound a little preachy in this section, I admit, and it's because I have felt first hand the damage that alcohol can cause, but only you know yourself when it comes to alcohol and other drugs, and only you can gauge your temptations. Gary Zukav writes that temptation is a dress rehearsal for a karmic experience

Alcohol – Author's story

I had a problem with alcohol for several years. The problem was that I couldn't seem to just have one drink. As soon as any alcohol entered my system I felt a compulsion to drink more to make the most of its effects. This started out as having a bottle of wine every night and as time went by turned into binges that lasted for days. The hangovers were so bad, the anxiety was so bad that I often thought I was going to die. I suffered at work, went from a top performer to struggling to do my job. Alcohol was certainly a catalyst towards divorce in a marriage that was already in trouble. In the end I had to go through multiple steps to overcome the disease of alcoholism. I read Allen Carr's book which worked for a while, then I got hypnotised. Twice. Then I didn't drink for almost a year until I forgot about not drinking on my birthday. Then I stopped drinking again for months at a time, would have one binge, and remind myself of why I stopped, then go for months of abstinence again. In the end the only way to stop is to keep learning and reminding yourself that you don't enjoy drinking enough that you don't ever want any. If you are going to try and enjoy the effects (and not just forget them) then the only way to do so is by exercising awareness.

of negativity, so you can avoid it in real life: 'Temptation is a gracious way of introducing a soul to his or her power'. Many of us are regularly tempted to drink alcohol. If you experience the temptation of wanting to drink and notice how that temptation physically feels with your senses, your Happiness Animal will not need to suffer. When you are tempted, what sensations do you feel and where do you feel them in your body? Do you feel tightness or tension around your forehead or a building of pressure behind your eyes?

**Time to define:
Karmic waves**
The real benefits of awareness and moderation are reducing the nasty side of karmic waves. If you think of karma as an infinite seesaw: the higher you go in excess, the harder and further back down it is going to hit you on the come down.

Awareness is exercising intuition

So far in this Chapter the focus has been on alcohol. Alcohol is the most socially accepted and pervasive of all drugs so it serves as a powerful example for all consumables with which you can exercise your awareness muscle. Exercising awareness is knowing what is good for you by noticing how your body feels, noticing what your body wants, and noticing how what you want impacts the strength of your Happiness Animal. If you have a craving for a certain food, what is it? Sometimes these instinctual cravings tell you what is good for you. Pay attention to what you want and try acting on instinct. There is a difference between listening to your thoughts ('I'm just going to have one drink to take the edge off the day') and listening to your instincts. Instincts are pure and authentic. Your thoughts, however, are determined by associations and attractions beyond your choosing. Put on your determinism glasses to check the source of your thoughts. Do you want something because of thoughts, thinking links and associations or do you want something because your awareness and your senses make you notice that you want something? Sometimes when I crave food, it is almost as if I can taste that food on my tongue, which creates the craving for it. Sometimes it is not as specific; it may be my body feels like it wants steak as opposed to fish or vice versa. Or if I notice my body feels stuffed or cold, I notice I feel like I want soup inside of me as opposed to an omelette. That's different from being subconsciously attracted to a bar of chocolate in the store with a shiny or sophisticated cover, or that's got '50% off' or 'buy one get one free' and when I put one piece in my mouth, the pleasure creates a desire for more pleasure, that ends in me feeling demoralized. And it's different to wanting a glass of wine because your friend just opened a bottle. Or because you think that glass of wine will 'take the edge off the day'. Brad Blanton advises the best way to tell the difference between what you are subconsciously attracted to vs. what your body is telling you it wants is to 'focus on becoming 'organismically self-regulating' That is, live by paying a lot of attention to immediate physical needs as a way of orienting yourself in the world. If you are thirsty, drink. If you are hungry, eat. If you are tired, rest.' In short, the best advice here is to stop thinking about what you think you want (or should want) and notice what you want.

Addiction - feeling powerless to deny the selfish ego fuel

Eckhart Tolle describes addictions as 'the wants of your personality that are resistant to the energy of your soul. They are aspects of your soul most in need of healing. They are your greatest inadequacies.' Beneath every addiction is an issue of power of the personality, your ego, your mask. If you sleep with a lot of women or men, it may be because your personality preys on weaker egos that are more shattered than yours, to feed your inadequate feelings of power. The same with alcohol addiction: it is triggered by feelings of inadequacy. Not inadequacy of your being which is always whole, but inadequacy of your ego, which is fighting for control of your being. It's mind vs. existence; happiness kryptonite vs happiness health.

Lose your addiction

Gary Zukav's advice in his book *The Seat Of The Soul* supports the approach that, as with fear, the way to overcome addiction is to first accept and acknowledge its presence. It is the feeling of powerlessness that causes a person to act towards their addiction. By acknowledging and becoming aware of your feeling of powerlessness, and your feeling of inadequacy, you become moderator of your own addiction. With the awareness that your feeling of inadequacy is a creation of your ego (a creation of your thoughts, thinking links and your imagination), and doesn't reflect any inadequacy you can notice with your senses, it swings control away from your ego and back to your conscious existence. It is at this moment of awareness that you gain the authentic power of choosing what you do next. The more you are aware that your ego is the source of your feeling of inadequacy and your addiction, the more you accept it, the less power it (and your ego) has control over your being. Accepting the source of your inadequacy completely disengages the power of your addiction as you increase the authentic power of your being. For example, if you feel the desire to go and get a bottle of wine for yourself on a Sunday night, what inadequacy in your ego could be causing that? If you are single, is it a feeling of loneliness and the associated thoughts of ego that you are not good enough because you are on your own? If you are in a relationship, is it because you have inadequate open and honest communication with your partner? So you feel the wine will help loosen the evening up? Do you feel alone in your relationship? Perhaps the wine will numb that feeling of loneliness? Are you dreading work tomorrow because your ego feels inadequate to face the office? Gary Zukav has some good tips for working through your feelings of inadequacy:

'As you work through your weaknesses and you feel levels of addiction and attraction, ask yourself the critical questions of the spirit:

1. If, by following these impulses, do you increase your level of enlightenment?
2. Does it bring you power of the genuine [internally authentic] sort?
3. Will it make you more loving?
4. Will it make you more whole?'

In the case of any action motivated by a feeling of inadequacy (of ego), leading to attraction and addiction, the answer to Zukav's questions is almost always no. Once you accept the no, the attraction of addiction is further diminished through your increased awareness. When you see that there are no benefits, you lose your desire. Seeing your ego for what it is – a mask – can also release your ego's power. First you have to accept it to be aware of it. Your ego is always prone to feelings of inadequacy because your ego isn't real so it needs real things to strengthen and reinforce its delusion of existence. Your ego or egos will always be your lesser self. Your authentic being, your existence, is not ego, although it can use ego as a plaything. For most adults though, the mind's ego is master and commander of the being, and master ego's orders come in the form of your thoughts. What exercising awareness in the case of addiction really comes down to is exercising awareness of your mind and your ego. As Zukav puts it: 'You stand between two worlds of your lesser self and your full self. Your lesser self is tempting and powerful because it is not as responsible and not as loving and not as disciplined so it calls you. This other part of you is whole and more responsible and more caring and more empowered, but it demands of you the way of the enlightened spirit: conscious life. *Conscious* life. The other choice is unconscious permission to act without consciousness. It is tempting.'

The lesser self Zukav refers to here is your ego – the unconscious mind's control over your existence. The full self is your conscious being. Ego is unconscious. Being is conscious. Accepting the temptation of your ego is exercising awareness of your ego, its inadequacies and its unhealthy attractions. This is strengthening your being, your conscious Happiness Animal. It is the key to self-control.

Exercising awareness with FAD (Food, Alcohol and Drugs (moralive 4.1)): the tempting way to self-control

Exercise for when you feel compelled to consume something that you know isn't healthy for your body, nor for your happiness, nor your authenticity.

Instructions
Pause before acting. Take a Being Time Out and do the following.

1. Notice the sensations in your body associated with your feelings and thoughts compelling you to consume. What feelings (e.g. tension in my forehead) are you feeling in different parts of your body?

_____

_____

_____

_____

2. What do you feel is your inadequacy? Try and define your source of feelings of inadequacy as specifically as possible. Are they sourced in fear of something? What are your thoughts associated with this fear?

_____

_____

_____

_____

3. How do you feel consuming will help with this inadequacy?

_____

_____

_____

_____

4. Before you consume, ask yourself the following four questions:

    A. Will it bring me power of the genuine [internally authentic] sort?

    B. Will it increase my level of enlightenment?

    C. Will it make me more whole?

    D. Will it make me more loving?

5. Now notice with your senses what your body wants. If your muscles feel tired, it could be sleep. If your throat is dry, it could be water. If you have pressure in your bladder or your bowels, maybe you want to go to the toilet. Write it down here:

6. Is what you wrote down in step 6 different to what your mind wants you to consume? The secret to releasing yourself from excess is to start living from what you notice you want rather than what your mind says you should want.

    _____

    _____

7. Now go back and repeat step 2. Focus on the physical sensations you are having that your mind is associating with the compulsion to consume. Rate your level of pain or discomfort of not giving into the compulsion to consume on a level of 1-10 with 10 being intolerable agony and preferring to die.

    _____

8. Reality test your pain/discomfort. Can you live with it? Can you survive it?

    _____

9. Allow yourself to fully experience and notice those sensations now. The more you allow yourself to experience them, the more they will have been experienced fully and therefore disappear of their own accord. The alternative, which is resisting those sensations, allows those sensations to persist. The only way to ease them is to allow yourself to experience each physical sensation individually and to stop resisting its perceived unpleasantness. Your mind is a drama queen. The sensations are never as bad as you think they are. It helps if

you notice when each sensation appears in your body and if you describe each sensation individually. Describe each sensation below now and then focus your attention on each in turn. Allow yourself to fully experience (and feel) each sensation.

_____

_____

_____

_____

_____

Exercising awareness with doing (moralive® 4.2): to do or to be, that is the question

The very simple test should be does whatever we are doing do us any good?
Away with every obstacle and leave yourself free to acquire a sound mind – no one ever attains this if he's busy with other things

Seneca

Nothing is *going to* make us free because only the present moment can make us free.
That realisation is the awakening
If you can neither enjoy or bring acceptance to what you do – stop.
Otherwise you are not taking responsibility for the only thing you can really take responsibility for, which also happens to be one thing that

really matters: your state of consciousness. And if you are not taking responsibility for your state of consciousness, you are not taking responsibility for life

Eckhart Tolle

There are limits to how many things you can do, but no limits to how much you can be you. You are your sensations and your senses. Exercising awareness in doing, enables you to exercise infinity in being. This is where your Happiness Animal can reach a whole new level. Awareness allows for slow progress, but without burning out or terminal collapse. It also ensures the direction of progress is chosen consciously, rather than pre-determined by your thinking links. Doing too many things in one day is a fast track into the vicious cycle of excess: If you spend more than what you need, more than enough, then you need to earn more than what was enough. Excess earnings demand excess activities, which lead to excess consumption, and alcohol and other drugs complete the vicious circle of excess. Enough has no such circle. Enough allows for linear growth, not a cycle that spirals you to oblivion. The best guide of what is enough to do in a day is nature. Day balances with night. The tide comes in for six hours, the tide goes out for six hours. When was the last time you worked for six hours in a day? This essential natural flow back and forth ensures your health. Exercising awareness to ensure your health, applies to all activities, not just those in the workplace.

When to exercise with awareness of doing (moralive®4.2)

Getting caught up – the rainbow reality

You say no to social events, to friends, lovers, family, to that weekend away, to that dinner, to that twenty-minute coffee, because you want to 'get caught up'. You say 'I have a few things I need to catch up on; I am so busy right now.' I have at least a couple of friends who, for several years, whenever I have asked how they are, have replied: 'I am so busy!' From outside their world looking in, it appears that they haven't known a life without being 'so busy'. No matter how many things you tick off your to-do list, do you find that you end up *thinking* of other things to add before you ever have an entirely blank list? Who decides that you need to catch up on your to do list? Who creates your to-do list? Is it your mind – your ego – or is it your authentic, present tense, noticing being? Trying to get caught up with a to-do list created by your mind, is much the same as trying to chase a rainbow. Your mind associates completing one task with something else, and bingo, you have another action on your to-do list. Your ego, like the rainbow, doesn't physically exist, so you are following a to-do list created by something that doesn't exist. Acceptance that the rainbow – like the ego created by your mind – is an illusion and getting caught up is also an illusion is a healthy way to exercise awareness. You are not putting yourself in a better position for tomorrow, you are just changing what you will be working on tomorrow for the same amount of time. For as much as you take out of your to-do list, it will fill up again. It's like trying to dig a hole in the sand with the tide coming in. But you can float in a boat and come back when the tide is out. What you can exercise awareness of, is how much attention and time that you give to your to-do list. Focus on how much is enough time to be a healthy amount of attention for one day. Don't focus on how much time everything in your to-do list will take. If you decide what is enough time to spend on your to-do list each day, you are in control of it. You can get back in your boat at the end of the day and sail away. If you are trying to catch up with the hours and minutes that the things in your to do list will take, then your to do list is controlling you, it is drowning you, and it's doing it through your mind. The tragedy is that almost everything that you perceive to be important in your to-do list now, will cease to be important in a few weeks, months or years. But in the same time, your relationships can suffer infinitely because of your attention being diverted to chasing rainbows, to fighting the incoming tide, to vanity and chasing after wind.

The Preoccupati

Illnesses, which are weaknesses in the body or the mind, can be caused by overactivity or being pre-occupied. You are so busy doing – and not being – that your body doesn't get a chance to look after itself. Instead, all of your energy goes into your mind and strengthening your ego by doing things that reinforce your ego's identity. Seneca called the preoccupied the 'occupati' and defined those occupati as those who spend their lives in useless or

Sen Says:
Unremitting effort leads to mental dullness and lethargy.

They are not at leisure whose pleasures involve a serious commitment. Thus each man ever flees himself but to what end if he does not escape himself? He pursues and dogs himself as his own most tedious companion. And so we must realize that our difficulty is not the fault of the places but of ourselves. The mind should not be kept continuously at the same pitch of concentration but given some amusing diversions.

Our minds must relax: they will rise better and keener after a rest. Just as you must not exhaust it, so constant effort will sap our mental vigour while a short period of rest and relaxation will restore our powers. We must indulge the mind from time to time and allow it the leisure which is its food and strength. We must go for walks outdoors so that the mind can be strengthened and invigorated by a clear sky and plenty of fresh air.

redundant activities and sometimes cannot even give a rational account of what they are doing. The occupati are the restless. You become restless when you are short of inner resources. When you are short of inner resources you seek more resources from outside. But no resources from outside are enough to satisfy your inner resource requirements. So the restless remain dissatisfied. The restless remain restless. When you look after your Happiness Animal through exercise there is less need to seek resources – distractions – from outside. Your inner resources are your Happiness Animal's muscles. The better shape they are in through exercise, the more satisfied you are with your inner resources. The human mind is naturally mobile and enjoys activity, but outside distractions are like an itch and an itch loves to be scratched. When you start talking about distractions you start to scratch the itch. Exercise of your Happiness Animal's awareness muscle is the cure to mental restlessness. When your awareness muscle is healthy you become less prone to any demoralizing distractions. Have you ever wondered, for example, why musicians stay inside their hotel when they are on tour in the middle of a beautiful city? 'Building slowness allows space for executive function – planning, remembering, inhibiting impulses, and creativity – to grow,' says the father of Positive Psychology, Martin Seligman in his book *Flourish*. Seligman advocates meditation, slow talking, slow eating, and not interrupting, as some of the ways to incorporate some slowness into your life.

The full diary

A full diary is an anti-awareness agent (AAA) of mass destruction. A full diary means not enough time to be you. Appointments, to-do lists, and a full diary are all AAAs that grow your ego at the expense of your Happiness Animal. A good place to start stemming the demoralizing anti-awareness flow is to ask yourself how much time is enough to have free from working hours, from appointments. Unless you have free time you don't have enough time to notice with your senses what the next right thing for you to do is. That's why a lot of people are unable to change problematic behavioural patterns like excess consumption, unless something major happens to shake up their life. It's not that they don't have time to think. It's that they don't have time to notice they are alive because they are spending too much time thinking.

The past – sniffing more stinky prawns

When the past is your model for how to live now, it takes you away from the present moment and leaves no time to notice, experience and feel the present. So it's critical to exercise awareness to prevent over-thinking about the past from limiting your present. (If you are having problems with this, do the exercise for tolerance of self, which helps with past obsessions such as regret, the kryptonite that poisons every muscle in your Happiness Animal.) It is critical to the health of your Happiness Animal to have some time to be free to notice what the next right thing to do is, based on your natural instincts in each moment, based on what your senses tell you to do now, and not based on what your mind and ego planned for you before this moment arrived. Brad Blanton's advice is worth listening to again here: 'Your own mind is not your friend. It is big brother inside of you. It considers itself to be who you are.' How much time you spend thinking, is how much time you give your mind and your ego, rather than your existence in the present moment. Thinking about the past too much is like going to an office where you used to work. You are no longer an employee there.

The 'done the guidebook' mentality

In Sydney, I've lost count of how many times I've heard English, German or French backpackers tell me, I want to *do* that, need to *do* that trip. What does *do it* mean? Check it off the list of places to see? Going there isn't the same as experiencing there. Cramming in as many places as possible at a destination does not make for a fulfilling holiday. Just as the human brain can only allow you to have a meaningful relationship with 150 people at a time (known as Dunbar's number), you can only have a meaningful experience with a limited number of places in a limited period of time. You can gauge what your own optimum is. Instead of running around to stand in front of a tourist attraction for a few minutes before running to the next, oversee some time in your holiday to rest. Don't plan every day. Allow yourself to explore. Exercise awareness with rest. This is the only way to avoid degrading your holiday experience to the level of a to-do list. It's time for you make some conscious choices…

PART I exercising awareness with doing (moralive®4.2): the conscious veto

Exercise for clearing your mind of distraction and moderating what gets into your to-do list. The more things you feel you should and shouldn't do, the further and further behind your expectations of yourself you fall, the more you shit on yourself, and the more demoralized you feel.

Instructions

1. Look at your to do list if you have one (if not skip to step 3). Mark only those items that are an absolute necessity to you and your family staying alive with an '**N**' for necessity. Mark the things you think you should do with an '**S**' for SHIT. One of the Golden rules of the Happiness Animal is that when you should on yourself, you shit on yourself. Shitting on yourself is fairly demoralizing. Mark those things you genuinely want to do with a '**W**' for want.

2. Look at your list again. Choose some of the '**S**' items to veto and cross them off your list. What remains is more of what you want or need to do.

3. Practise this for the next week: every time you have a thought to do something, ask yourself if it is something you want or need to do. If it isn't, veto it. If you can notice the origin of the

thought –what previous thoughts caused you to have that thought? Be aware that you are noticing yourself having the thought to do whatever it is, and you are consciously choosing to veto it.

PART II (from a Harvard Health Report on Positive Psychology)

To keep the burden of choice from robbing you of pleasure, go on a choice diet. For choices of no great consequence, limit the amount of time or number of options you'll consider. Cut off your opportunities for second guessing: stop looking at car or employment ads after you've made a commitment; go ahead and wrap or mail that gift; wear and launder your new pants so they can't be returned. When critical medical or financial choices need to be made, that's the time to put your Maximizer tendencies to work. But for the many small choices you make each day, try to narrow your choices quickly and make your decisions confidently.

Exercising awareness with time and money (moralive®4.3): Time isn't money and money isn't time

Life is short, art is long

Hippocrates

It is not that we have a short time to live but that we waste a lot of it
Many are occupied by either pursuing other people's money or complaining about their own. Wealth however modest, if entrusted to a good custodian, increases with use, so our lifetime extends amply if you manage it properly

Seneca

You can only lose something you have but you cannot lose something that you are

Eckhart Tolle

Planning to earn by planning to learn

Planning to earn more than enough, by spending on learning to get a qualification that will get you extra income? Planning to earn by planning to learn? Does this apply to you or to anyone you know? When you're not working, you're studying, so that when you work more in the future, you will earn more in the future? How much free time does that leave available to you now? What if you change your mind about what industry you want to work in? What if, once you have the qualification, you realize it's not something your new employer really cares about? When expectations are not met, you get frustrated or angry. We know from chapter 3 that expectation is the mother of disappointment, yet you still plan based on expectations of the future. You do to earn, you learn to do, and then do more to earn more, but when do you learn what is enough for happiness? When do you learn the risk of poor health through lack of exercise of your awareness muscle? Einstein said that everything (including your life, your job, your plans, your learning) should be made 'as simple as possible, but no simpler', and that is a good way to exercise awareness with everything. At a simple level, you can plan to do things with the intention of being happy, or, you can plan to do things with the intention of gaining money. Choose your intention wisely. Financial ambition is a subclass of greed which thrives on the poor health of your Happiness Animal. It often requires you to sacrifice the health of your honesty, kindness, courage, awareness and tolerance muscles.

Sen Says

Let us aim to acquire our riches from ourselves rather than fortune.

Living is the least important activity of the preoccupied man.

How few days have passed as you have planned, when were you ever at your own disposal; when your face wore its natural expression; when your mind was undisturbed; how much you have lost through groundless sorrow, foolish joy, greedy desire, the seductions of society, how little of your own was left to you.

You act like mortals in all that you fear and immortals in all that you desire. What can be above the man who is above fortune? But nobody works out the value of time: men use it lavishly as if it cost nothing. But if death threatens these same people, you will see them praying to their doctors. How alarmed would be those who see only a few years ahead, and how carefully they would use them!

To a wise man every place is his castle. There is no evil in poverty as anyone knows who has not yet arrived at the lunatic stage of greed and luxury which ruin everything.
We must not send our desires on a distant hunt but allow them to explore what is near at hand.

How much lighter is the pain of not having money than of losing it. How much happier is the man who owes nothing to anybody except the one he can most easily refuse, himself. The ideal amount of money is that which neither falls within the range of poverty nor far exceeds it. Poverty can turn to riches by practising economy.

Noblesse oblige

As Brad Blanton puts it, 'although cultural humanity has been on earth for some 2 million years, the very concept of jobs is only about 500 years old.' My point: A 9-5 or 8 hour a day job is not necessary to your existence. OK, but we've all got to make a living right? Right, and there is a way to make enough money, so you cover your needs, your $40,000 USD a year or whatever it may be without sacrificing the health of your Happiness Animal. There is a way to earn what you need without being any less of you, in fact in a way that allows you to be true and authentic. You can earn in the spirit of Noblesse oblige – sharing your authentic talents that you possess in a job that exploits your talents for the good of all. Exercising responsibility for your talents rather than pursuit of money is one of the surest ways to ensure the health of your Happiness Animal. Noblesse oblige really means the responsibility to share who you are. What everyone is, regardless of financial position, is an authentic being. The obligation for happiness is to share that being with other beings at work and in society. One of the ways to ensure you can do this is to exercise awareness in how much your activities are in line with your authentic talents, and not simply activities you struggle with that you are not naturally talented at, purely with the end goal of financial gain.

The ego is empty

It is a tale
Told by an idiot, full of sound and fury
Signifying nothing

Shakespeare

Eckhart Tolle, in *A New Earth* sums up the importance of job titles and job roles as nothing more than labels your ego collects like a kleptomaniac: 'those who do not attempt to appear more than they are but are simply themselves stand out as remarkable and are the only ones who truly make a difference in this world. Their mere presence – simple, natural, unassuming – has a transformational effect on whoever they come into contact with. When you don't play roles it means there is no ego in what you do. There is no secondary agenda, pretending, protection or struggling in yourself.'

When you are not focused on roles, you are focused on whatever scenario you are in. You are most powerful, and your Happiness Animal is healthiest when you are completely you. But don't try to be you. You don't have to do anything to be you. You are you already. The best that you can do is to express your essence fully through your authentic expression and through the creation that leads to. What exercising awareness with time and money comes down to is becoming aware of roles so they don't mask your authenticity. It is accepting that more money and a promotion to a new role won't make you superior to anyone else. All attachment to a role or money will do is reduce you to a more plastic, demoralizing, empty existence where your ego will constantly be looking for ways to strengthen itself and looking for weaknesses in others to bolster its feeling of superiority. A rule of thumb is this: The greater your attachment to money, the greater your attachment to your ego, the greater your attachment to being unconscious (not living through your senses). To exercise awareness with ego, all you need to do is to notice the thoughts and emotions you have as they happen. Notice if your thoughts are related to an attachment to ideas or expectations. If the answer is yes, they are of ego origin. You can exercise noticing the difference between thoughts of ego origin (imagination) and thoughts of sense origin (anything you notice using your five senses) e.g. seeing something beautiful that makes you feel physical sensations you can notice and describe in sensory language.

Don't forget to breathe

If you struggle to notice your thoughts, you will find it easier if you become conscious of your senses with the help of a breathing exercise (or try the exercises on pages 53-55). If you only remember one tip for exercising awareness, remember this: You cannot consciously breathe and think at the same time. Take regular 'breathers' throughout your day: take one to three breaths and notice the feeling of the air going in and out of your body, how fast you are breathing in and out. Doing this will give you some space from your ego's thoughts of money, job roles, to-do lists, and your ego's fear of running out of time. And so will the following exercise...

Exercising awareness of time and money (moralive® 4.3)
PART I

Exercise for identifying what is enough when it comes to work and to money

Instructions

1. How many hours of work would you like to accomplish in a working week? **Tip**: if it's over 40 you may have a problem

    _____

2. What do you consider to be enough hours for you to work a week?

    _____

3. How many activities would you like to accomplish in a week in addition to your work?

    _____

4. How many hours would a week do you want to spend on those activities?

    _____

5. How much money do you want to earn as a minimum in a working week?

   _____

6. What do you consider enough money for you to earn in a working week? **Tip**: once you cover basic needs (estimated at $40000 USD a year in the USA) any increase in your cash levels will not have an impact on your happiness

   _____

PART II

For whenever you feel dominated by thoughts of money or all the things you still have to do at work. This also works as a relaxation and grounding-in-the-present-moment technique for any scenario.

7. Become conscious of the feeling of the air going in and out of your body as you breathe.

8. How many seconds do you pause between the end of the in breath and the beginning of the out breath?

   _____

9. How many seconds do you pause between the end of the out breath and the beginning of the in breath?

   _____

10. Repeat the above for at least three breaths.

Exercising awareness with desire (moralive®4.4)

People cease to possess everything as soon as they want everything for themselves

Seneca

And as to the form that may be taken by knowledge, one of the best is knowing when one has had enough. Also known as temperance

Christopher Ricks

On the new Earth, enjoyment will replace wanting as the motivating power behind people's actions. Wanting arises from the ego's delusion that you are a separate fragment that is disconnected from the power that lies behind all creation. Through enjoyment, you link into that universal creative power itself

Eckhart Tolle

There glowed for him in fact a kind of rage at what he wasn't having; an exasperation, a resentment begotten truly by the very impatience of desire

Henry James

What's the difference between following your desire and following your intuition? Desire is normally caused by distraction or attraction. Desire is determined by external stimuli. Intuition is determined by internal feelings. As a result your desires are often inauthentic whereas your intuitions are authentic: they are of you. The exercise of awareness with desire (or temperance) moderates your reactions, keeps anger to specific resentments, rather than generalized abstractions, and helps you to know how much pleasure is healthy before it becomes unhealthy.

When to exercise awareness with desire (moralive®4.4)

The pleasure of distraction

Desire often stems from dissatisfaction, and pleasure is only a distraction from unhappiness. Some pleasure has nothing to do with exercising your Happiness Animal and some does. By exercising your awareness muscle you become aware of the difference. There are the pleasures of happiness and love, but also, the pleasures of distraction for the unhappy – that's where addiction comes into play: addiction to sex, drugs, alcohol, pot, violence, food, porn, video games – the list goes on. I call these pleasures 'empty pleasures' and the pleasures of love and happiness 'filling pleasures'. Unless they are connected to the umbrella of happiness, by default they are empty pleasures. But what if you aren't addicted and you just enjoy the things on the empty pleasures list? That's fine as long as you accept that those pleasures won't have as much an impact on the health of your Happiness Animal as filling pleasures. If you apply the empty vs. full concept to your work environment, some pleasure will be connected to the umbrella of happiness and some pleasure will be empty. If your work allows you to exercise any of the five muscles of your Happiness Animal while working, you will experience more filling pleasure at work. Some pleasure fills you with energy, and some drains you. Some pleasure strengthens your Happiness Animal and some demoralizes you. By exercising awareness you learn to identify the difference so you choose more of the pleasure that makes you happy. When your job, your life, your pleasure and your happiness are all intertwined, then you are in the running for the Happiness Animal Olympics.

Your cheating mind

Short-term pleasure can be a weapon against your Happiness Animal. Exercising awareness with relationships is one of the healthiest ways to ensure fidelity. However, it's not easy. Excess in other areas can make it harder to exercise awareness here. As you have seen, excess in one area necessitates excess in another area of your life, always at the expense of your Happiness Animal. Viagra for someone who has no erectile dysfunction is a sign of excess. It's ok not to get excited sexually by every woman or man. It is natural. I'm not going to beat about the bush. It's critical for your relationships present and future: **a lack of exercise of awareness in any area of your life will increase the chance of you cheating on a spouse, lover or other**. The source problem of all of this is the greed of your ego, motivated by a desire to grow beyond social expectations. An ego is always out to grow itself. How many drunken kisses that demoralized you can you count? How many times did Ko give into his demoralizing desire for either alcohol or women? How many times did one lead to the other as the alcohol numbed his senses, blurring the distinction between who he was and was not attracted to? What is more than enough, is at the expense of your Happiness Animal always. Exercising awareness can even help your Happiness Animal when you are mourning. When you exercise, you notice what is enough mourning and when is the right time to move on after a loss or the end of a relationship. This may sound harsh, but an excess of mourning is the result of an ego trying to grow itself through pain, and it's always at the expense of your Happiness Animal. With enough mourning, by contrast, you move into a state of gratitude for the other's life, and for their impact on your life. This moving from a state of mourning to a state of gratitude strengthens your Happiness Animal.

Luck be a lady tonight: when pessimism prevails

The expectation of luck and fortune is an excess. It's a misleading passion puller that leads into the vicious cycle of expectations of success. Expectation of luck is happiness kryptonite. Oddly enough, when it comes to luck, pessimism is the healthiest approach. British philosopher, Alain de Botton, advocates listening to sad songs to cheer you up, and to exercise a healthy level of pessimism every day. The irony is, the lower your expectations of the day, the greater your chance of success. De Botton says that the most common cause of failure in the bedroom, as well as in life, is the expectation of success. If you have performance anxiety in the bedroom, your best shot is to tell your lover that you are a mediocre lover so that she has low expectations of you. If you start by telling your potential mate that you are a fantastic lover and that sex with you will be mind-blowing, you set yourself up for the pressure of expectation of a mind-blowing performance, and for failure. The moral of the story: exercise your Happiness Animal with awareness towards optimism, use of ego, and blowing your own trumpet. After all, if you blow your own trumpet, no one else will want to.

Exercising awareness of desire (moralive®4.4): the tempting way to self control

Exercise for when you feel compelled to do something you know isn't healthy for your relationships, nor for your authentic being, nor your Happiness Animal.

Instructions:
The next time you feel a compulsive desire to cheat on a partner you love, take a time out for your being and do the following.

1. Accept that you are attracted to other people than your partner. If the other person is flirting with you or making physical (sexual) advances towards you, tell them the following, in your own words.

    I accept I am attracted to you, AND, I also accept that I am in a relationship with someone I love so as long as I am in that relationship I want to respect that love.

2. Notice the sensations in your body associated with your feelings compelling you to cheat. What feelings (e.g. tension) are you feeling in different parts of your body?

_____

_____

_____

_____

_____

3. What do you feel is your inadequacy? Try and define your source of feelings of inadequacy as specifically as possible. Are they sourced in a feeling that you are not getting enough attention/affection from your current partner? Is it that you don't feel you can communicate fully with your partner? When was the last time YOU initiated an open and honest conversation with your partner?

_____

_____

_____

_____

4. How do you feel cheating on your partner will help with this inadequacy?

_____

_____

_____

_____

5. Before you cheat, ask yourself the following four questions:

    a. Will it bring me power of the genuine [internally authentic] sort?

    b. Will it increase my level of enlightenment?

    c. Will it make me more whole?

    d. Will it make me more loving?

6. Now notice with your senses what your body wants. If your muscles feel tired, it could be sleep. If your throat is dry, it could be water. If you have pressure in your bladder or your bowels, maybe you want to go to the toilet. Write it down here:

_____

_____

_____

The secret to being faithful to the one you love is that you start living from what you notice you want rather than what your mind says you should want, and you honestly communicate what you notice you want to the one you love.

Exercising awareness with conformity (moralive®4.5): keeping up with convention

It is better to be despised for simplicity than to suffer agonies from everlasting pretence

People with fortune and vice tempt others to imitate them by their own public example

Seneca

Social proof is a flame to the human mind moth, and it leaves a fire trail of destruction across the path of enough. If there is one type of awareness exercise that is critical to all others it is for you to exercise awareness in how much you conform to the expectations of your society and your culture. 'Cultures are only habitual mind-sets with a lot of emotional attachment,' said Brad Blanton. Social conformity makes you predictable, inauthentic, a silenced you. If you silence your truth, you can only lead a dishonest, unhappy existence. Exercise awareness in conformity to ensure you stay true to you.

When to exercise awareness with conformity (moralive®4.5)
Social proof has heavy artillery aimed at your authentic existence. Social proof is a current, a proponent against authentic existence. Social proof speaks the language of shoulds and should nots. You should get that laptop, that phone, you should live there. You should buy a house. You shouldn't rent. You should get a job. You should have some kids. You should cut the hedge, and mow the lawn. You shouldn't get that savings account. You should shop there. You should buy her that perfume for Christmas; you should get the new IPAD. It's

easy to fall into a pattern of these kind of social obligations and imagined social contracts to do things a certain way around certain people. But here's the thing: the more things you feel you should and shouldn't do, the further and further behind your expectations of yourself you fall, and the more demoralized you feel. The antidote is awareness of determinism, combined with the exercise of your Happiness Animal's muscles. Yes I told you those determinism glasses would get some more use. The determinism glasses of awareness grant your authentic being, your Happiness Animal, immunity against social proof.

When giving is too much

The social proof of giving and gifts is another lethal AAA (anti-awareness agent). Making sure that you 'spend enough' on someone can us struggling to have enough money for ourselves. It leads to us increasing our credit card debt, and then we find ourself working to excess, and then self-medicating with whatever slippery excess bucket we slide into. If you can't afford it, it's healthier

Sen Says: Only a mind that is deeply stirred can utter something noble and beyond the power of others. When it has scorned everyday and commonplace thoughts and risen aloft on the wings of divine inspiration, only then does it sound a note nobler than mortal voice could utter.

When mixing with people, in place of the ideal we must put up with the least bad. In choosing our friends, take care to find those who are the least corrupted. Mixing with the sick is how disease starts. A companion who is agitated and groaning about everything is an enemy to peace of mind.

Two things must be mingled and varied, solitude and joining a crowd: the one will make us long for people and the other for ourselves, and each will be a remedy for the other.

to give your honesty and courage instead of that expensive gift. Create something authentic for the person instead, with your own hands – a creation from yourself to them. And remember that the ultimate gift is the gift that takes away: the gift of your compassion.

The Sex Bomb AAA

With the advent of Viagra and personal lubricants we are now having sex with people we wouldn't naturally have sex with. It is regularly assumed that if you hang out with and kiss someone enough, the next step is sex. It's ok to exercise awareness in getting to know someone to find out if you are physically attracted to them enough to want to have sex with them, rather than taking Viagra or getting 'drunk enough' because sex is the 'done thing'. Don't listen to your mind over your biological chemistry that tells you naturally who you want to sleep with. Sex to boost your ego is doubly demoralizing. Natural sex will make you and your Happiness Animal feel more alive.

Moderation in moralizing

> People carry roses, make promises by the hour
> Bob Dylan

Moderation and awareness in promises is important. Yes, promises are another AAA. A promise can also take the form of a statement you make about your personality. Because Ko had told Juliette that he didn't drink, he felt it impossible to be honest about his excess and cravings because it would mean his word was broken. It would mean that he was no longer perfect. He was attached to the idea of being perfect because he had a weak awareness muscle. His awareness muscle was weak because it had not been exercised, but rather had been poisoned by moralizing. Ko's moralizing about his own self-image was making promises by the hour. Promises that he could not keep. What Juliette wanted was Ko to be honest with her. She wanted a man she could trust. When people think of moderation they normally think of it as being a restriction. Sometimes the thing you need to moderate is restriction itself, and the most poisonous restriction of all is moralizing. Moderation is based on listening to your honest intuition, whereas restraint is moralizing and chastising yourself with restriction, and tightening your mind's spring. Moralizing is an activity of your ego. Moderation and awareness are an exercise of your Happiness Animal. At some point your moralizing spring is bound to break or rebound with extreme force. It's the same extreme force that sprung load Ko's canon of excess. 'We all have the disease of moralizing and the secret of the good life is learning how to manage the disease like one manages herpes or diabetes, and other incurable but somewhat controllable diseases,' says Brad Blanton. You manage the disease of moralizing by exercising awareness of your shoulds and should nots, and by wearing your determinism glasses when noticing and accepting your thoughts. But even with determinism glasses on, it takes courage to disobey social norms, and courage to not give into the pull towards the crowd. It takes courage to stand face-to-face with the crowd and acknowledge the social proof at work. It takes courage to be you when social proof calls you out. That's why the chapter about courage follows this final exercise for awareness...

Exercising awareness with conformity and moralizing (moralive 4.5): how to stop shitting on yourself

Exercise for recognising your shoulds and should nots, to minimise how much you shit on yourself. Every should and should not you attach importance to, demoralizes you. Every should and should not is about as good for your Happiness Animal's health as taking a shit on yourself before you go out the door.

Instructions

1. At home practice replacing the word 'toilet' with the word 'should' – even put a sign on the toilet door that says should.

2. On your phone or in a notepad, start a 'should shit log' for the next week starting right now. Every time you notice yourself saying the word 'should' write down 'I shit on myself' with the time and date.

3. What are your favourite limiting beliefs that your self imposes on your existence? (e.g. I don't know enough about this, I don't have time.) Write them down below.

_____

_____

_____

_____

_____

_____

4. For every limiting belief you notice yourself saying over the next week, write down 'I squirt on myself' in your 'should shit log'.

5. Write down how you normally shoot yourself in the foot. (E.g. by making excuses, prioritising something financial over something you want to do, or by getting distracted.)

_____

_____

_____

_____

_____

Every time you notice yourself shooting yourself in the foot, write 'I constipate myself' in your 'should shit log'.

6. After a week of entries, re-read your 'should shit log'. Congratulations you have now identified the bullshit of your ego existence. Now flush it down the toilet.

Animal Advice

- When you should, you shit on yourself.

- Self-imposed restraint isn't healthy for your Happiness Animal, nor is moralizing.

- Be more, do less, create more, buy less, notice more, think less.

- Moderation means to oversee and be aware of.

- There is no link between alcohol and happiness, but there is a link between alcohol and depression.

- If thirsty, drink. If hungry, eat. If tired, rest. Use your senses.

- Very simple test: does whatever we are doing do us any good?

- If you can neither enjoy or bring acceptance to what you do – stop.

- There's a limit to how much you can do & no limit to how much you can be you.

- It's OK to say no.

- Social conformity makes you predictable, inauthentic, a silenced you.

Chapter 9

moralive®5: courage

There is nothing fearful except fear itself. It is not that we have fears in the daylight but that we have entirely created darkness for ourselves. If you can look directly at things they often cease to be frightening

It is not because things are hard that we lack confidence but things are hard because we lack the confidence in the first place

Seneca

Creating is the place where the human spirit shines its brightest light

Robert Fritz

Animal's Anecdote

The waiting room

Leo picked up the photograph of his friend and long-term hairdresser, Elise, from his desk. The picture was of Elise sticking her tongue out at Leo's cheek. It was her birthday party tonight and he needed an excuse not to go. He put the photograph back down and stared into the blank surface of his desk. Leo's thoughts drifted back to his daily recurring memories of a drunken night in Darwin. He'd been in a bar and a couple of men had started harassing him. A woman - Leo's memory displayed her with light brown hair, skinny and tall - had come up to him and said 'let's get out of here'. He had no recollection of their conversation but within minutes they were naked in a backpacker's swimming pool. He couldn't remember the act, but he was 90% sure he'd had sex with the woman either in the pool or in his room or both. But what was of most concern to Leo was what he imagined the woman had said afterwards. Fear told him she might have said something along the lines of 'you should get yourself checked up'. Or 'my boyfriend will kill us both if he finds out about you'. It was hazy but Leo had never been afraid of boyfriends. Over time the memory had become a Chinese whisper. His uncertainty of what events took place was what fuelled the fear in his lower chest and guts. Two months after Darwin, he'd gone to the doctor's for a check up and had come back all clear. The doctor had told him 'you need to wait six months to be absolutely certain for HIV though'. It was two and a half years later and Leo was buckling under the weight of silent what ifs, made heavier by the toxic lead of his imagination.

Hey. Happy Birthday. I'm really sorry but I don't think I can come to the party tonight, I'm not feeling well. Leo sent the message to Elise. Thoughts of dancing without alcohol, and having to interact with people in a place with loud music, and loud drunken voices shrank Leo. He imagined himself to be a discarded old sock, a creature of filth and shadow with no muscle. He wanted to hide in a drawer, so no one would see his shadow and his filth. He'd sent the text to Elise so he didn't have to call her and face a unpredictable conversation where he might not know what to say, and he'd be stranded in the conversation, exposed. Leo looked on his wall and saw another photo of Elise and himself from three years ago when they'd been at a concert together. He noticed his smile was real. There was no tension in his face. Then he looked in the mirror at his furrowed forehead and his joyless eyes. This fear had been hanging over him for two and half years. For the first time Leo realized that it had taken up so much of his attention that he was no longer able to enjoy his life, and yet here in the photograph he could see that he had the capacity for real joy. He was a lonely alien with a sick secret. And even if it killed him, he had to face this secret. A life in the darkness was no life at all.

Leo opened the door to the medical practice. He gave the receptionist his name and took a seat. The waiting room lived up to its name. Leo could feel the front of his stomach tense at the thought that had been haunting him. The thought came back stronger at each new haunting. Shallow breathing, his jaw clamped shut and acid in his throat. He was shit scared. But he had to eliminate doubts from his mind about his health. 'Mr Leo,' he heard a woman's voice call out, breaking the 20 minute torture between impending doom or freedom. The fear could be confirmed or destroyed in an instant by the doctor.

'Hello,' said Leo.

'So what can I do for you' said the doctor, oblivious to the weight that was hanging in the balance in Leo's thoughts.

'I'm here for some test results,' said Leo

'OK, lets have a look. So, Chlamydia-negative, HIV-negative, Gonorrhoea-negative. All negative,' said the doctor.

Leo's expression remained motionless. A new fear driven by hope arose. 'Is that the test from last week?' asked Leo.

'The third of May. Yes, that's last week. Well it's all good news. You made the request for this test some time ago, is that right?' said the doctor, the corners of her mouth flexing upwards.

Leo breathed out and smiled at the doctor. 'I don't think I have seen you here before have I? It was nice to meet you.'

Leo shook the doctor's hand. He opened the door and his heart's long-term tenant, fear, slowly began to make its exit. Leo boarded a bus to the city.

'I'm invited to a party on Crown street tonight.' said Leo to Debbie, the receptionist at his office building.

She smiled at Leo. The whites of her eyes were always clear, and wide. Leo liked Debbie.

'Really, what's that for?' asked Debbie

'It's for a new salon that's opening there. My hairdresser invited me and it's her birthday so it's two parties in one. But I think if I go, there's going to be a lot of pressure to drink.'

'You know it's a lot harder than people think. I found the first couple of months very hard. People don't understand, but then you get used to it and I've been off the booze for a year now,' said Debbie.

'Congratulations, sorry, I would give you a hug but the desk is in the way.'

Leo reached across the desk and shook Debbie's hand.

'On New Year's Eve someone got very angry with me because I wouldn't drink,' Leo said.

'Sometimes you have to remove yourself from the situation. I had to do that with a group of girls the other day – I was invited to a lunch but I had to make up an excuse to cancel. I knew that if I went, it wouldn't end well,' said Debbie.

'Yeah, I wouldn't go if it wasn't my friend's birthday.'

'Don't drink,' said Debbie.

'Nope I won't. I don't like myself when I drink, even after one glass I don't feel myself,' said Leo.

'It's not good. Everyone says they'll just have one but as soon as you've had one, you've opened the flood gates. Maybe you shouldn't go?' said Debbie.

After work, when Leo reached the turning for Crown street, he saw a bus was pulling in at the bus stop that would take him home, so he didn't have to face the noise of the party. He started walking towards the bus before he realized he was letting his imagination create more imaginary fears. 'It's just a party, what's the worst that can happen?' he said out loud. He laughed. Leo felt a new confidence and trust in himself, a relaxed sensation across his body like the feeling of having had a satisfying day's physical work. He went to the party and gave, Elise a kiss on the cheek and a hug. The loud music beat him with self-consciousness. He felt his shoulders rising up the sides of his neck and his stomach compressing. He noticed the tension, he stood still allowing himself to experience the feelings in his body – what he thought was 'nervousness', 'uncomfortableness'. The longer he focused on feeling these feelings, the more he realized they were just sensations in his body, and the less he felt the sensations. Then he stuck out his tongue at Elise, smiled, and began to dance.

Animal Analysis

If you are not afraid, you are dangerous

Osho

Courage is the acceptance of fear. Courage is to do the opposite of social norms, if one's intuition doubts the validity of those norms. Courage is consciously following one's intuition. To be an individual while belonging to a family and wider group of people is the greatest courage of all. Courage, like the other four muscles you have already read about in *The Happiness Animal*, is universal to all human beings. We are all born with a muscle for courage, but our education has wasted it away.

Your existence precedes your thinking. You exist before you think about existing, and you have to learn to think to be unhappy. You are taught to think to compare yourself against others, labels, roles, ranks, and egos in a competing society. It takes courage to accept that this is the status quo and it takes courage to challenge it. Unfortunately, you are up against your left-brain, which according to Osho, 'is a coward'. A coward has no respect for his own being, only for his ego. The coward follows his fears but the courageous person looks them square in the eyes. The tragedy for the coward is that almost all fear is imagined and almost always relates to something other than the present. Yet the present is all you can know. The future is an unknown, not a reality. The only fear that is

Time to define Courage vs. bravery. Courage is not the same as bravery – bravery is repression of fear and acting in spite of it. Courage is accepting fear. 'Fear accepted becomes freedom…The only way to be fearless is to accept fear.' (Osho)

useful is fear of natural danger that you can notice with your senses, and where harm is likely if you pay no attention to the trigger object of your fear: a cliff edge, or a rattlesnake. As you begin this chapter of exercising your own courage muscle, listen to these words of Bob Dylan's biographer, Christopher Ricks, in *Dylan's Visions Of Sin*: 'As difficulties become greater we must attack them with more spirit. We all whistle to keep our courage up. This is an achieving of courage, not a lapsing from it. And what we whistle, we may sing.'

Exercising courage with acceptance of fear (moralive®5.1)

Awareness liberates. Unconsciousness enslaves. Courage – acting with awareness and intention – liberates you from the bondage of unconsciousness. The first step to tackling fear is to check whether you have a case for tolerance or courage. Decide whether you are best off exercising your tolerance or your courage muscle: You can begin by using the reality testing in moralive®3.1 to test whether your fears are imagined or real. If your fears don't disappear when you reality test them, then you have some exercise equipment for your courage muscle. The next thing to do is identify your fears and accept them as your fears. It could be a fear of sickness, a fear of death, a fear of having sex, a fear of public speaking or a fear of being exposed. Accepting these fears is the first step of exercising the courage to take responsibility for your Happiness Animal.

When to exercise courage with accepting fears (moralive®5.1)

Looking directly at fear necessitates noticing the source of that fear, so that you are ready to respond to it at the source. Necessity is the mother of

Oddly enough – courage has no future or past. Courage only exists now. Fears can be of the future, but courage only exists in the present moment.

dealing with things. If you are underwater, necessity forces you to notice that you are underwater and you need to move to the surface to breathe. If you are afraid of someone, go towards that person and notice with your senses, how your body feels about talking to that person. Keep your descriptions specific to what you can sense e.g. my right hand is trembling, my stomach muscles are tightening. Stay with the sensations in your body. What is the source

Time to define: responsible

Responsible means ready to respond.

of your fear of this person? Is there something physical you can detect in their body that you are afraid of? Identify the source of your fear. Stay with the sensations in your body and if you decide to talk to the person, you can even tell the person that you were afraid of talking to them. Tell them how you physically feel when you are talking to them. Stay with them until you feel the fear disappear. Could it be that all you are afraid of is sensations? Whatever the sensations, you are exercising the courage to look into the source of your discomfort. I recently had a fear of picking up a moth that was inside my girlfriend's apartment (and that she was terrified of). I put my hand next to the moth and let it sit there noticing how I was feeling. I could feel tension in my stomach and my chest. Then, I picked up the moth and focused all my attention on it, staying with the sensations in my body. After a few seconds of focusing on the moth, I noticed my body relaxing and I put the moth down outside. Author and former fighter pilot, Waldo Waldman says that 'by experiencing fear, we become more human. Fear teaches us that we are not perfect nor are we superior to anyone else. It makes us more compassionate as we realize the frailty of life and emphasises what truly is important in our lives'. The key is in allowing yourself to experience the fear fully by facing it head on, and accepting it rather than running from or avoiding it. That is courage.

Responsible being

Courage to accept your fears is the courage to take responsibility for yourself. Being responsible means being ready to respond in the present moment to your reality, whatever that reality may bring. Once fear is accepted, you become free of the fear's unconscious control of your existence. By acknowledging your fears, you see them more objectively. Your fears often remain, but you cease to be afraid of them. The more you exercise your courage muscle by identifying and accepting your fears, the closer you get to the ideal of accepting all fears. The closer you get to that ideal, the closer you are to a state of fearlessness. The exercise of identifying and accepting your fear, prevents your fear's dominance over your Happiness Animal. As Osho says in his book, *Courage: The Joy of Living Dangerously,* 'one of the fundamental laws of life is this: whatsoever you hide goes on growing'. We have already seen this to be true with shame, which needs silence and secrecy to grow. So exercise exposing your fears instead of hiding them. Notice them, accept them, and I guarantee you they will shrink. With enough exercise, as your courage muscle becomes stronger and stronger, your fears will weaken and wither.

The grim reaper – the sum of all fears

Leo was afraid of going for a sexual health check-up. Why? Because he has a fear of being diagnosed with an illness that could reduce his lifespan. Why is he afraid of that? Because he is afraid of death. Try this with any fear and get to the root of it: ask yourself why you are afraid of anything, anyone, or any course of action. And then keep asking why you are afraid of that until you get to the root of your fear. The capital fear (from the Latin 'caput' meaning head) is the fear of death. It drives all our fears.

Oddly Enough When you don't understand what it is you are afraid of, fear controls your subconscious. To understand means to stand under. Your understanding your fear is to see it standing under you as you rise above it.

Fear of being alone

Meditation is one way to release the fear of being alone. If you are afraid of being alone, go deep into the fear and ask yourself what reasons are causing you to be afraid. Focus on the fear. Look straight at it. Close your eyes if it helps you feel the fear. Notice the bodily sensations you have when you experience the fear. The more you allow yourself to experience the full sensations of the fear, the less you will find the fear in you. Meditation – or just consciously breathing – is a good way to identify your fears, accept them and accept your self, and feel good about the peace it brings. Once you have done this alone it is time to get back to being courageous with others. While you can improve your Happiness Animal's health by facing your fear of being alone, you will also be exercising your Happiness Animal to feel healthier around others.

No worries mate

Behind every worry is a fear. If I am currently worried about money and how little I have, I ask myself: Why am I worried? Maybe I have a fear of either losing or not having any money, or maybe I have a fear of not being able to pay back what I owe? I may have a fear of being enslaved to a corporate job. I ask myself: why am I afraid of having no money? The answer is I am afraid I won't be able to afford to live. Why am I afraid I won't be able to afford to live? Because I am afraid of dying. Or, if my fear is that I won't be able to afford to pay my credit card bills this month, then I ask myself: Why am I afraid of not paying my credit card bills? Because I have a fear of getting into trouble with the credit card companies. Why am I afraid of getting into trouble with the credit card companies? Because I am afraid they will punish me. Why am I afraid of being punished? Because I am afraid of going to jail. Why am I afraid of going to jail? Because I am afraid that I won't be able to live. Why I am I afraid of not being able to live? Because I am afraid of dying. Just articulating this fear helps you to see it and as soon as you see it, it stops confusing your thoughts, and dominating them. What you have to do is identify the causes behind your worry in simple articulation, rather than vague imaginative language, which has no boundaries. Whenever you have a worry again, just ask yourself as it comes up: What is the fear behind this? Then accept it. Specifics are a lot easier to manage than your imagination. By identifying and accepting your specific fears, you tame your imagination so that rather than it being a wild dark horse that always runs away from you, it becomes a reliable stallion you can ride on the back of to make new journeys possible. First you need to break your imagination in with some reality testing. If you need a refresher in reality testing re-read the section in moralive®3.3 (page 165). Then do the exercise below.

Exercising the acceptance of fear (moralive®5.1)

Exercise for becoming aware of and accepting your fears

Instructions

Make a list of your fears, and accept that these are your fears. Make a list of the bodily sensations associated with those fears. A while ago my list might have read:

1. **Name of fear:** Fear of losing money.

   I notice these sensations with the fear: It's a hollow feeling in my stomach and like reflux is coming into my throat.

   Root of fear: Fear of not being able to survive without money – fear of dying.

2. **Name of fear:** Fear of not having a job.

   I notice these sensations with the fear: It's a feeling of someone squeezing the front of my head.

   Root of fear: Fear of not being able to survive without money – fear of dying.

Now do the same for your fears. Do this exercise with as many fears as you want. The more you exercise, the more you increase the strength of your courage muscle, and of your fearlessness.

1. **Name of fear:**
   I notice these sensations with the fear:
   Root of fear:

2. **Name of fear:**
   I notice these sensations with the fear:
   Root of fear:

3. **Name of fear:**
   I notice these sensations with the fear:
   Root of fear:

4. **Name of fear:**
   I notice these sensations with the fear:
   Root of fear:

5. Now go back and read your fears one by one. This time notice the feelings you associate with your fear again. Keep noticing those feelings. The longer you stick with the sensations, noticing the specifics in your body, the more those bodily sensations will get processed by your body and diminish. Don't try and diminish or avoid them. Accept them and be aware of them and they will disappear. It won't take more than a few minutes for each bodily sensation to diminish. By looking head on at your fears you become less and less afraid of them and you reduce their power over you.

Exercising courage with the unknown (moralive®5.2): courage to risk giving up what you know for what you don't

Courage will come to you. Just start with a simple formula: *Never miss the unknown.* Always choose the unknown and go headlong. Even if you suffer, it is worth it – it always pays. You always come out of it more grown up, more mature, more intelligent

Osho

To begin with you will need courage to reject all that has been imposed on you – all that you 'know' already. What you 'know' is only what you 'know' in your mind. Your thoughts are decided by what you 'know'. It takes courage to drop the mind for what you don't yet know. Encouraging and nurturing your curiosity – rather than vetoing it – is a great tool for this, and exercising tolerance can help a lot. Think back to any memories you have of playing as a child. Think about how you used to explore places. How much more fun were birthday parties as a child than as an adult? So many new corners to hide in, so much exciting new territory to charter and explore outside. Allow the child in you to play and explore again. Play like no one's watching.

When to exercise courage with the unknown: (moralive®5.2)
Habits are what you know. Routine is also what you know. You can use courage to break unhealthy habits simply by doing the opposite of what you know, what you normally do.
Osho says the known is 'the dead' because once something is known it ceases to change and evolve, whereas the unknown is the living and it continues to evolve and change. To have the courage for freedom you need to have the courage for uncertainty. He says that it is best not to call it uncertainty, but to call it wonder. And it is better not to call it insecurity, but to call it freedom.

Drop knowledge and recover your inner sense; your innocence

Your imagination uses what your mind thinks it 'knows'. Unless you can notice something with your senses, you don't know shit. Falling into the habit of using your mind rather than your senses for knowledge is falling into living in a demoralizing imaginary world, and it's demoralizing because you are disconnected from existence. But combined with the exercise of the veto power of awareness, your courage empowers you to let go of the 'knowledge' of your imagination. Often what your mind thinks it 'knows' is what the crowd 'knows'. You have adopted views and public opinions on one side of the

Sen Says
Troubles press harder on the person who runs away from them. Fortune falls heavily on those whom she is unexpected. The man who is always expecting her easily withstands her.

fence or the other. Whether it's vaccinations, caged eggs, antibiotics and medicines, nuclear power, climate change, dairy, wheat, fat, carbohydrates, or alcohol this is domesticated knowledge, not natural knowledge. Society has tamed your mind's knowledge. Living on tame knowledge demoralizes your Happiness Animal in as much as it imprisons you in your mind of domesticated knowledge. Osho says that if you reach higher and risk views, or ask questions that take you further away from your settled routine, you become wild again, and your nature becomes closer to the natural animal world: 'The moment you are no longer afraid of the crowd, you are a lion.'

The courage to abandon hope and the courage to accept doubt

Leo summoned up the courage to face the unknown when he went to get his test results from the doctor, but while he was with the doctor a new kind of fear struck Leo. The source of the fear was both doubt and hope. Doubt that the doctor had given him the latest test results. Doubt that he was all-clear, hope that he was all-clear. Doubt and hope are intrinsically linked. It is possible that the more you have hope the less you doubt in a particular moment, but like a seesaw, doubt can come slamming down at any time. Hope and doubt are on opposite ends of an unhealthy seesaw. Hope that your investments will rise based on good news can swing instantly to doubt that you will lose all your money when you see the share price slam down. Hope is a less reliable version of an expectation. Attachment to hope lays a lot of disappointment eggs that can hatch on you at any time. The shells of hope are even more fragile than the shells of expectation. It is healthy to plan certain courses of action, but treat your plans objectively rather than personally. Be nonchalant and carefree without attachment to outcomes. If you plan based on your intentions for the year, the nuts and bolts of the specific actions you take won't matter. Your intentions can remain the same for the year regardless of what happens during that year. If your intention is to be kind to your family, and you plan to take them on a trip, but then realize you don't have enough money, you can adapt your plan to do something kind for your family that doesn't require money. You can either experience existence or your can avoid experience by remaining locked in your mind of thinking links, attachments to hopes and expectations. Accept that there are doubts as to whether your plans will work out. Accept that you and your intentions will remain in existence regardless of external constraints. You are, no matter what isn't. The courage to be without expectation is the courage to truly live.

Exercising courage with the unknown (moralive® 5.2)

Exercise for fear of uncertainty, the unknown and for facing emptiness Based on an exercise by Osho in *Courage: The Joy Of Living Dangerously*

Instructions

Make it a point before you go to sleep to close your eyes for twenty minutes.

1. Focus on a feeling of emptiness while your eyes are closed.

2. Focus on falling deeper and deeper into your emptiness.

3. Accept the emptiness. Let it be there inside of you or all around you.

4. If fear arises – let that be there too. Notice the feeling of your fear and stay focused on noticing the emptiness.

5. You may tremble with fear but don't reject this space that is being born there in the emptiness.

6. Continue doing the above steps for two to three weeks at bedtime. Within that time you will be able to feel the beauty of the emptiness inside you and all around you. Once you have touched that beauty, fear will disappear on its own accord. Do not try to fight the fear or the emptiness at any point. All you have to do is notice and accept with your eyes closed.

The courage to take action (moralive®5.3)

Do it, irrespective of the results, and your boredom will disappear

Osho

The courage of action is the courage to do without focusing on an expected result. It is the courage to do things for the sake of doing them. It is the courage to follow your instinct after accepting your fear of what other people might think. When you act for the intrinsic reward of doing what you are doing, you will never be bored. Doing something with a goal in mind but doing it for the reward of the activity itself is what Mihaly Csikszentmihalyi's state of *flow* is all about. When you play chess you play for the reward of playing chess itself. The game is only playable if there is the goal of winning, but regardless of whether you win or lose the enjoyment is in the playing. When you play a song, you are not trying to get to the end of the song. Human beings are the only animals that feel boredom outside captivity, and it is because we have unlearned the natural habit of playing for play's own intrinsic reward. Play is mocked, and called 'childish' by a society modelled around earnings targets, cost savings, material gains, new condos and KPIs. But we live in a world where children are often smarter than their parents. Exercising your courage muscle to take action that is not motivated by financial and material gains is exercising the courage to live.

When to exercise courage with action (moralive®5.3)

Decision time

When making decisions for your wellbeing, it is critical that you remember the myths about what makes you happy. You can exercise your awareness and courage muscles to veto the influence of money, power and prestige in your decision making. Your actions, like those of a child, can be those that you want to do for their own intrinsic reward, and what your unmasked being wants to do free from external motivations or dependencies. Osho says that the goal of life is play. Plato says that 'life must be lived as play'. We must have the courage to take risks with our actions if we are to be happy. Being comfortable with 'security' is about as healthy for your Happiness Animal as watching television is for the health of your body. Security is a generalization. You can't notice security with your senses. Security doesn't exist. When you are bored, you are bored with your self. You are bored with non-existence. It means you have not acted honestly in accordance with your authentic being, and with what that authentic being sincerely wants to do. You have acted in a way that disrespects your existence by not listening to who you are. It's time you gave your existence some respect.

Exercising courage with action (moralive®5.3)

Based on Dr Martin Seligman's 'Signature Strengths Test'.

Exercise for building the courage to do what you are naturally talented at doing.

This exercise is pure applied positive psychology, developed by the founder of Positive Psychology, Dr. Martin Seligman. Millions who have done this exercise have already felt the benefits. Seligman says, in the book *Flourish*, that the purpose of this exercise is to 'encourage you to own your signature strengths by finding new and more frequent uses for them. A signature strength has the following hallmarks:

- A sense of ownership and authenticity ('This is the real me').
- A feeling of excitement while displaying it, particularly at first.
- A rapid learning curve as the strength is first practised.
- A sense of yearning to find new ways to use it.
- A feeling of inevitability in using the strength ('Try to stop me').
- Invigoration rather than exhaustion while using the strength.
- The creation and pursuit of personal projects that revolve around it.
- Joy, zest, enthusiasm, even ecstasy while using it'.

Instructions
You will need access to the internet for part of this exercise.

1. Take the strengths test here (it takes a few seconds to register first): https://www.authentichappiness.sas.upenn.edu/testcenter Click on the link for VIA Survey for character strengths.

2. You will get your results immediately. Print them out for reference.

3. Review your strengths. Were there any surprises for you? Which strength surprises you?

   _____

4. Look at your five strengths one at a time and ask yourself, 'is this one of my signature strengths?'

5. What is your number one signature strength?

   _____

6. Does your strength correspond to one of your Happiness Animal's muscles? Which muscle(s)?

   _____

7. Create a designated time in your schedule when you will exercise one or more of your signature strengths in a new way either at work or at home or in leisure – just make sure that you create a clearly defined opportunity to use it. For example: If your signature strength is creativity, you may choose to set aside two hours one evening to begin working on a screenplay, a book or crafting a home-made gift for someone. Focus on the signature strength in a way that allows you to exercise your

corresponding Happiness Animal's muscle as much as possible.

8. How did you feel before engaging in the activity of using your signature strength?

_____

_____

_____

_____

_____

9. How did you feel during the activity?

_____

_____

_____

_____

10. How did you feel after the activity?

_____

_____

_____

_____

_____

11. Was the activity challenging or easy?

_____

12. Did time pass quickly? Did you lose your sense of self-consciousness?

_____

13. Do you plan to repeat the exercise?

_____

Exercising the courage to love and trust (moralive®5.4)

Sen Says

As a rose can't live without the rain so a heart can't love without risk of pain

We are afraid of the masks people wear but not only people but things must have their masks stripped off and their true features restored.

Anonymous

The root of the word courage is 'cor', which is the Latin word for heart. Courage for love is the courage for trust. Love, like courage, is the polar opposite of fear. Fear is a feeling of no contact with existence, hence the reason why the sum of all fears is the fear of losing existence, of dying. Love is a feeling of bonding with existence. Love can only happen when there is no fear present. That's why love and courage, if not intrinsically linked, are one and the same. Exercising your courage muscle is exercising your power to love and be loved, to trust and be trusted.

When to exercise the courage of love and trust (moralive®5.4)

Having the power to create your life the way you want it with the help of others and then be able to enjoy what you have done with them depends on your courage to complete the past

Brad Blanton

I open this passage with Blanton's quote, as completion is the best way to begin exercising the courage of love and trust. Just as you'll do your muscles damage by running a marathon without warming up first, you will do your courage muscle damage without warming up first. The warm up required here is getting complete with your past by expressing your resentments and appreciations to those people you resent from your past. Otherwise you will find those resentments being triggered in your new relationships and preventing your appreciation, trust and love in those new relationships. Unexpressed resentments are an obstruction to new love. This is an exercise in the courage to tell the truth. Go back and review the exercise in moralive®1.3 'Express yourself'. Are there people from past relationships you still need to get complete with by first releasing your unexpressed resentments and appreciations?

Love the world and overcome your fear of the world
To love, you cannot meditate on your own. Once you have accepted your existence and your fears, your next step is to face the world with your existence. Only in moments of love for the world will you experience no fear for the world. If love is not allowed to flow from you to others, it becomes fear in you. Fear deteriorates the health of

your Happiness Animal. Exercising courage with love improves that health and it also sharpens your intelligence and ability to face uncertainty and insecurity. While love sharpens your intelligence, fear limits and numbs it. So how do you love the world? Dr. Rick Hanson, a neuropsychologist and author, has some good advice: 'In terms of the aspect of love that is about caring for, this means to me a combination of cherishing, protecting and nurturing the world. You naturally cherish what you love. Cherishing something, you want to keep it safe; once it's protected, you want to help it flourish. For a minute, an hour, or a whole week, touch natural and human-made things around you like you truly cherish them. If you cherished an orange or a cup, how would you hold it? Pick one thing and focus on helping it grow and thrive. Perhaps a plant, or a business, or a project at a local school, or a collaboration among some friends, or a fix-it repair at home.'

Courage to risk a broken heart

If you are afraid of a broken heart, you will not be able to experience love. Accept the risk that someone else can break your heart. Accept your fear and it will disappear. Without vulnerability you cannot experience love. It takes courage, but the way to be vulnerable in an intimate relationship is simply to be you, say what you notice to the other person and give them your complete honesty. Vulnerability is exposing your existence, not protecting that existence with ego. It is exercising the courage to hide no part of your existence. The rewards of being in love are infinite. Your Happiness Animal thrives. Being in love makes you more courageous, kinder, more tolerant and more honest and you don't even notice you are exercising your muscles. And love also has its biological benefits. A study described by Dean Ornish in his book, *Love and Survival, the Scientific Basis for the Healing Power of Intimacy*), monitored ten thousand men who had no previous history of angina. Those men who reported the feeling the warmth of love from their wives experienced half the angina rate compared to men who felt their wives didn't give them any love. To be able to feel the love from your spouse, you first have to be vulnerable in front of your spouse.

During the writing of this book, I had to spend time away from my girlfriend for up to four months at a time, and at time when our relationship was still in its infancy. I could only stay in the USA on a tourist visa for a maximum of six months before I'd have to leave and spend a few months back in the UK to reset the visa. Gina and I had only been together for less than a year, and the second time I left the USA, Gina naturally felt some doubts about whether I'd actually return. Initially she kept those doubts to herself. What I, oblivious to what was going through her mind, started to notice, was her reducing her contact with me week by week, until she was barely speaking to me and always seemed busy when I asked if she'd like to Skype. I began to worry that she didn't want me to come back. What I imagined was her pushing me away was actually her trying to protect herself. Thankfully she told me what had been going on:

I'm so sorry if you feel like I have been pushing you away, now or before you left.

I think I have been preparing myself for the off chance that you might not come back and I'm sorry. That's not right to you because I love you so completely but I haven't let myself, if that makes sense.

Exercising the courage to love (moralive®5.4)

Exercise for loving the world and increasing your vulnerability.

Instructions

Pick something or someone to protect each day. Pick up an insect from the street or the sink and move it to the side of the road or put it outside. Let a stranger stand under your umbrella in the rain. Stop a door from slamming into someone. Tell the person behind you if there is a slippery surface or a loose cobble that they could trip on. Before the end of each day aim to have protected something or someone.

If you are in an intimate relationship, write a letter to your partner where you open up about all your feelings for them and your greatest fears. Tell them everything you have been too afraid to tell them about how you feel. If you are afraid that they will leave you, tell them what makes you feel that way. Work on the letter over a few days. Put it in an envelope and post it to them even if you live together. If you are not in an intimate relationship, you can do this exercise with your best friend.

Exercising the courage to create (moralive®5.5): from the courage of vulnerability comes the courage to create

The ego is always coming out of fear. A really fearless person has no ego. The ego is a protection, an armour

Osho

Courage is about putting our vulnerability on the line. If we want to live and love with our whole hearts and engage in the world from a place of worthiness, our first step is practicing the courage it takes to

own our stories and tell the truth about who we are. It doesn't get
braver than that

Brené Brown

The courage of vulnerability and humility is the courage to be authentic, to reveal your true nature to the world, exposing yourself with no protection of masks, roles, job titles or responsibilities. It is the courage of your innocence – your inner sense – with the ego removed. Your ego is a creation of fear, and it was created as part of your misguided attempt to protect your vulnerability from the world. The more you have ego in your life, the less you have authenticity, honesty, and courage, the weaker your Happiness Animal, and the weaker your existence. Exercising vulnerability is exercising the courage to connect with existence. You need to exist before you can create.

When to exercise the courage to create (moralive®5.5)

When you become an idea
When you find yourself wearing a mask of expected words and behaviour, risk the false for the true. When you feel a pull to conform to what others are doing, remember that the crowd is not pulling you, it is you who is being pulled by the idea of who you are – the idea that you should be like them, or that you should be a certain way. Osho said 'personality is bogus, but individuality is substantial'. Having the courage to be vulnerable is having the courage to be a substantial individual – an individual of substance. Once the truth is exposed through the exercise of your honesty muscle it becomes stronger as the

Sen Says
There is also another not inconsiderable source of anxieties if you are too concerned to assume a pose and do not reveal yourself openly to anyone

untruth of ego loses its power over you. Your individuality is your reality. Make it substantial. In group settings remember to accept your fear of not conforming and you will exercise the courage to be an individual and add to existence with your true presence. Exercise the courage to ignore the expected formalities of a social context. Formalities are for egos, not for courageous beings. Act out of your innocence, your inner sense. Don't worry if the egos around you find you naïve as a result. Don't worry about the result. Your goal is to connect with your existence. Drop the idea of you, because you are not an idea. You exist.

The courage of humility

People full of fear make others afraid by pumping more air into their ego. 'The greatest fear in the world is the opinion of others,' said Osho. Don't let that fear jeopardise your existence. Don't starve your reality by fattening your unreality, fattening the ego you have been presenting to the world. Humility is not thinking less of yourself. It is thinking of yourself (your ego) less. It is you noticing what exists more than thinking about how to exist. Trust your inner sense. When you catch yourself pretending – stop. Ask what would the real you do if you stopped caring about what any other person thought of you? What other people think of you is none of your business. I remind myself of this essential truth by repeating the mantra of Gestalt therapist Fritz Perls:

Oddly Enough

'The root of the word courage is cor – the Latin word for heart. In one of its earliest forms, the word courage had a very different definition than it does today. Courage originally meant to speak one's mind by telling all one's heart.

Over time, this definition has changed, and, today, courage is more synonymous with being heroic. Heroics are important and we certainly need heroes, but I think we've lost touch with the idea that speaking honestly and openly about who we are, about what we're feeling, and about our experiences (good and bad) is the definition of courage. (Brené Brown)

'I do my thing and you do your thing.
I am not in this world to live up to your expectations,
And you are not in this world to live up to mine.
You are you, and I am I,
and if by chance we find each other, it's beautiful.'

The courage to use your mind as an instrument of creation

In *Practicing Radical Honesty*, Brad Blanton advocates 'a way to use your mind to keep yourself from falling back to the neurotic survival skills of the mind. You do it by living into a vision of the future, creating in the present from the future, rather than having the present be a reaction to the past.' With a little practice in exercising awareness in vetoing thoughts that pop into your mind, and noticing through your senses rather than being unconsciously led through your thinking links, you can start to use your mind as a plaything for creating your life. If you create based on the intentions that allow you to exercise any of the five muscles of your Happiness Animal – and by consciously using your imagination as a tool – you can start to plan a life that will benefit the health of your Happiness Animal. For example: you start by doing a stream of consciousness exercise, or noticing vs. imagining with the exercise of moralive®3.5. Once you are in a conscious state of noticing using your senses, you can create something new using your mind as the tool. The only requirement is that you are aware that you are using your mind and your personality as a tool to help shape what you create. Let's try it now...

Exercising the courage to create (moralive®5.5)

Exercise for creating using the courage of implementing your life purpose. Based on an exercise by Phil Laut.

1. Below, list fifteen characteristics of your self. You may have previously considered some of them to be negative, but you can transform them in developing your life purpose. You may be intelligent, humorous, joyful, driven, slovenly, weird, whatever. Make sure you have fifteen. Have some fun with this exercise. If you are taking it seriously, one of your characteristics could be 'serious'.

1_____   6_____

2_____   7_____

3_____   8_____

4_____   9_____

5_____   10_____

6_____   11_____

7_____   12_____

8_____   13_____

14_____   15_____

If you didn't put fifteen down, get back up there and finish!

2. Now circle your five favourite personality characteristics. Do it quickly – don't think too much, or your ego will start to take over.

3. Referring loosely to the five favourite personality characteristics you just circled, make a list of fifteen actual behaviours that are ways you enjoy expressing these characteristics. For example, if one of your characteristics was generosity, then the behaviour you perform in the real world that exemplifies generosity could be 'feeding the homeless by working in a soup kitchen on Sunday mornings'.

a) _____

b) _____

c) _____

d) _____

e) _____

f) _____

g) _____

h) _____

i) _____

j) _____

k) _____

l) _____

m) _____

n) _____

o) _____

4. After you have completed a list of at least fifteen activities, pick your five favourite activities and circle them.

5. Write a brief statement (twenty-five words or so) of your vision of an ideal world. Write this vision in the present tense and in terms of how you want it to be rather than how you want it not to be. Begin your statement this way:
   'An ideal world is one in which...'

   _____

   _____

   _____

   _____

   _____

6. Now you are going to cut and paste your life purpose together. It's easy and fun. Here you go.
   The purpose of my life is to use my (list the five general characteristics you circled)

   _____,

   _____,

_____,

_____, and

_____

by (list the five specific behaviours)

_____,

_____,

_____,

_____and

_____

to bring about a world in which (copy in your ideal world statement)

_____

_____

_____

_____

_____

_____

Congratulations! You now have a good draft of a life purpose statement of your own. You can now edit it a bit. After you edit and/or revise it, type it up and print it, or copy it neatly. You can put it in your purse or wallet and carry it around with you. If you're on a bus or in a bar or at a party and you strike up a conversation with somebody and they ask you what you do for a living, whip that puppy out and hand it to them. In fact, carry a few extras so they can keep one if they like. This is the beginning of the conversation you generate that has you creating the kind of world you want to live in with the help of a whole bunch of other people. Because I don't know exactly what you wrote, I'll review a sample life-purpose statement in case you want an example to follow while you are revising yours. You can work on a life purpose statement like you would work on a poem or a song. Polish it and make it sing, make it move people, make people cry when they hear it. Write a song from it. Make a poster from it. Write it on the wall next to the telephone. Put it on the refrigerator.

At the time of writing here is my life purpose statement as an example:

The purpose of my life is to use my kindness, curiosity, creativity, childishness, grit, and love of company by talking to strangers, writing books, giving talks, providing personal training for happiness, being curious, living with loved ones, and being present with all people to bring about a world in which people thrive by noticing each other with their senses, by telling each other the truth, by giving warmth to others, by paying it forward, by anticipating others needs with empathy, asking questions of each other, and loving each other without fear of doing so.

You can see that in my statement there are seven specific behaviours. In your own statement, add or subtract whatever makes this more powerful for you. Play with this to make it as clear and inspiring for you as possible. Make it inspiring to other people as well. Phil Laut, who created this exercise, says: 'It is possible that several iterations will be required before you have a statement of purpose that you will like well enough to write on a slip of paper and carry around with you. Some of the benefits that you can expect are that thinking and behaviour that do not support your purpose will be more evident to you and goal setting and decision making will both be easier. The statement and expression of your purpose is derived from your values. Without a clear sense of your purpose all of the education you receive and all of the improvements that you make in yourself serve only to make you a more productive slave to someone else's purpose.'

This exercise has multiple benefits and engages your honesty, courage, moderation, and kindness muscles: while you are exercising your honesty muscle in authentically defining yourself, you are also defining the areas of your life that bring meaning to you so that you can plan your career and your life in a way that grows your authenticity, and in a way where you will give your creativity to the rest of society. This exercise helps you be more of you.

- Accept your fear and it will disappear.

- Drop the idea of you, because you are not an idea. You exist.

- Courage – acting with awareness and intention – liberates you from the bondage of unconsciousness.

- Courage to accept your fears is the courage to take responsibility for yourself.

- Behind every worry is a fear. Identify the fear and accept it.

- Drop knowledge and recover your inner sense – your innocence.

- The courage to be without expectation is the courage to truly live.

- Your ego is a creation of fear, and it was created as part of your misguided attempt to protect your vulnerability from the world.

- If you are afraid of a broken heart, you will not be able to experience love. Make yourself vulnerable by sharing your feelings and fears with the people that matter.

- You need to exist before you can create.

Chapter 10 – Conclusion

Happiness Animals

Nature endowed us with noble aspirations just as she gave certain animals ferocity. She gave us a spirit that takes us in search of life of the greatest honour

The only thing that belongs to a man is his spirit. The perfection of his reason is that spirit. All that reason demands is that we live in accordance with our own nature .

Seneca

The spirit Seneca talks of is your Happiness Animal. The perfection of reason Seneca talks of is the exercise of your five Happiness Animal's muscles. If you exercise enough it becomes natural. It is in your nature to have freedom from the chains of your thinking links. Freedom from thought is the freedom of awareness, and with it comes the choice of intention. Your Happiness Animal has five intentions to choose from, five muscles to exercise, and every exercise of those five muscles benefits the health of your Happiness Animal. So go forth, and choose your intention. Your Happiness Animal's health also contributes to the health of humankind. Indeed, a little exercise has far reaching consequences, not just for you but for the survival of every living being on this planet. As you exercise, global happiness increases as global ego decreases.

Ego: the fool's gold of happiness

Eckhart Tolle said that the 'stronger the ego, the stronger the sense of separateness with people'. The more honest you are, the more your ego diminishes, and the stronger your sense of togetherness with other people becomes. The actions of honest intentions that involve any of the five muscles of your Happiness Animal don't just benefit you – they benefit all human beings. And not just human beings. You can exercise kindness towards all living beings, even if it's rescuing a beetle from the middle of the road. If you adopt an abandoned pet from a shelter, or just rescue a moth from the shower, all these things will make you feel more alive, less separate from existence, and happier. And it is never too late to begin exercising the muscles of your Happiness Animal – in the words of Osho: 'A man dying with awareness is born with awareness.'

Reality checking the ideal of happiness

It is true that throughout the researching and writing, as well as the experiences that led up to this book, I experienced the polar opposite of exercising the five muscles of my own Happiness Animal. I experienced extreme unhappiness when I demoralized my spirit by doing the opposite of exercising my Happiness Animal's muscles. This 'demoralizing exercise' was necessary for me to truly understand, through experience, the nature of each of the five muscles and to be able to troubleshoot ways in which these muscles could be exercised. I don't believe that anyone is happy all the time, but I do believe that with exercise, anyone that feels demoralized or unhappy, can exercise – and strengthen – their Happiness Animal. The more you exercise the stronger an Animal you will be. And just like your biceps, once that muscle has built up, it won't disappear overnight. Every obstacle you encounter every day is an opportunity to be happier by using that obstacle as the exercise equipment for your Happiness Animal's muscles.

At the beginning of the book, I asked you to make a list of the top five things that would make you happier than you are now. Before you go back and check what you wrote, fill out the *Pens with Benefits* on the following page.

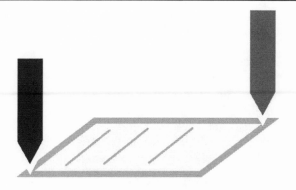

Pens with benefits

Instructions

Use the space below to make a list of the top five things that would make you happier than you are now. Spend no more than one or two minutes on this.

1. _____

_____

2. _____

_____

3. _____

_____

4. _____

_____

5. _____

Look at your list above. Do your five answers relate to something internal e.g. an intention (i.e. non-material, non-monetary), or are they dependent on external things? Start with a total of 100% and deduct 20% for each of your answers that relates to getting something external. What % are you left with? Your thinking is now_____% happy. Now, go back and compare what you wrote today with what you wrote when you were just beginning this book (page 25). Is your % higher or lower than it was when you began this book? What other differences are there between what you wrote at the beginning of the book compared to what you wrote now?

Living Social

No one can live happily who has regard to himself alone

Seneca

You can only be a happy person if there are other people around to connect with. You exercise your Happiness Animal, not just for your own benefit, but for the benefit of the whole of humanity. Global Happiness Animal health increases in multiples, the more it is distributed the more it flourishes exponentially. One Happiness Animal literally inspires another: The word inspiration means 'in spirit'. The origin of the word animal is 'anima' meaning spirit. You strengthen Happiness Animals by inspiring – putting spirit into. A study by the University of Warwick has shown that a 30% increase in one spouse's happiness boosts the other

Oddly Enough
If there was a cause to explain the purpose of our existence other than solidarity – to connect well with others – then it would have been discovered by now. There is not a definite point to our existence other than to be one. We are all one universe, one existence.

spouse's happiness: 'It is significantly greater than the effect of owning a house outright; it can completely offset the non-[financial] cost of unemployment; it is equal to not having to spend around two months in the hospital,' says British researcher Nick Powdthavee. As you exercise your Happiness Animal, you improve the lives of other people.

Egoism excites egoism in others. Altruism excites altruism in others. It's the rules of attraction: people mirror each other's behaviour. Science proves that mirror neurons exist in the brains of every human being. The exercise of kindness, tolerance, awareness, courage, and honesty leads to solidarity, which in turn leads to long term personal benefit as well as benefit to others. The key point here – and it's obvious really when you think about it – is that we will be happier if others around us are happy. **You can strengthen the Happiness Animal in others in many ways but it begins by being social.** Here are some examples of how help someone else strengthen their Happiness Animal:

- You could ask them if they want to collaborate with you on a project.

- You could get together to express gratitude to a mutual friend.

- You could tell them what you appreciate about them.

- You could be honest with them and ask them to be honest with you about anything.

- You could ask them what they are afraid of and then face it with them, with curiosity head on.

- You could find out what specifics are making them unhappy, asking them to notice what thoughts they are having and what bodily sensations they notice.

- You could agree to tackle the source of their unhappiness with them after you have empathized with their feelings e.g. you can empathize with a generic feeling of shame, guilt, fear, anger.

- You could help them by agreeing to own some of their problems with them (you get to exercise compassion and they feel recognized and accepted at the same time).

- You could give them the warmth of your smile and your hugs.

The Happiness Animal Is

To be or not to be, really is the question. Shakespeare was right again. Aristotle said that 'men become builders by building houses, and harpists by playing the harp'. What Aristotle could have added is that 'you become happy by existing well'. You are well when you are kind, kind when you are honest, honest when you are courageous, courageous when you are aware, aware when you are tolerant. Here's the best thing: whatever you want to do that uses any of the five muscles will strengthen your Happiness Animal. Your Happiness Animal is your spirit. See then that your spirit is well exercised, for it is the source of your happiness.

Afterword

When I had the idea in 2001 for *The Happiness Animal*, I had no idea it would turn out in 2013 to be the most educational experience of my life, and would take me on three years of journeys both physical and mental to meet new places and new faces. I discovered happiness is not in conforming, nor is it in common sense. No five senses are the same. What I create and what I give by being true to my senses is the most valuable creation I can offer existence. Happiness is connecting well with existence. I discovered that a strong connection exists by being honest, being kind, being aware, being curious, being loving, and being courageous.

Happiness is being well.

Will Jelbert.
26th December 2013.

For Happiness Coaching & Personal Training for Happiness visit: www.happinessanimal.com or email the author: w@happinessanimal.com

<u>Acknowledgments</u>

Time for me to exercise some more gratitude to:

My parents for encouraging me, supporting me and not judging me for abandoning my corporate career to research and write this book. And for exposing me to people and books from an early age including *Self-control and how to secure it, by Paul Dubois,* a book that I pinched from your bookshelf in 2001, the book that planted the seed in me for creating the *The Happiness Animal.* Thank you, **Paul Dubois**.

Nicolette Houben for her support over the last two years, not just in editing the manuscript, but also in project managing the creative team and our guerrilla marketing at the Sydney Opera house.

Irene Macias for her artistic flair and for creating the book trailer.

Anthony Vu for the illustrations that appear inside this book, and for producing the original book trailer.

Alejandra Moreno and **Yifei Zhao** for assisting the animator.

Rob Wetton for his enthusiasm and editing on the first draft.

Sue Hines, publishing director at Allen & Unwin for providing the encouragement and knowledge to make this book publishable. **Leon Nacson,** Managing Director of Hay House Australia and **Gideon Weil,** editor at Harper Collins for expressing their confidence in the book.

Jamie, an incredible client who inspired me to continue the application of *The Happiness Animal* to the world of coaching. And all my **clients** for testing and evaluating the book's exercises.

Huda Serhan, Jacques Wisdorff, Davy Luscombe, Vidya Khan, Malissa Trojan, Sadie Oliver for their unconditional words of support and belief in the value of *The Happiness Animal.*

Brad Blanton, for coaching me in the exercise of my honesty muscle, and for bringing me back to my senses when I got mindjacked.

Laura Stratton at Animal Assisted Therapy Programmes of Colorado, for helping me to exercise my awareness muscle.

Thousands of Facebook followers who provided their feedback, ideas, support and enthusiasm for the book before it even existed.

The staff at the **Don Adan café** in Mosman, Sydney, and **Aviano coffee** in Cherry Creek, Colorado, for providing me with writing fuel.

John Jelbert, my brother, for his support and graphic design work.

And last but not least, **Gina Montoya**, for providing creative and marketing support, and for creating *The Happiness Animal* website, but most of all for trusting me and loving me. Your warmth makes me feel more alive.

<u>References</u>

Blanton, Brad. *Radical Honesty: How to transform your life by telling the truth.* Dell Publishing, 1996.

Blanton, Brad. *Practicing radical honesty.* Sparrowhawk Publications, 2000.

Ferrucci, Piero. *The Power of Kindness. The Unexpected Benefits of Leading a Compassionate Life.* Tarcher, 2007.

Furedi, Frank. *On tolerance.* Continuum, 2011.

Osho. *Courage.* St. Martin's Griffin, 1999.

Muller, Wayne. *A life of being, having, and doing enough.* Harmony Books, 2010.

Gilbert, Daniel Todd. *Stumbling on happiness.* A.A. Knopf, 2006.

Haidt, Jonathan. *The happiness hypothesis.* William Heinemann, 2006.

Brown, Brené. *Daring greatly.* Gotham Books, 2012.

Seligman, Martin E. P. *Flourish.* Nicholas Brealey Pub., 2011.

Csikszentmihalyi, Mihaly. *Flow.* Rider, 2002.

Bloom, Paul. *How pleasure works.* Vintage, 2010.

Rubin, Gretchen Craft. *The happiness project.* Harper, 2011.

Fritz, Robert. *Creating.* Fawcett Columbine, 1991.

Hamilton, David R. *Why kindness is good for you*. Hay House, 2010.

Carlson, Richard. *Stop thinking & start living*. Element, 2003.

Zukav, Gary. *The seat of the soul*. Rider, 1990.

Tolle, Eckhart. *A new earth*. Penguin, 2006.

Epictetus. And Sharon Lebell. *A manual for living*. HarperSanFrancisco, 1994.

Walsch, Neale Donald. *Conversations with God*. G.P. Putnam's Sons, 1996.

Seneca, Lucius Annaeus and Robin Campbell. *Letters from a stoic*. Penguin, 2004.

Seneca, Lucius Annaeus and C. D. N Costa. *Dialogues and letters*. Penguin Books, 1997.

Seneca, Lucius Annaeus and Aubrey Stewart. *L. Annaeus Seneca on benefits, addressed to Aebutius Liberalis*. George Bell and Sons, 1887.

Dubois, Paul. *Self Control and How to Secure it*. Funk and Wagnalls, 1909.

Dubois Paul. *L'éducation de soi-meme*. Masson. 1909.

Aurelius Antoninus, Marcus and Staniforth, Maxwell. *Meditations*. Penguin Books, 1986.

Ince, Susan and Ronald D Siegel. *Positive psychology*. Harvard Medical School, 2011.

Seligman, Martin E. P. *Authentic happiness*. Free Press, 2002.

Benjamin, Daniel J., Ori Heffetz, Miles S. Kimball, and Alex Rees-Jones. 2012. *What Do You Think Would Make You Happier? What Do You Think You Would Choose?* American Economic Review, 102(5): 2083-2110.

Belk, Russell W. *Three Scales to Measure Constructs Related to Materialism: Reliability, Validity, and Relationships to Measures of Happiness in NA* - Advances in Consumer Research Volume 11, eds. Thomas C. Kinnear. Association for Consumer Research, Pages: 291-297, 1984.

Kasser, Tim and Ryan, Richard. M. *A Dark Side of the American Dream: Correlates of Financial Success as a Central Life Aspiration.* Journal of Personality and Social Psychology 1993. Vol. 65. No. 2, 410-422

Mogilner, C. *You'll feel less rushed if you give time away.* Harvard business review 90, no. 9 (2012): 28.

Grace Chou, Hui-Tzu and Edge, Nicholas. *They Are Happier and Having Better Lives than I Am: The Impact of Using Facebook on Perceptions of Others' Lives.* Cyberpsychology, Behavior, and Social Networking. February 2012, 15(2):117-121.

Pacifica, 438 U.S. at 748.

Houseman, Barbara. *Finding your voice.* Routledge, 2002.

Pennebaker, James W. *Opening up.* Guildford Press, 1997.

Misztal, Barbara A. *Trust in modern societies.* Polity Press, 1996.

Helliwell, John F, Richard Layard and Jeffrey Sachs. *World happiness report 2013.* Sustainable Development Solutions Network, 2013.

Grewen, Karen M. PhD, Anderson, Bobbi J. Girdler, Susan S. PhD, & Light, Kathleen C. PhD. *Warm Partner Contact Is Related to Lower Cardiovascular Reactivity.* Behavioral Medicine. Volume 29, Issue 3, 2003: pages 123-130

Lyubomirsky, Sonja. *The how of happiness.* Penguin Books, 2008.

Doty, James. *Is Being Compassionate Healthy?* Stanford Institute for Neuro-Innovation and Transformational Neurosciences SINTN Newsletter. August 2011, Issue 5: page 9.

Zautra, Alex J. Fasman, Robert. Davis, Mary C. Craig, Arthur D. (Bud). *The effects of slow breathing on affective responses to pain stimuli: An experimental study.* PAIN - April 2010. Vol. 149, Issue 1, Pages 12-18.

Ramacharaka. *Science of Breath; a Complete Manual of the Oriental Breathing Philosophy of Physical, Mental, Psychic and Spiritual Development.* Yogi Publication Society, 1905.

Saks, A. M., & Ashforth, B. E. (1996). Proactive socialization and behavioral self-management. Journal of Vocational Behavior, 48, 301–323.

Laut, Phil. *Money Is My Friend.* Vivation Pub., 1989.

Cronin, Melissa. *Smiling At Strangers Eases Loneliness, Feelings Of Ostracism, Study Says.* The Huffington Post. 25 May 2012.

Griffin, Forest. *Got Fight?: The 50 Zen Principles of Hand-to-Face Combat.* William Morrow Paperbacks, 2010.

Made in the USA
Middletown, DE
06 February 2015